Employment and Work Relations in Context Series

Series Editors

Tony Elger and Peter Fairbrother

Centre for Comparative Labour Studies,

Department of Sociology,

University of Warwick

The aim of the *Employment and Work Relations in Context Series* is to address questions relating to the evolving patterns and politics of work, employment, management and industrial relations. There is a concern to trace out the ways in which wider policy-making, especially by national governments and transnational corporations, impinges upon specific workplaces, occupations, labour markets, localities and regions. This invites attention to developments at an international level, tracing out patterns of globalization, state policy and practice in this context, and the impact of these processes on labour. A particular feature of the series is the consideration of forms of worker and citizen organization and moblization in these circumstances. Thus the studies address major analytical and policy issues through case-study and comparative research.

YOUNG PEOPLE IN THE WORKPLACE

Job, Union and Mobility Patterns

Christina Cregan

MANSELL

London and New York

First published 1999 by
Mansell Publishing Limited, *A Cassell imprint*
Wellington House, 125 Strand, London WC2R 0BB
370 Lexington Avenue, New York, NY 10017-6550

British Library Cataloguing-in-Publication Data
A catalogue record for this book is available from the British Library.

ISBN 0 7201 2327 5

Library of Congress Cataloging-in-Publication Data
Cregan, Christina, 1948–
    Young People in the workplace: job, union, and mobility patterns / Christina Cregan.
        p. cm. — (Employment and work relations in context)
    Includes bibliographical references and index.
    ISBN 0–7201–2327–5 (hb)
    1. Youth–Employment–Great Britain. 2. Trade unions–Great Britain. I. Title. II. Series.
HD6276.G7C74 1998
331.3'4'0941–dc21
                                                      97-50238
                                                          CIP

Typeset by York House Typographic Ltd.
Printed and bound in Great Britain by The Cromwell Press Ltd, Trowbridge, Wiltshire

CONTENTS

List of Tables   vi
Acknowledgements   viii

1   The Thesis   1
2   The Post-war Youth Labour Market in Britain   10
3   The Survey: Early School-leavers, 1979–81   21
4   Jobs, Apprenticeships, and Wages   34
5   Young People and Promotion: A Mutual Dependency
    Analysis   61
6   The Free Rider Problem: A New Theory of Trade Union
    Membership   78
7   Trade Unions: An Empirical Account   93
8   Young People and Instability: Job-swapping and Quits   115
9   The End of the 1979–81 Survey: Themes and Patterns   137
10 The Youth Labour Market in Britain at the End of the
    Century   147
11 Jobs, Unions and Stability Patterns at the End of the
    Century   169
12 What is the Youth Labour Market? Conclusions and Policy
    Implications   187
Appendix 1   The Logit Model   205
Appendix 2   Data Dictionary   207
Appendix 3   England and Wales Youth Cohort Series   210

Bibliography   211
Index   229

LIST OF TABLES

3.1	16-year-old school-leavers entering employment in 1979	22
3.2	Change in unemployment rates in Britain, 1979–82	23
3.3	Changes in unemployment and vacancies in London, 1979–81	24
3.4	Borough of residence of interviewees in survey	27
3.5	Occupation of head of household	28
3.6	Ideally, what kind of job would you like when you leave school?	29
3.7	Ethnicity of interviewees	29
3.8	Response rates (cumulative)	30
4.1	Commuting times	40
4.2	Job information	45
4.3	Logit model: gaining work	48
4.4	Job location and place of residence	52
4.5	Logit model: gaining an apprenticeship	54
4.6	Male attitudes to job before and after they started work	56
4.7	Regression: level of income (1)	58
5.1	Job progressions (1)	72
5.2	Logit model: gaining a job with prospects	74
5.3	Job progressions (2)	74
5.4	Formal training	75
5.5	Regression: level of income (2)	76
7.1	Reasons for union membership (1)	95
7.2	Reasons for union membership (2)	98
7.3	Reasons for union membership (3)	99
7.4	Reasons for union membership (4)	100
7.5	Reasons for union non-membership (1)	101
7.6	Reasons for union non-membership (2)	103
7.7	Logit model: joining a trade union (1)	107
7.8	Logit model: joining a trade union (2)	111
8.1	Stability patterns	121

8.2   Separation frequency   122

8.3   Reasons for leaving first full-time job   127

8.4   Logit model: quit behaviour   132

9.1   Regression: change in income (1)   141

9.2   Regression: change in income (2)   142

10.1 Participation rates (per cent) of early school-leavers   148

ACKNOWLEDGEMENTS

I am indebted to Ray Richardson for allowing me access to a most valuable data-set and for his strong encouragement in the early days. Stewart Johnston, Alan King and William Jones provided expert statistical information. I would like to thank the Department of Industrial Relations at the London School of Economics for providing me with facilities for research, and the Faculty of Economics and Commerce at Melbourne University for awarding me a research grant. I am grateful to the University of Otago for allowing me continuing access to its computer facilities. Stewart, Madeleine and Phil have been very supportive, and the Cregans, Willises and Mullens provided outstanding hospitality and friendship. In particular, however, I owe a great deal of gratitude to Peter Fairbrother and Tony Elger for their insight and careful scrutiny. All errors, of course, are my own.

1 THE THESIS

Introduction

Over the last two decades, the lack of labour market opportunities for young people has been an issue of constant concern to successive governments. Youth is highly represented in low-skill work and its unemployment level is about twice that of the labour force in general. As a consequence, there has been a variety of state interventions to help provide remedies. The aim of this book is to challenge those policies that have as their basis an assumption that most young people lack a work ethic. It will be argued, first, that early school-leavers do not necessarily display immature labour market behaviour merely by virtue of their age and inexperience. Labour market immaturity can be defined as a transient, aimless, or erratic attitude to work as reflected in job search behaviour, patterns of instability and attitudes to trade union membership. Second, it will be proposed that opportunities available for youth may consist not just of the low-skill jobs of the conventional youth labour market model, but also of those which offer training and prospects. The availability of such occupations is closely related to context, culture and policy and, in turn, affects the labour market behaviour of participants. Finally, it will be contended that if a large part of the school-leaving cohort enters the labour market and sufficient job and training opportunities are available, then the resulting matching process will engender mature or purposeful, rational behaviour in many young people, even in the occupations and industries in which youth is generally represented.

This book will empirically substantiate the arguments by an analysis of the characteristics of the British youth labour market in the second half of the twentieth century. It will demonstrate that in the post-war years, the idiosyncratic nature of this market lent it a heterogeneity which, since the end of the 1970s, has largely disappeared, leaving many young people with the prospects either of dead-end work or of unemployment following an extended period of schooling or training. The arguments have important contemporary policy implications in this changing context. If youth is not essentially immature in terms of labour market behaviour, then the raising of the school leaving age will have little effect on attitudes to work without the provision of meaningful job opportunities which will help engender labour market purposefulness, no matter what the age of labour market entry.

Most studies of the British youth labour market have been carried out in separate disciplines, notably economics and sociology. This book will attempt to draw together their explanations and findings. The terminology relating to young people will be employed as it is customarily used in British work (e.g. Ashton *et al.*, 1982; Ashton and Maguire, 1986b). 'Youth' will refer to 16- and 17-year-olds, and the term 'young adults' will be employed to embrace 18–24-year-olds. The terms 'young people' and 'youngsters' will be employed generally.

The Youth Labour Market

It is conventionally accepted that, at any given time, the labour market for youth consists of certain occupations and industries where many young people, and sometimes other groups, are represented. Most of these jobs are unskilled and offer no training or prospects. Many youngsters are said to work in them during their transition to the adult labour market when they 'move from childhood to adulthood' (Garonna and Ryan, 1991, p. 3), becoming accustomed to work and taking on informed and responsible attitudes. This viewpoint is expressed in many separate strands of the literature. Young people are said to need a time of adjustment (Ashton, 1975; Smith, 1975; Springhall, 1986); they experience a floundering period (Hamilton, 1990); they undergo a moratorium stage (Osterman, 1980); they suffer a period of disorientation (Gilman, 1975; Glickman, 1975); they struggle with the acquisition of the social roles required in the work setting (Von Maanen, 1977).

Freeman and Wise (1982) argued that supply factors are determinants of this situation. That is, many young people, relative to other age groups, do not wish to have a stable occupation with steady hours. The basis of this viewpoint lies in the assumption that there are distinctive youth-based characteristics determined by age. Lack of responsibilities, commitments and skill combined with parental contribution to expenses leads to a willingness to work for low pay. An immature attitude, risk propensity, a low replacement ratio (i.e. the ratio of net income out of work and in work), and the shock effect of initial exposure to the workplace lead to a temporary attitude to jobs until a purposeful outlook is adopted. These traits are manifest in terms of a carefree approach to job search, and a weak commitment to the workplace demonstrated by high separation rates and a low level of union membership. However, Osterman (1980) claimed that demand factors are also crucially important because employers recognize these general characteristics and consequently offer low-paid work to most young people, excluding youth from career jobs and those which offer training opportunities. From this viewpoint, the transition period consists of adjustment to the world of work by confinement to a sector where there are no entry ports to long-term jobs and where immature behaviour is inconsequential. Participation in the youth labour market of unskilled work is therefore seen as a transient and interim stage, part of a growing-up ritual before entry to the adult labour market where jobs with training and prospects are available and a responsible approach is desirable.

The high representation of youth in some jobs is not questioned because the evidence is overwhelming. For example, in a European study, Marsden and Ryan (1986) found that some sectors employed few young people, while others employed many of them. They also reported a strong similarity in the industries that were large employers of young people in six countries, including Britain. However, the arguments proposed in this book challenge the explanations for this situation, which suggest that most youth is confined to such sectors because it demonstrates age-related traits of purposeless behaviour. Although youth has a distinctiveness, it is argued that this is not necessarily based on traits of immaturity. First, not all age-linked characteristics of young people have negative implications. Young people are recipients of the most recent schooling techniques and ideas (Garonna and Ryan, 1991); they are relatively optimistic in outlook;

they have no entrenched attitudes. Thus, they provide a 'clean slate' on which up-to-date training and loyalty to the company can be written.

Second, if early school-leavers consist of the minority who drop out of high school, one might expect a generally maverick attitude to work. However, in a situation where early school-leavers constitute the majority of the age group, and therefore represent a wide range of abilities, many of the young people are not unreliable or irresponsible by nature. Although their inexperience does mean they need to adjust to the labour market, much of their behaviour may have a different source of motivation than that proposed by exponents of youth fecklessness. That is, they may be receptive to adjustment to the labour market by means of job-shopping to gather information in a situation of uncertainty by purposeful behaviour (Johnson, 1978). This process will equally be facilitated by a low replacement ratio and will also result in high instability rates. The transition period from this viewpoint, therefore, is one in which information is gathered about wages, jobs and the labour market in a situation where some employers may be keen to offer ports of entry to longer-term jobs and where matching is facilitated by means of rent-seeking behaviour.[1]

In summary, the distinctiveness of youth in terms of age, inexperience and a willingness to work for low pay allows for both erratic and purposeful behaviour. From both viewpoints, however, youth will display relatively high separation rates, and it may be that some employers prefer more stable employees. The transition to work, therefore, may largely be concentrated in certain sectors and jobs. Thus, the youth labour market is likely to consist of a conventional low-skill framework in which, however, heterogeneity may be manifest. It is contended that the level of this manifestation and therefore the character of the youth labour market are, in large part, context-based. It is argued that where, first, the norms and legislation of society permit a large range of youth to leave school at the earliest opportunity and, second, jobs and training opportunities are available, the outcome is mature labour market behaviour on the part of many early school-leavers. Much of their instability, therefore, indicates rent-seeking activity for those ignorant of the workplace and perhaps their own talents and aspirations. Clearly, there is an interaction between these two features because it is argued that the existence of job opportunity and heterogeneity affects patterns of individual behaviour. Where training and prospects are available, even within a restricted sector of jobs and industries, these become major determinants of labour market maturity. Where they are unavailable, young people of any ability level may react against dead-end work and display traits of aimlessness.

The importance of such assertions lies in the policy implications in the current economic and political circumstances as they affect young people at the beginning of the twenty-first century. Unemployment and structural changes, which have occurred particularly since the 1970s, have more than proportionately affected youth relative to many other groups. While Conservative government strategy for nearly two decades continued to provide youth training and changed its scope to embrace the effects of structural change, nevertheless it made an important departure from previous policies. There was an emphasis on strategies that brought about the virtual disappearance of the 16-year-old youth labour market (Payne and Payne, 1994). Until the end of the 1970s, most young people in Britain left school at 15 or 16 and gained employment. By the mid-1990s, less than 10 per cent of 16-year-olds gained work. The increase in some further and higher educational opportunities can be seen as partly responsible for this change. But the decline in job opportunities, financial assistance for youth training, and the abolition, in 1988, of unemployment and social security benefits for under-18-year-olds are generally held to be other important causes.

If 16-year-old young people are thought to be unreliable by virtue of their youthfulness, then policies which keep them within the family and school or college until they are older and better-equipped educationally for the workforce can only be seen in a favourable light. However, if age *per se* is not the crucial factor but rather it is the homogeneous and dead-end nature of available jobs which is the major cause of a transient attitude, then the provision of meaningful work and training become crucial factors. If most young people now postpone their leaving age until 18, and are faced with jobs which offer no prospects, then, it is argued, labour market immaturity will still be manifest, but in a group who have become adults by reaching the legal majority.

The Investigations

The argument will be supported in the following way.

The post-war period

By an appraisal of existing literature, it will be established that the post-war period in Britain provided a context of opportunity and heterogeneity through to the 1970s. During the 1950s and 1960s, there was job opportunity both in general and in areas that required skill. The law that allowed young people to leave school at 15 (16 after 1972) meant that school pupils could be available for work and training at this age, and the successful, historical tradition of apprenticeships, especially in the area of manufacturing, meant that many employers regarded youth as sufficiently responsible for long-term skill acquisition. In this situation, the emergence of institutional, legal and cultural norms meant there was a range of jobs available, some with training opportunities. Unsurprisingly, most young people left school at the earliest opportunity. This does not contradict existing theory but merely enriches the flavour of its British setting by providing context-related detail.

It will be demonstrated that such a situation engendered labour market maturity in many early school-leavers as manifested in attitudes to job search, quit behaviour and union membership. This will be carried out by examining a survey that took place at the end of that period. Investigations of a data-set consisting of responses from 2000 early school-leavers who entered the labour market in 1979, will specifically examine these propositions in the final years of that period. In retrospect, the two years of data collection marked an important watershed. For the first time since the war, young people began to experience the declining levels of job opportunity which have persisted thereafter. Moreover, these years marked the beginning of fundamental changes in government policy because 1979 was the start of nearly two decades of Conservative rule. Thus, the time of the survey proved to be a turning point for Britain and its young people.

Several investigations of this survey will be carried out, linked to the main argument. It will be demonstrated that, in this post-war context, jobs, training and promotion opportunities were available, and that there was some evidence of a matching process via youth search and employer selection. Gender segregation was apparent and there was group disadvantage in the form of race, inner-city residence and household unemployment. With regard to quit behaviour and job-swapping, it will be established that most young people were stable throughout the survey, probably as a response to increasing unemployment. Although a transient immature attitude was apparent for a minority, for others there was evidence of a rational decision-making process in which purposeful behaviour was apparent. With regard to unions, unsurprisingly, most youths did not join but, for many, this was because they were not asked rather than through age-related transient views. Clear and positive attitudes were found in those who did join. Finally, it will be shown that, in such a context of heterogeneity, skill acquisition, ability and purposeful behaviour in the form of job-swapping and union membership were important influences on wage increases for some young workers.

The Conservative era: the 1980s and 1990s

It will be shown that although changes were occurring by the end of the 1970s, the two decades or so after 1979 marked an era in which opportunities for jobs in general and skill acquisition in particular became more scarce. By an analysis of important youth research projects of the 1980s and 1990s, it will be demonstrated that, after evolving gradually over 25 years, the youth labour market changed in a radical way with the advent of Conservative rule. By the middle of the 1990s, the school-leaving age for the majority was 18. There were fewer jobs, training opportunities had decreased and jobs of non-standard hours were a growing phenomenon. Although the craft tradition survived to some extent, the youth market was losing its idiosyncratic features and converging to a model of unskilled work and unemployment.

It will be demonstrated that labour market patterns apparent in the 1979 survey investigations were still in evidence but with different implications in the changing panorama. In this situation of job and training scarcity, a matching process was identified but group disadvantage in the form of gender, race, inner city residence and household unemployment had more profound consequences. For 16-year-old school-leavers, some heterogeneity of work was still apparent but the market now was much smaller. The 18-year-old leavers, however, faced an even more homogeneous set of jobs, and high unemployment persisted for them. For some youth in unskilled work, patterns of instability and labour market immaturity associated with the conventional youth model were more likely to arise. Thus, there was evidence of quit behaviour associated with aimlessness, lower union membership and an end to job-swapping as a means of workplace betterment.

Policy Implications

Finally, it will be proposed that, as some of the characteristics of the youth labour market can be engineered, help for young people in these circumstances can best be brought about by state intervention in a context where market mechanisms and labour institutions are constrained. If youth is not unreliable *per se*, then the provision of work and of jobs with training and prospects will result in the emergence of a largely responsible workforce, with opportunities for the rent-seeking activities of job-swapping. This has clear implications for market efficiency. It will be maintained that the provision of a transition period comprising a mix of non-standard hours and on-going education via day-release to jobs will provide a different kind of training ground in the absence of full employment opportunities of work of standard hours.

The Structure of the Book

The book will reflect the thematic sequence presented above. Chapter Two examines the characteristics of the post-war youth labour market. The following six chapters investigate the survey. Chapter Three examines its context and describes the data-set and method of investigation. Chapters Four and Five are concerned with the issue of heterogeneity through investigations of job and training opportunities and determinants of income levels. Chapters Six, Seven and Eight examine employee purposefulness in the form of attitudes to union membership and stability patterns. Chapter Nine draws empirical and theoretical conclusions from the whole sequence. Chapter Ten analyses recent research on the youth labour market and discusses changes which have occurred in the last twenty years. Chapter Eleven examines employee behaviour and attitudes in the new context. The final chapter proposes policies which might help young people in the light of the character of the youth labour market which has been made apparent from the investigations.

Note

1 'Rent' is a technical term in economics which refers to the returns to the supply of an input which is fixed. However, in recent years there has been a tendency to extend the use of the word to include all payments, e.g. wages which are above the minimum required to make, say labour, available to the firm or industry. For the employee, therefore, rent-seeking is the search for the greater surplus, a higher wage (other things being equal).

2 THE POST-WAR YOUTH LABOUR MARKET IN BRITAIN

Introduction

The aim of this chapter is to demonstrate that in post-war Britain, although young people were highly represented in low-skill jobs and certain industries, nevertheless opportunities for skill acquisition and responsibility were clearly available to early school-leavers. The latter comprised the majority of their age cohort and thus exhibited a range of abilities. These are not new propositions. Some writers suggest that institutional and legal factors are important influences so that, for example, the apprenticeship system lends a distinctive character to the British youth labour market (Kerckhoff, 1990; Marsden and Germe, 1990; Blanchflower and Lynch, 1992). It will be argued in this chapter that the economic, institutional and legislative context of the post-war years led to a situation in which a heterogeneity of jobs was apparent for early school-leavers, though changes were occurring by the end of the 1970s.

The Post-war Youth Labour Market in Britain

In the first three decades after the Second World War, most young people left school at the earliest opportunity and most of them gained work, some of it in the form of long-term training opportunities. Until 1972, legislation permitted youth to leave school at 15. This age was raised to 16 in September of that year. Up to the late 1970s, the legal minimum was the normal age for leaving school. Although there was a rise in the number of 16–18-year-olds going on to further or higher education in the 1960s, in 1971/2 about 78 per cent entered the labour market, and for most of the 1970s this proportion remained constant, with less than one in five school-leavers staying in the education system (Department of Education and Science, 1980). 'About 800,000 16–18 year olds leave school each year, and most depart at 16' (Department of Education and Science, 1980, p. 151).

The major reason for this situation was the availability of work, some of which offered career prospects. The post-war decades in Britain were, for the most part, marked by a boom in consumer demand and persisting low levels of unemployment. Between 1969 and 1979, the average rate of unemployment was 3.9 per cent (Waddington and Whitston, 1995). Moreover, employers could select from a group with a very wide range of abilities, from those with no qualifications at all, to those with CSEs and/or GCEs.[1] This was, at least in part, because only a minority of young people had the option of continuing in meaningful education. Although there had been a university expansion in the 1960s, the UK still had a relatively low rate of participation at tertiary levels: 'the proportion of 16 year olds in Britain who stay on at school is low by OECD standards' (Micklewright, 1989, p. 25). Moreover, most sixth forms only provided places for the academic training which was required for entrance to higher education (Roberts, 1995).

It was unsurprising, therefore, that some young people were considered suitable for training opportunities. In particular, the day-release system for apprentices to colleges of further education was an important characteristic of the British youth labour market. Its roots lay in large part in the historical basis of the British manufacturing tradition and craft union strength (Keep and Rainbird, 1995). Manufacturing offered the largest number of apprenticeships and, within that sector, engineering had two-thirds of male apprenticeships (*Department of Employment Gazette*, 1982b). About 40 per cent of young males entered the British system of apprenticeships during the post-war period (Metcalf and Richards, 1983), almost half of them within the manufacturing sector (*Department of Employment Gazette*, 1982b). Young females faced less advantage. Eight times as many males as females held apprenticeships at the end of the 1970s and only 20 per cent of the females were 16 or 17 (*Department of Employment Gazette*, 1982b). Moreover, there were different and fewer training opportunities in 'female' work. Hairdressing and beautician work accounted for two-thirds of the much smaller number of female apprenticeships (*Department of Employment Gazette*, 1982b). Young women were less likely to receive training than young men, and when training was available to females, it was generally of shorter duration (Metcalf and Richards, 1983).

Nevertheless, in Britain in the post-war decades there was a range of ability among early school-leavers and of jobs. In this context, many young people were considered to be reliable workers by some employers. It is likely that exigency fostered such an attitude. The post-war consumer boom in Western Europe following the war years produced a need for labour in the 1950s which made young people, along with immigrants, welcome into the labour force. Moreover, apprenticeships demonstrated to employers the ability and stability of many in this age group. Major institutions like the Civil Service had ports of entry specifically geared to school-leaver examinations for the better qualified 15–16-year-old age group as well as older groups. The Post Office, insurance companies, banks and building societies 'have a long-standing preference for recruiting young people then promoting internally. They are not alone' (Roberts *et al.*, 1987). Thus, opportunity and heterogeneity in the labour market encouraged young people to leave school early, and most of them did so to take advantage of such a situation.

The timing of the workplace transition from childhood to adulthood was a product of this post-war job availability: findings from his analysis of youth in Britain over the period 1860–1960 prompted Springhall (1986) to conclude that adolescence is 'a cultural definition' (p. 235). Unsurprisingly, therefore, in a 1968 investigation, a government advisory body reported that two-thirds of parents felt that 15 was the right age for their children to start work, and that half of them were completely opposed to raising the school-leaving age (Schools Council Inquiry, 1968). Ashton and Field (1976) claimed that up until the 1970s, despite competition from other groups and exclusion from some areas of work, youth had a smooth continuity of experience from school to work. As economic growth persisted throughout the 1950s and 1960s, stable youth labour market patterns emerged in which norms and traditions could prevail.

However, changes were occurring which began to make an impact on the youth labour market during the 1970s. For example, there was a rising birth rate from 1955 to 1965 which, over the 1970s, resulted in a steady increase in the youth population aged 16–19 as a percentage of the total civilian labour force. It rose from 12.6 per cent in 1971 to 14.8 per cent in 1983, when it reached its zenith (Deakin, 1996) even though there was also an overall growth in the labour supply in the 1970s.

Moreover, job opportunities were declining as recession and structural change made an impact on Britain. In the mid-1970s, unemployment began to rise consistently. The industries in which youth had been traditionally represented in the post-war decades were exactly those industries which experienced the greatest number of net job and apprenticeship losses over the 1970s. In particular, in the latter half of the 1960s, manufacturing started to decline in terms of numbers employed and, by the end of the 1970s had reached immediate post-war levels. Employment in manufacturing as a percentage of the civilian population decreased by 16 per cent between 1960 and 1979 (OECD, 1991). Formal training in all manufacturing industries peaked in 1968 at under 450,000 to fall back to 240,000 in 1980 (*Department of Employment Gazette*, 1982a), and between 1971 and 1978 the proportion of craftsmen and skilled operators halved, from 20.6 per cent of the labour force to 10.7 per cent (MSC, 1980). The decrease in training opportunities particularly affected young males, who were much more likely to undertake apprenticeships than females.

A major effect of the decline in manufacturing, skilled work and craft apprenticeships was to increase competition for unskilled work in other areas, particularly in the service industry, which had been steadily expanding since the 1950s (Nolan and Walsh, 1995). Lacking skill and training, young people faced competition from workers with similar characteristics. Early school-leavers from previous cohorts who had not gained stable employment became competitors of the current leavers. Older workers, especially perhaps those with redundant skills and experience, could compete with young people for similar jobs, and there was an increase in their supply as fewer than average people reached retirement age due to a trough of births in the 1914–18 period (Atkinson and Rees, 1982). Moreover, in the 1970s women joined the workforce in growing numbers. Metcalf and Richards (1983) noted the trend in increased economic activity rates among married women, which rose from 42 per cent in 1971 to 57 per cent in 1979. They also reported a rise in the proportion of economically active young females, aged 20–24, in the 1970s, reflecting the later age of marriage and the falling birth rate (until 1977). Yet this must not be overestimated. Deakin (1996) indicated that the overall proportion of women in the total civilian labour force rose by just 3 per cent, from 36.3 per cent in 1971 to 39.3 per cent in 1978, and Hakim (1995) reported that the increase in economic activity rates of females from about the late 1950s was due to the substitution of full-time for part-time work. She claimed there was 'absolutely no increase in the volume of female employment, measured in full-time equivalent numbers' (Hakim, 1995, p. 431) in the post-war period up to 1987.

Moreover, the distinctiveness of youth, in terms of its willingness to accept low pay, was becoming less apparent in the 1970s and despite lower rates overall, youth wages were rising relative to those of adults,[2] reducing their competitiveness. In 1949, among male manual workers, those aged under 21 earned well below half the adult rate, but by the beginning of the 1980s they earned over 60 per cent of it (Metcalf and Richards, 1983). Throughout the 1970s, youth earned a relatively high percentage of adult pay (Ryan, 1987). According to Metcalf and Richards (1983), this started to become a problem in the mid-1970s in terms of its effects on youth unemployment. Wells (1983), analysing New Earnings Survey data, 1948–79, also concluded that the fall in the employment of young people in the 1970s was associated with rises in their earnings relative to adults. McClure (1979) claimed that the earnings of the lower paid, including the young, rose rapidly relative to the rest of the labour force during 1976–7, partly as a result of Labour government legislation. Moreover, trade unions in Britain have historically aimed to link young people's pay to adult rates (Ryan, 1987) and the effect was increased by the Family Law Reform Act of 1969, which lowered the age of majority from 21 to 18. Thus, some unions began negotiations for the adult rate of pay, not normally payable for males until 21, to be paid at 18, compressing and raising rates for those between the ages of 16 and 17. In fact, Wells (1983) reported that the unemployment effect seemed to be concentrated in the under-18 age group. By the later years of the 1970s, youth unemployment, in fact, was higher and increasing at a faster rate than that of the rest of the population, and this was largely because recruitment fell (Makeham, 1980).

Decreasing opportunity for this age group particularly affected youth from the racial minorities in Britain. Partly as a response to the post-war tight labour market in Britain, most West Indians immigrated to Britain in the early 1950s though, since the 1960s, immigration had slowed down dramatically (Smith, 1977), while the Asian wave, from the Indian subcontinent, did not reach its peak until the early 1960s. Nevertheless, the 'first waves of UK born West Indians were just beginning to reach school-leaving age in the 1970s' (Sillitoe and Meltzer, 1985, p. 1). Although the 1968 Race Relations Act, which made discriminatory practices illegal, was strengthened in 1976, the young minority groups were disadvantaged relative to the white population. School-leavers rely heavily on adult contacts in the labour market, and Sillitoe and Meltzer (1985) reported that West Indian school-leavers had less well-informed parental guidance than their white counterparts. This was unsurprising as West Indian and Asian households were over-proportionately represented among the unemployed and unskilled. In the late 1970s, the unemployment rates of non-whites were between two and three times those of whites: in 1977/8 over 11 per cent of those of minority origin born in the UK were unemployed (registered or otherwise), compared to 4–6 per cent of whites (NDHS, 1978). Mayhew and Rosewell (1978) examined a male sample from the 1971 population census and reported that non-whites were crowded into undesirable, low-paying occupations, and had more difficulty than whites in obtaining higher-status jobs. Smith (1976) also indicated that blacks and Pakistanis were more likely than whites to be in manual rather than professional and managerial work. Moreover, in general, ethnic minority adults had been in the labour market for a shorter period than whites: about 80 per cent of persons of West Indian origin born in the UK were under 30 compared to about 30 per cent of the white UK population (NDHS, 1978).

Unsurprisingly, the increase in youth unemployment was reflected in the rise in the proportion of 16-year-olds staying on at school after the mid-1970s (Department of Education and Science, 1980). In 1976/7, 30 per cent of 16–18-year-olds were studying in schools and further education colleges (Booth, 1981) and by 1979, some 50 per cent of 16-year-olds continued in full-time education or training, just over half for GCE A-levels, the rest for repeats of earlier exams or to undertake vocational courses. This trend was clearly, at least in part, a response to decreasing opportunity. Only a little over 45 per cent had entered their first employment by December 1979 (*Department of Employment Gazette,* 1982b). Female full-time education participation rates were traditionally lower than males. Throughout the 1970s, this remained the case and by 1980/1 the rates for females were 48 per cent and for males 54 per cent (*Labour Market Quarterly Report,* 1996). Clearly, at least in part as a response to their relatively disadvantaged situation, black and Asian participation rates in education were higher than those of whites. The Swann Committee of Enquiry (Swann Report, 1985) investigated six Local Education Authorities with high concentrations of ethnic minorities in 1978/9 and 1981/2. It found that, in those areas, the participation rates of South Asians in full-time secondary education after the age of 16 were nearly double those of whites, while those of Afro-Caribbeans were 60 per cent more than whites.

Nevertheless, youth still had some advantages over its competitors in the labour market. First, there is evidence that employers had views about the kind of work in which youth should be employed. For example, Ashton et al. (1982) found, at the end of the 1970s, that some employers felt that young people could be trained into the culture of the firm more easily than adults. A Confederation of British Industry (CBI) survey in Wolverhampton at the beginning of the 1980s (CBI, 1983) asked employers their main reason for hiring young people: 77 per cent said it gave them the opportunity 'to mould beginners from scratch'. Raffe (1992) wrote of the insistence of employers in that period that they recruit 16-year-olds straight from compulsory schooling in preference to slightly older groups.

Second, young workers might have been more prepared than many adults to offer themselves for casual, temporary, or seasonal work as they have less responsibility and fewer commitments, or for lower incomes because their reservation wage was lower.[3] Bradshaw et al. (1987) calculated that the average replacement ratio for British teenagers had been significantly less than for adult unemployed. Moreover, although school-leavers could obtain supplementary benefit in their own right subject to a means test, and unemployment, sickness, and disability benefits were also available to youth who met the eligibility requirements, Layard (1982) argued that the amount of benefit was small relative to youth earnings and was not usually a deterrent to job search.

Third, some legislation had the effect of making young people preferable to other unskilled workers. For example, the Employment Protection (Consolidation) Act of 1978 excluded 16- and 17-year-olds from redundancy payments, which employers had to pay after at least two years' service by an employee after the age of 18. Consequently, those firms who feared uncertainty, or who did not want to finance expensive recruitment, might have been more tempted to take on early school-leavers than their substitutes.

Fourth, trade unions are important labour market institutions and a low proportion of young people are union members compared to adult workers so fewer of them have recourse to union protection. In the post-war period, Metcalf and Richards (1983), analysing unpublished data from the National Training Survey for 1975, concluded that over half of males aged 25–62 were in unions but only 19 per cent of teenage males. Although these figures do not control for other influences, nevertheless, based on this crude observation, employers anticipating declining demand might have preferred to recruit young rather than adult male workers.

Fifth, the stability of the post-war period meant that customs and traditions emerged which persisted into the 1970s. Roberts *et al.* (1987) reported that some employers claimed they could hire older workers for the same tasks but took on youth through traditional practice from earlier times. Ashton and Maguire (1986a) also reported the existence of custom and practice.

In fact, although change was occurring in post-war Britain, and at an increasing rate in the 1970s, nevertheless there were strong continuities apparent over the period. In general, early school-leavers took up jobs in a labour market characterized by low-skill work but where training opportunities were also apparent. Heterogeneity remained an important feature of the post-war British youth labour market and, although educational participation rates were increasing, the vast majority of young people who left school at 16 gained work.

The Character of Youth Jobs in Britain in the Post-war Decades

In such a situation of continuity, stability, and heterogeneity, the British youth labour market has been described as segmented (e.g. Ashton *et al.*, 1982) or stratified (Roberts *et al.*, 1987). This viewpoint suggests that, in some instances, the market does not clear; i.e. freedom of mobility between occupations and/or industries is constrained or impeded and thus the entry and/or exit of labour is restricted. This situation is particularly apparent where legislation, institutions, and customs impose age restrictions on recruitment. Consequently, there are said to be identifiable youth jobs or sectors in which many youth work and/or form a high proportion of the workforce.

It is conventionally accepted that, because of its lack of training and experience, youth takes up low-skill work and is restricted to certain industries. This was certainly the case in post-war Britain. The industrial sectors in which work for youth was available were manufacturing, distribution, transport, and communications, together accounting for 60 per cent of first-time entrants (MSC, 1977). Moreover, there were clear traditional gender differences apparent within these industrial groupings. In manufacturing, young men (under 20) were heavily represented in mechanical engineering and metal goods, with young women in textiles and footwear. In the service sector, both were highly represented in distribution, with males also in construction and miscellaneous services, and females in insurance, banking, and finance (Makeham, 1980). Nevertheless, Marsden and Ryan (1986), in a comparative study of European countries, reported that although some sectors employed few young people and others employed many of them, 'in Britain ... youth exclusion is not even approached in any sector' (p. 85). This was seen to be caused largely by the effects of the apprenticeship system, which acted as an entry port to long-term careers.

The basic framework of low-skill work but with the availability of some jobs with training and prospects was also reflected in the occupations available to youth. Ashton *et al.* (1982), unsurprisingly, found that most professional, administrative, and managerial jobs were closed to 16-year-olds. They claimed that many firms refused to consider youths at all because they thought that young people were irresponsible, they might disrupt production processes through inexperience, or that the cost of training them was too high. They also reported that physical requirements barred some youths from jobs. With regard to legislation and the exclusion of young people, Metcalf and Richards (1983) indicated that the Factories Act of 1961 had the general effect of precluding young persons from shift systems which begin before 6 a.m. and end after 10 p.m. (2 p.m. on Saturdays). In the same way, the Employment of Women, Young Persons and Children Act (1920) prohibited them from being employed in night work. Ashton and Maguire (1986a) proposed that age restrictions with regard to gaining driving licences of different categories excluded youth from many jobs and that, in the absence of legal regulations, custom and practice was important, for example, with regard to working with dangerous machinery. Gender segregation was apparent in occupations also: the largest group of males (40 per cent) took up apprenticeships, mainly in manufacturing, while a similar proportion of females entered clerical jobs (Metcalf and Richards, 1983).

Yet although high proportions of youth were represented in certain jobs and industries, this did not mean that there was a sector exclusively reserved for youth; there is evidence that some employers hired both youths and other low-skill workers. For example, Ashton *et al.* (1982) found both young and adult workers in semi-skilled and unskilled manual jobs and clerical work. In fact, Roberts *et al.* (1987) reported that only apprenticeships and other traineeships were unequivocal 'youth jobs' in Britain. In 1979, 89.5 per cent of male apprentices were 16 and the rest 17 (*Department of Employment Gazette*, 1982b). This was not the conventional unskilled youth job, but a training position, institutionally determined, which endowed its participants with advantage. However, in terms of segmentation analysis, if important entry ports are only available at the age of 16 or 17, then recognizable segments or strata emerge and persist in terms of later career patterns. This is because if these opportunities are not taken up in the early years, young people may well be excluded from rewarding work in adult life.

Overall, although many young people worked in low-skill areas, the effect of the heterogeneity apparent in the British youth labour market was to allow some young people access to jobs in which adults worked. This seems in large part to have been brought about by the institution of apprenticeships, for the most part exclusive to young people. These not only allowed access to long-term career training, but probably persuaded employers that some early school-leavers were sufficiently mature to offer them work with prospects.

Conclusion

In summary, during the first three decades after the Second World War, many jobs were available to young people, usually in traditional areas segregated by gender. Most youth left school at the earliest opportunity to enter the labour market. Changes, however, were already occurring in the form of increasing unemployment, structural shifts, and the increase in women workers. Nevertheless, at the end of the 1970s, many young people still left school at 16 and most of them gained work, many with training opportunities particularly in the form of apprenticeships for males. It was in this context of the last years of opportunity at the end of the post-war era, that the survey took place.

Notes

1 Certificates of Secondary Education (CSEs) were associated with the former secondary modern schools, and General Certificates of Education (GCEs) with the grammar schools.
2 Rubery (1995) outlined the laws which could raise the wages of the low-paid, who included many working youths. For those workers who did not bargain collectively, and this included many young workers, Schedule 11 of the 1970 Equal Pay Act (implemented in 1975) allowed them to seek imposition on the employer of a requirement to at least match the 'general level' of pay for comparable workers. Wages Councils provided minimum rates in certain low-pay industries. The Fair Wages Resolutions of 1946 required government contractors to pay fair wages, usually interpreted as at least equal to minimum rates of the relevant industry-level agreement.
3 That is they were more willing to take a job at a lower wage than adults would require, than remain unemployed.

3

THE SURVEY: EARLY SCHOOL-LEAVERS, 1979–81

Introduction

The main focus of this work is an analysis of a survey of 2000 early school-leavers, white and non-white, male and female,[1] carried out in London boroughs over the years 1979–81. The investigations of this data-set will attempt to establish the link between the characteristics of the labour market and the experience, behaviour, and attitude of its participants. Within the general framework of the conventional youth labour market of unskilled work, evidence of heterogeneity and purposeful behaviour is sought. The analysis will be carried out by examinations of job search, the matching process, instability patterns, and attitudes to union membership. This is an introductory chapter to these empirical enquiries. It outlines the context of Britain and London in the survey years of 1979–81 and describes the data-set and the methods of analysis.

The Context of the Survey: 1979–81

In 1979, after the post-war decades, just less than half of 16-year-olds left school at that age (*Department of Employment Gazette*, 1982b). Unemployment for 16–19-year-olds was just 8.7 per cent for males and 8.6 per cent for unmarried females, though 15.4 per cent for married women (*Labour Force Survey*, 1979). The employment situation was as follows (see Table 3.1). About a third of both males and females worked in manufacturing. Distributive trades and other services were also

Table 3.1 *Sixteen-year-old school-leavers entering employment in 1979: distribution by industry and occupation in England and Wales*

	Per cent male	Per cent female
INDUSTRY		
Agriculture, forestry and fishing	4.3	0.9
Mining and quarrying	2.0	0.1
Manufacturing	37.4	35.1
Construction	14.9	1.3
Gas, electricity and water	1.3	0.5
Transport and communication	3.4	2.7
Distributive trades	14.7	26.0
Other services	22.0	33.3
All industries and services	100.0	100.0
OCCUPATION		
Management	0.9	0.2
Professional and related (excluding science)	0.6	1.6
Literary, artistic and sports	0.5	0.5
Professional and related in science	8.8	0.6
Clerical and related	5.0	32.9
Selling	6.2	18.2
Security and protective services	4.0	0.3
Catering, cleaning, hairdressing and other personal services	3.4	12.5
Farming, fishing and related	4.9	1.4
Material processing, making, repairing and related	37.6	17.8
Painting, repetitive assembling, product inspecting, packaging and related	4.9	7.7
Construction, mining and related	8.2	0.2
Transport operating, materials moving/storing and related	6.1	0.5
Miscellaneous	8.9	3.6
All occupations	100.0	100.0[a]

Note: Sample numbers were: 19,286 males, 13,896 females.

[a] Throughout, percentages are subject to rounding errors.

Source: *Department of Employment Gazette* (1982b, pp. 117 and 119).

important for both genders, though construction was for males only. With regard to occupational patterns, clerical was the most important for females and material processing for males (though only about a third in each case entered those job types); sales and catering/cleaning/hairdressing were important for females but not for males; material processing was important for females also but not to the same extent as for males. Moreover, young males gained more opportunities for skill acquisition than young females. For 16/17-year-old labour market entrants in 1979, 31 per cent of males and 42 per cent of females received no training at all, while 36 per cent of males and 6 per cent of females were in positions which offered over two years of training (*Department of Employment Gazette*, 1982b).

The 16-year-old early school-leavers of 1979, however, formed the last cohort which experienced such job opportunity in the twentieth century. Over the next two years, unemployment in Britain increased at a much higher rate than previously. Using January figures for Great Britain, total unemployment rates doubled. Youth unemployment

Table 3.2 *Change in unemployment rates in Britain, 1979–82*

Category	January 1979 (%)	January 1982 (%)
All males	7.1	15.3
All females	4.2	8.8
Males under 18 years old	10.8	23.1
Females under 18 years old	12.0	22.0

Source: Department of Employment (DE) Gazette (1983, p. s59).

rates, which were considerably higher, also doubled (see Table 3.2). Hart (1988) reported that between 1951 and 1981 unemployment rates for young people under 18 years increased from about 1 per cent to about 25 per cent and that about half of this increase occurred during the final two years. Moreover, between 1979 and 1981, unemployment for 16–19-year-olds nearly trebled to reach 23.8 per cent for males and 21.2 per cent for unmarried females, while it doubled to 30.5 per cent for married women (Labour Force Survey, 1979, 1981). With reference to race, where official figures are only available for all labour market participants, by 1981 unemployment estimates for non-whites were double those for whites.[2]

London in 1979–81

The survey was carried out in London, in the three inner city areas of Tower Hamlets, Hammersmith, and Lambeth, and the two outer areas, Hounslow and Bromley. The capital city had been prosperous relative to Britain in general in the post-war years. However, it was claimed that 1979 was 'the last good year for London' (MSC, 1982d). In Greater London, the numbers of school-leavers registered as unemployed more

Table 3.3 *Changes in unemployment and vacancies in London, 1979–81*

Numbers of London school-leavers unemployed	
September 1979	7475
September 1980	15,490
September 1981	24,039
Vacancies at London careers offices: average monthly stock	
1979	9343
1981	1427

Source: MSC (1982a)

than trebled over two years (MSC, 1982a) (see Table 3.3). Moreover, the numbers of young people (16–19) unemployed as a proportion of total unemployment in London also rose: from 15 per cent in October 1979 to 20 per cent in October 1981. Vacancies at London careers offices fell dramatically throughout the same period (see Table 3.3). The average monthly stock of vacancies in 1979 was nearly 10,000 but by 1981 it was under 1500, or less than a sixth of this (MSC, 1982a). A complete set of borough figures was not produced in 1979 but the London Labour Market Review (MSC, 1981) reported that rates of unemployment in inner London, especially in the east (including Tower Hamlets), were nearly twice as high as outer London. The London Employment Review (MSC, 1984) explicitly maintained that unemployment in the Greater London Council area was worst in Tower Hamlets and Lambeth, two of the inner-city areas in the survey.

Nevertheless, there were still many employment opportunities for young people in London in these years. Buck and Gordon (1986) reported that London had traditionally provided major entry points for young people in a wide range of white-collar jobs and in the lower stratum of the service industry. They claimed that both these types of job were over-represented in inner London. According to a Manpower Intelligence Unit Report, approximately one-fifth of Great Britain's total services employment at the time of the survey was based in the West End and the City of London and those parts of Camden, Islington, Lambeth and Southwark which border on central London. Westminster, for example, employed over half a million people, and like the City offered office jobs in insurance, banking and public administration and also typical youth work in hotels, restaurants, entertainment and shops. New construction opportunities in Dockland were becoming available in 1979 (MSC, 1981). With regard to manufacturing, the London Employment Review (MSC, 1984) reported that the decline of several traditional industries in the East End – docks, engineering, clothing and paper – had been offset by the rise of the new light engineering and electronics industries of the outer areas, especially West London. It also maintained that Hounslow was not only part of this West London complex, but also contained a flourishing service industry in the airport at Heathrow, connected services and resultant communications networks (MSC, 1984). A Manpower Services Briefing Note (MSC, 1982b) maintained that with regard to thriving and diverse manufacturing and service industries, Hounslow had no equal among London boroughs.

London school-leavers, however, faced strong competition from other workers. A relatively high proportion of adult unemployed in inner London had few skills (MSC, 1984). Certainly, large sectors of cheap state housing in the inner city made it attractive to low-paid, unskilled workers or those on benefits, and hindered relocation elsewhere (GLC, 1980). Moreoever, Buck and Gordon (1986) reported that the relative availability of work in London had attracted young workers from outside the region. Although between 1961 and 1981 the population of inner London fell by 28.5 per cent, from 3.5 million to 2.5 million, this trend concealed large movements both in and out, and the only age group to demonstrate a net inward movement was the

15–24-year-old group. Some entered higher education but others were from the provinces, looking for jobs in competition with local school-leavers (MSC, 1984).

Finally, the high cost of commuting might have provided a problem for relatively low-waged school-leavers, so young people in each borough faced competition from adults more able and willing than they to commute within the London area and from residents of areas outside London. For adults, there is ample evidence to suggest that London, with its vast commuter transport systems, not just in the inner city but to the outskirts and further, is one single labour market. An MSC report claimed that more people in employment in London worked outside their borough of residence than worked inside it. The small City of London had less than 5000 residents but over 300,000 jobs. Over a third of London jobs were in central London. Commuting was particularly high from outer boroughs with large residential populations and good communications to central London. Up to 15 per cent of jobs in London were taken by non-London residents (MSC, 1984).

With regard to race, the majority (about three-fifths) of the economically active population of England of minority ethnic origin lived in the South-East, and mainly in London (NDHS, 1978). According to Landau (1983), in 1979 the population in the Greater London area consisted of 82.8 per cent whites, 3.3 per cent West Indian/Guyanan, 1.1 per cent African, 3.6 per cent Indian and 0.9 per cent Pakistani/Bangladeshi, giving a total of 8.9 per cent non-whites.[3] These ethnic groups were concentrated in a small number of boroughs. Over half of West Indians and Africans were dispersed throughout south London, including Lambeth. Over 75 per cent of Asians lived in outer London, in the cheap housing areas of north-west London and Hounslow (NDHS, 1978). Unemployment figures are available for Greater London in 1979, and demonstrate ethnic differences: Landau (1983) estimated that while the unemployment rate for whites (of all ages) was 3.3 per cent, for West Indians/Guyanans it was 11.3 per cent, for Africans 10.1 per cent, for Pakistanis and Bangladeshis 6.1 per cent and for Indians 4.9 per cent. However, the rates capture the age factor as well as ethnicity (see Chapter 2) so they must be interpreted carefully.

The Data

The panel data-set consisted of a survey of a single cohort of white and non-white 16-year-old London school-leavers, males and females. It was conducted by professional interviewers from Social and Community Planning Research and took place in five stages over the period March 1979 to December 1981. The population from which the sample was taken comprised fifth-form pupils of early school-leavers from state-maintained schools (except for special schools) in three inner-London boroughs – Tower Hamlets, Hammersmith and Lambeth – and two

Table 3.4 *Borough of residence of interviewees in survey*

Location	Males	Females	All
Inner city			
Tower Hamlets	195 (21%)	194 (26%)	389 (23%)
Hammersmith	134 (15%)	118 (16%)	252 (15%)
Lambeth	192 (21%)	142 (19%)	334 (20%)
Sub total	521 (57%)	454 (60%)	975 (58%)
Outer city			
Hounslow	258 (29%)	172 (23%)	430 (26%)
Bromley	131 (14%)	133 (18%)	264 (16%)
Sub total	389 (43%)	305 (40%)	694 (42%)
Total	910	759	1669[a]

[a] Throughout, any figure less than the 1672 of the sample total is a result of missing data problems.

† Any discrepancies in numbers throughout the text are a result of missing data problems.

outer London boroughs – Hounslow and Bromley (see Table 3.4).

Excluded were those known to be leaving at Easter or returning to school. The Department of the Environment sent a letter to all head-teachers asking them to list eligible pupils. This constituted the sampling frame. The sampling procedure was as follows. First, the lists for each school within a borough were ordered geographically and the names sorted into separate lists for males and females. Second, a systematic random sample was selected from each list so compiled by taking a random start number and a fixed interval to generate the required number of individuals of each gender in each area. This procedure yielded a total of 8066 names. The target sample was 250 of each sex for each borough. Of this total, 1922 agreed to take part, but there were no statistical differences between borough representation rates.

Some of the young people, after leaving school initially, decided to return, and they were excluded from the investigation. For the most part, this was a working-class sample (see Table 3.4): of the 1672 who remained, there were 1604 parents who provided a head of household occupation; 67 per cent came from homes where the head of household was a manual worker,[4] and the largest group, 44 per cent,

Table 3.5 *Occupation of head of household*

Occupation	
Managerial/professional	289 (18%)
Other non-manual	242 (15%)
Skilled manual	368 (23%)
Semi-skilled/unskilled manual	705 (44%)
Total	1604

comprised children of unskilled workers (see Table 3.5). In fact, lower socio-economic backgrounds will clearly form a relatively large proportion of the 16-year-old school-leaver population. In 1980 'over half of those whose fathers worked in professional or managerial occupations remained in full-time education beyond the minimum leaving age compared with less than a third of those whose fathers worked in manual occupations' (*Social Trends*, 1981, p. 62). For the most part, males and females demonstrated significantly different attitudes to the labour market (see Table 3.6).

A large majority of males wanted skilled manual work. Female tastes were more varied though over half sought clerical work. When they gained work, the females were concentrated into three occupations: shop assistants, clerks and typists. The males tended to become manual workers: motor mechanics, construction workers, assembly workers and general labourers.

Table 3.6 *Ideally, what kind of job would you like to do when you leave school?*

Job category	Males	Females
Skilled manual	732 (81%)	129 (17%)
Unskilled manual	35 (4%)	35 (5%)
Clerical	73 (8%)	435 (57%)
Other non-manual	51 (6%)	140 (18%)
Don't know	18 (2%)	22 (3%)
Total	909	761

At the start of the survey, non-whites comprised about 15 per cent of the sample and so were highly over-represented for London. This was even more the case for Britain in general where they only formed 5.9 per cent of the total population (NDHS, 1978). However, the West Indian population of Britain had a high proportion of young people (see Chapter 2) so the survey sample is likely to be representative of black youth in London at that time. Nevertheless, the Asian group may well be under-represented as it formed the largest ethnic minority group in London at that time (NDHS, 1978) (see table 3.7).

Table 3.7 *Ethnicity of interviewees*

Ethnic group	Males	Females	All
White	739 (82%)	673 (89%)	1411 (85%)
Black	128 (14%)	51 (7%)	179 (11%)
Indian subcontinent	25 (3%)	18 (2%)	43 (3%)
Oriental	0 (-)	3 (-)	3 (-)
Other	13 (1%)	12 (2%)	25 (2%)
Total	904	757	1662

Sixteen per cent of those who entered the labour market did not find work immediately they left school. This is similar to official figures for London for 1979, though higher than national rates.

Five interviews were conducted, each in the young person's home, and carried out by the survey staff of Social and Community Planning Research. The first interview took place with the parents; the remainder with the school-leaver. They occurred at the following times: March 1979 (parent and child); March 1979 (child); July 1979; March/April 1980; November 1980; and November/December 1981. The drop-out

Table 3.8 *Response rates (cumulative)*

Ethnic group	*	July 1979 (Base year: 100%)	March/April 1980	Nov/Dec 1980	Dec 1980/ Jan 1981
Asian	m	25	19 (76%)	17 (68%)	13 (52%)
	f	18	15 (83%)	13 (72%)	11 (61%)
	all	43	34 (79%)	30 (70%)	24 (56%)
Black	m	128	108 (84%)	104 (81%)	83 (65%)
	f	51	44 (86%)	35 (69%)	23 (45%)
	all	179	152 (85%)	139 (78%)	106 (59%)
White	m	739	642 (87%)	617 (83%)	548 (74%)
	f	673	588 (87%)	540 (86%)	467 (69%)
	all	1412	1230 (87%)	1157 (82%)	1015
Other	m	13	12 (92%)	11 (85%)	8 (62%)
	f	15	12 (80%)	12 (80%)	9 (60%)
	all	28	24 (86%)	23 (82%)	17 (61%)
Total	m	910	786 (86%)	754 (83%)	656 (72%)
	f	762	664 (87%)	605 (79%)	513 (67%)
	all	1672	1450 (87%)	1359 (81%)	1169 (70%)

* Number of respondents: m = male, f = female.

rate was as follows (see Table 3.8): white response rates decreased by 13, 18 and 28 per cent (cumulative rates); blacks by 15, 22 and 41 per cent; and Asians by 21, 30 and 44 per cent. The decline in response rates is important and needs comment. There were no significant differences in drop-outs from the beginning of the survey figures between genders or ethnic groupings until November 1980, when significantly more (p < 0.01) white women relative to black women continued to respond. By the following year (November/December 1981), there were a number of differences. The following groups were more likely to respond: white women relative to black women (p < 0.005); white men relative to black men (p < 0.05); white men relative to Asian men (p < 0.05); and, most interestingly, black men relative to black women (p < 0.05). These figures probably partly reflect their employment status of each particular group at the end of the survey as the unemployed were less likely to respond.

In general the sample is representative of London early school-leavers in the years 1979–81. (See Richardson, 1983, for a discussion of the representativeness of the full sample.) It is also representative of Britain except for two characteristics: youth unemployment was higher and blacks were over-represented. These features, however, can be seen as strengths in a situation where youth unemployment and the labour market disadvantage of racial minorities were both increasing.

In summary, the characteristics of the data made it possible to investigate a single cohort, all of the same age and the same educational background, who left school at the same time, were from the same socio-economic group, had access to one large labour market, and possessed no initial skill label.

Method of Investigation

For the most part, particular issues are investigated by the use of logit analysis, although ordinary least squares analysis is employed where appropriate. The richness of the data-set means that simple patterns are best observed by such techniques. The findings, however, will be discussed in close relation to the theory and context, and the material presented in an accessible form.

Logit analysis has been used because, for the most part, each dependent variable, or feature to be explained, is in dichotomous form: for example, to be employed or not employed. The independent or explanatory variables are items taken from the data-set which proxy aspects of a general model of causation: for example, traits like race or sex. The impact of each of these on the probability, say, of being employed or not, is measured, controlling for (or taking account of) all the other proxies or variables in the model.[5] Unless stated to the contrary, the variables are dichotomous, usually based on a positive response to a question (1) or otherwise (0). The questions are taken directly from the survey questionnaires. In order to simplify the presentation, the variables are described fully in the Data Dictionary in Appendix 2. For purposes of clarity, the prediction regarding each result, in terms of the expected direction of the relationship between the dependent and the independent variables, is recorded in parenthesis after the description of each explanatory variable for every model. Predictions are made with a formal 'ceteris paribus' assumption which, for the sake of readability, is not explicitly stated.

Following Clark and Summers (1982), Richardson (1983) and Lynch (1985, 1987), the term 'unemployment' will be used to embrace the state of being without work. In most instances, information regarding unemployment registration was not available. In any case, school-leavers accustomed to parental support might not bother to register in the early stages. Moreover, there was a concern to capture the 'out-of-work' rather than the technically unemployed. This book is concerned with youth in the workplace so, for the most part, neither the unemployed nor those who undertook training schemes are the objects of analysis. Lynch and Richardson (1982) and Lynch (1985, 1987) undertook in-depth studies of the unemployed in this data-set, and reference will be made to those findings.

Notes

1 Terms used to describe racial groups and males/females must be used carefully. In the British literature, the term 'black' is often used to refer to all groups, including Africans, Caribbeans and Asians from the Indian sub-continent, who might define themselves in this way. However, the survey provided mutually exclusive categories of identification, consisting of white, black, Asian, Oriental and other. Consequently, to avoid confusion, the term 'black' will be employed to refer to those who are likely to have categorized themselves in such a way: mainly those of West Indian/Guyanan (Caribbean) and African origin. The terms 'West Indians', 'Africans', 'Asians', etc., will refer to those of that origin, whether born in the UK or not. Most blacks, in fact, are likely to be of West Indian origin because they formed the largest proportion of the black population in London at that time (NDHS, 1978; Landau, 1983). The terms 'non-whites' and 'ethnic minorities' will refer to all of those groups who do not classify themselves as

white. The term 'immigrants' will refer to all those not born in the UK. When reporting empirical work, the definitions of the relevant author will be used.

With regard to males and females the term 'sex' refers to biological differences whereas 'gender' refers to the manner in which cultures define or constrain such differences (Siann, 1994). Thus, in general, 'gender' will be used regarding labour market identity. In the regressions, following Lightbody and Durndell (1996), 'the independent variable "sex" always refers to the biological sex of the subjects and the ascribed sex/gender of a hypothetical individual' (p. 134).

2 17.2 per cent of non-white males and 15.8 per cent of non-white females were unemployed, compared to 9.7 per cent and 8.7 per cent respectively for their white counterparts (*Labour Force Survey*, 1981), but figures for non-whites included more young people, whose unemployment rates were higher than those of adults.

3 The rest were 'Don't know' or 'No response'.

4 The occupational categories developed by Stern (1981) specifically for this data-set, and used in all the studies generated from it (e.g. Lynch and Richardson, 1982; Lynch 1985, 1987), were employed to determine the socio-economic status of the head of household. The first interview, in March 1979, was carried out with the parents or guardians, who were asked 'Who is the head of the household?' In 81% of the cases, the answer supplied was the father. There was no specific information about the occupation of the mother. However, only 29 per cent of the mothers held full-time jobs while 41 per cent held part-time jobs and 25 per cent did not work outside the home. Thus, in most cases the primary wage-earner held a manual occupation.

5 For a more technical account see Appendix 1.

4 Jobs, Apprenticeships and Wages

It has been demonstrated that, in the post-war period in Britain, the youth labour market did not consist wholly of unskilled work, but also provided training opportunities for young people. The existence of a hierarchy of jobs, with a wide range of school-leavers chasing them in a situation of increasing unemployment, means that a matching process must occur where employees seek the jobs they value most highly, and employers seek the most appropriate workers. If all jobs are not homogeneous and some are gained by purposeful search, then a rational pattern of causation will be apparent. The aim of this chapter is to identify a mature process of search on the part of early school-leavers in a situation of labour market heterogeneity.

Two investigations will be made about jobs, one concerned with gaining work of any kind, the second with gaining a job with general training opportunities. If there is a hierarchy , with unemployment at the bottom, unskilled work above joblessness and skill or career opportunity at the top, then a similar pattern is expected in both sets of results. Those who are unsuccessful will be pushed down the queue, and squeezed out into unemployment. A third investigation deals with determinants of income levels in the first job. Wage results should reflect any heterogeneity of job and individual characteristics and thereby denote the availability of ports of entry to longer term work.

Literature Review

There were several important studies of labour market entry for youth in Britain in the pre-Thatcher decades (Carter, 1962, 1966; Maizels, 1965, 1970; Roberts, 1968, 1984; Ashton, 1973; Brannen, 1975; Willis, 1977; Thomas, 1979; Clarke, 1980a; Ashton *et al.*, 1982; Dex, 1982; MSC, 1982a; West and Newton, 1982). However, many of the studies are empirical and therefore unconcerned with the provision of a theoretical base,[1] and there have been very few works which have focused on the direct move from school to work.

Nevertheless, there are several distinct theoretical viewpoints in the literature which can be applied to early school-leaver experience. The early work was carried out in an era of job availability and consequently was focused on the determinants of gaining different job types. The important occupational choice[2] literature, which developed in the USA in the 1950s (Ginzberg, 1951; Ginsburg, *et al.*, 1951; Super, 1957), lent itself easily to socialization arguments because choice was based on self-concepts which are not purely subjective, but develop out of a person's experiences within objective structures (Ginzberg *et al.*, 1951). Blau and Duncan (1967), for example, in their seminal work, claimed that occupational success was the outcome of a lifelong process in which 'ascribed status at birth' (p. 20) was one of the fundamental components.

There is a widely recognized association between the occupation of parents and those of children (e.g. Goldthorpe and Llewellyn, 1977), and most British work on occupational choice developed this theme. Most studies were concerned with the reproduction of the status quo, stressing the continuity of experience from school to the workplace in terms of social class. Choice was the result of socialization processes which took place prior to starting work, whereby young people replicated the values embodied in their home and school experience, prompting Roberts (1968), in fact, to proclaim the term a misnomer. For example, Ashton and Field (1976) claimed that choice was derived from the initial frame of reference of family and school which directs the school-leaver to different bands of occupations. They argued that it is through their experiences within these social structures that young people gain impressions of the opportunities available to themselves in the labour market. Thus, the overall result was smoothness and continuity of experience through the home, the school, and work.

Some writers saw this continuity of experience as deliberately engineered to reproduce the existing social order. Bowles and Gintis (1976), in a US work, argued that there was an almost perfect symmetry between socialization at school and accommodation to work. Bordieu and Passeron (1977) claimed that this was because the education system maintained the hegemony of the upper middle class in society by equipping it with 'cultural capital'. This took the form of socially ratified instrumental knowledge in a system which made the school experience alienating to out-groups, especially the working class and non-whites.

Most of the theory, especially the US work, is concerned with the entire range of youth and it is unsurprising that a wide range of occupational outcomes can be linked with broad definitions of social class. However, the character of manual jobs and the narrower range of divisions within them posed difficulties for theorists. Roberts (1975) suggested that occupational choice literature was not applicable to the kinds of jobs taken up by working-class youth because the career of the typical industrial worker could hardly be seen as the opportunity for self-actualization or the implementation of a self-concept. Nevertheless, he insisted there were important subdivisions within working-class jobs in which occupational outcome was a result, not of choice, but of socialization processes which took place prior to leaving school (Roberts, 1968). Following this theme, Ashton and Field (1976) proposed that the career outcome of working-class youth was a result of the replication of the values embodied in their home and school experience. As a consequence, upwardly aspiring manual youth headed for short-term manual careers via apprenticeship or clerical training and the 'rough' headed towards unskilled labouring jobs.

There is one important British work, however, which is concerned with early school-leavers, whose crucial theme is the contradiction of the existence of differences in manual working-class work: the assertion of homogeneity. Willis (1977), in a British study based firmly within the class tradition, also emphasized continuities between school and work. Yet, despite the subtitle of the work, which asserts that 'working class kids get working class jobs', it is a very different kind of continuity, presented within a theme of control and resistance in the context of deskilled work. Some of his arguments may now be thought of as romantic, nevertheless the case-study work gives a convincing flavour of the boredom that can be experienced at school and the manual workplace that is absent from abstract quantitative empirical work. Thus, from this viewpoint alone, it deserves serious consideration.

Essentially, this work does not emerge from the tradition of choice and socialization so the link between home and work is not apparent. Clearly, then the school is not seen as any kind of sifting or sorting agent as a means of reproducing the status quo by the allocation of 'appropriate' levels of qualifications to different social groups. Instead, Willis presents the school as an analogy of the workplace. The continuities of experiences depend on the similarities of the features of the respective institutions and the participants' reactions to them. The crucial basis of his argument is that all manual work, skilled and unskilled alike, is homogeneous and alienating. Consequently, knowledge, in the form of examination passes, does not lead to satisfying work. Therefore, teachers offer an unfair exchange of knowledge in return for respect and control. In Willis's study, most pupils were unaware of this and consented to the exchange, but some schoolchildren resisted this teacher control and won a 'space' from the school in which to practise their 'diversions'. They took little interest in schoolwork, examinations and job search activities, rejecting teacher and vocational advice. Thus, they gained unskilled jobs, often by chance.

Those who did realize they were offered an unfair exchange at school did so because they possessed a class-based 'penetration' of the nature of manual labour. However, their insight led them to 'limitations' because they were imprisoned in jobs with no future as they possessed no examination qualifications. Nevertheless, they coped with the boredom and harshness of the workplace better than their peers whose expectations were higher and disappointment correspondingly greater. This is because, in the context of the unfair exchange between capital and labour at the workplace, their diversions became a way of dealing with the same kind of boredom they experienced at school. For these pupils then, the school was the 'site' of a different kind of learning than that envisaged by teachers.

Continuities are said to be apparent in both school and workplace in the form of the boring nature of work, the unfair exchange, and the method of resistance by diversions. The function of the school seems merely to be to extract respect and control as ends in themselves, so the response of diversionary tactics is a product of a failure to elicit these features, a fortuitous by-product for the 'lads'. These arguments do not rest easily within Marxist notions of hegemony, and there are some internal inconsistencies (such as the claim of the limitations of not having exam passes in a homogeneous world). Moreover, the determinants of 'class-based' penetration are not explored. Nevertheless, the empirical work is a unique account of early school-leaver attitudes before and after initial entry to the labour market.

In his empirical study, Willis surveyed several small groups of British male early school-leavers in the same town in the Midlands in the early 1970s. The main case study concerned twelve non-conformist, i.e. anti-authoritarian, non-academic boys who attended a single-sex working-class secondary modern school in the middle of a council estate which was built between the two world wars: a school with a good reputation.[3] His methods of enquiry involved techniques of formal and informal observation and participant observation, regular group discussions and personal interviews. The studies were carried out simultaneously during the last five terms of school attendance and the first twelve months of work. The major concern of the studies lay in eliciting the attitudes and personal experience of the youths themselves, but interviews were also conducted with teachers, career officers, parents, managers, foremen and shop stewards. Willis's main finding was that conformists in school gained skilled work, while the anti-authoritarian youths were likely to gain unskilled or semi-skilled work, often by accident and without purposeful job search.

The problem with the findings is that they do not unequivocally support his explanations. Disruption at school amongst most 15-year-old low-achievers seems unlikely to be the result of political foresight about workplace alienation and the mental/manual split. The non-conformists numbered among them some of the bored and least able who were likely to be unsuccessful in exams. A more intuitive interpretation of his nonetheless compelling empirical account is that these young people were disruptive both at school and work because they were not achieving. They may well form a maverick group, unstable by proclivity, who displayed purposeless behaviour both at school and work.

In summary, most of the studies on labour market entry assumed a heterogeneity of job opportunities because they were concerned with the entire range of young adults. Some British authors suggested that there was variety among manual occupations. Willis's work, however, suggests the reverse. It deals with male early school-leavers and claims that those who take up manual jobs only have unskilled, homogeneous work available to them, no matter what the skill title.

However, regardless of assumptions about types of jobs available to working-class youth, there is an important problem with most of the studies concerning initial labour market entry. The possibility of not gaining work at all was rarely considered. This is because these models were constructed at a time when levels of unemployment were such that young people's expectations could be translated into jobs more easily than in recent times (Furlong, 1987). In a context when unemployment was beginning a steady rise, Roberts (1975) pointed out the limitations of the literature on choice. He claimed that working-class individuals rarely choose jobs but take what is available, so local opportunities and their own educational qualifications were more important than their aims.

Unsurprisingly, demand factors, employer selection of individuals by the use of screens and signals, and employee search for jobs in a situation of decreasing opportunity became important factors as unemployment increased rapidly. Indeed, the search for employment *per se*, rather than occupational outcome, became one of the major foci of British empirical work after the 1970s (Makeham, 1980; Layard, 1982; Main and Raffe, 1983a, 1983b; Lynch, 1983, 1985, 1987; Richardson, 1983; Lynch and Richardson, 1982). In general, these studies utilized a market forces approach via the mechanisms of a search process. The model on labour market entry will attempt to utilize this framework to embrace the relevant aspects of the choice and socialization literature, in the context of increasing unemployment, in order to investigate employment outcomes generally. In doing so, it will take account of any heterogeneity apparent in both individuals and in jobs. This approach does not challenge the conventional view of the youth labour market as offering many low-skill jobs, but suggests that some entry ports to longer-term work were apparent in Britain at the end of the 1970s.

Investigations

The aim of these investigations is to examine the existence of purposeful job search and a matching process. This will be carried out by investigating the determinants, first, of gaining a job and of gaining work with general training opportunity, and second, of wage differences in these jobs.

Gaining Work: The Model

If all available jobs are homogeneous and alienating and individuals are unconcerned about work, then jobs will be gained by accident as Willis (1977) argued. However, in a situation of heterogeneity, individuals compete with one another for scarce resources in the form of jobs generally, and of skilled jobs within that category. Two distinct groups will be considered: employers and job-seekers, who interact by means of a matching process for jobs generally, and within those, for jobs with training opportunities.

Job Characteristics

The demand for youth labour may differ from area to area, and because of youth's reliance on the parental home young workers may be restricted to local areas. In particular, beginning workers cannot afford independent flats, houses or a car (Roberts, 1984). They may rely on the financial 'home subsidy' offered by living at home (Casson, 1979) and they may also still need the psychological support of parental care: Bradshaw *et al.* (1987) reported that 90 per cent of teenage workers were unmarried and lived at home. In London, the cost of commuting by public transport might have provided a problem for relatively low-wage school-leavers. At the initial interview in summer 1979, the young people were asked how much time they already spent travelling or were

Table 4.1 *Commuting times. How long a journey to your job from home do you travel/would you be prepared to travel?*

Journey time	Males	Females	All
Up to 15 mins	259 (37%)	174 (29%)	433 (34%)
16 to 30 mins	249 (36%)	225 (38%)	474 (37%)
31 to 45 mins	117 (17%)	108 (18%)	225 (18%)
46 to 60 mins	48 (7%)	60 (10%)	108 (8%)
61 to 90 mins	25 (4%)	24 (4%)	49 (4%)
Total	698	591	1289

prepared to spend to travel to work (see Table 4.1). Only about a third of the young people at the outset of the surveys regarded London as a single labour market, as travelling time even between the inner areas and the outermost boroughs was likely to exceed an hour in peak times, even in 1979. The majority (two-thirds) were only willing to travel for up to half an hour. As almost all of them (99 per cent) lived at home, they were restricted to local labour markets in which adult commuters could compete with them for jobs.

From the figures in Table 3.1 and the discussion in Chapter 2, it emerges that most of the industries and occupations in England and Wales that recruited young people in 1979 were relatively more available in central London as a whole than in any single area of outer London. The City and West End provided more work for the school-leavers from each of the inner-city areas than either of the suburbs could provide for their respective young residents. Jobs which offered apprenticeships in the traditional areas of manufacturing and engineering were also located in the inner areas and were more quickly and conveniently accessible to inner-city than to outer-city residents.

Employee Characteristics

In 1979, most young people left school at 16 and individuals from such a wide range of an age cohort have different aptitudes and tastes. These characteristics can be used by employers to distinguish between individuals. If some firms have a range of different opportunities available, then a rational employer seeks workers considered to be most appropriate to the organization, i.e. workers who will contribute the highest marginal revenue product of which ability, effort, and attitude are sources. However, Spence (1973) maintained that hiring is an investment for the employer, which takes place under conditions of uncertainty. In particular, the main problem for employers is to find adequate proxies to signify the presence of these characteristics. Thus, they build up a system of signals and indices by which they relate observable traits to what they believe to be productivity potential.

Signals are traits subject to manipulation by the individual, for example, a qualification which recognizes ability and effort. Examinations are particularly important for employers of school-leavers because there are no previous full-time work records and therefore no skill label. Moreover, national exams are a uniform measurement of work productivity potential. A contemporary survey (Gordon, 1984) reported that most employers of school-leavers recruited on the basis of 'exams to be taken' because exam results are not announced until after the end of the school year (August), i.e. after many of these youngsters were questioned about job offers and acceptance decisions. However, many jobs available to school-leavers may merely involve a capacity to understand and follow instructions so some employers might use informal and subjective measures, perhaps by making judgements of the suitability of the applicant by means of interview techniques. In fact, when questioned, 87 per cent of those who gained a job in this data-set said they had been interviewed.

Indices are traits which cannot be altered by the individual, such as skin colour and sex. Regardless of whether jobs are dead-end or not, the exercise of prejudiced tastes by employers (Becker, 1971) may result in discrimination. Firms might carry out such recruitment policies because either managers are prejudiced or they feel that their existing employees or potential customers are prejudiced. If the law were not wholly effective, then non-whites would be at the lower end of queues for work, in terms of both skilled jobs and employment in general. However, this argument is not really relevant with regard to gender because young males and females wanted jobs for the most part in different occupations.

The range of employee characteristics do not merely act as signals and indices to employers in their quest for appropriate workers, but cause employees to direct their own search for certain types of work. They want occupations on the basis of personal tastes and relative incomes in those occupations (Robertson and Symons, 1990). For example, some may have a deep preference for a certain type of job or income level for which they are prepared to wait. Certainly, most of the males in the sample were looking for skilled manual work. Thus, as in 1979 unemployment was increasing and training opportunities were decreasing, those school-leavers who were prepared to settle for any kind of job might have been more successful in obtaining work in general, but less successful in obtaining skilled relative to unskilled work. However, there is no doubt that some youths would display an uncommitted attitude to work or a taste for unemployment of some duration.

Theory suggests that socialization processes are important factors which help to direct young people in their choice of occupation or employment status. Much of the literature which dealt with the work-place destination of youth was concerned with the reproduction of the status quo. However, few studies dealt directly with early school-leavers and a largely working-class sample. Willis (1977) reported that the anti-authoritarian – those who perceived the reality of the workplace – were more likely to gain unskilled work, or in this context, fail to find any job. Roberts (1968) and Ashton and Field (1976) suggested that there were divisions within the working class which meant that those from unskilled backgrounds would be more likely to take up unskilled work, or in the context of the late 1970s, fail to find work at all. In a context of persisting unemployment, those from households with unemployed parents or members were likely to have lower expectations of obtaining any work.

Matching Process: Search and Information

If there is a range of both jobs and searchers, a matching process must occur because individuals and employers operate with imperfect knowledge. The matching of workers to jobs and organizations is carried out by a joint process of search and information-gathering. In the context of high unemployment, most search with regard to the unskilled is carried out by prospective employees. In the economics literature, job search is said to incur the cost of gaining information, thus providing capital, the investment in which leads an individual to a higher wage than would be apparent in its absence (Stigler, 1962). The main idea was that individuals searched sequentially for jobs, choosing the one which offered the highest wage.[4] In fact, people look for jobs rather than consider a set of wage levels, especially in a situation of unemployment, and the latest literature takes this into account (e.g. Van den Berg, 1990). If some school-leavers carry out purposeful search, nevertheless the process for youth is constrained in several ways. Young people with no direct full-time work experience and relatively few friends in work might best obtain jobs through contacts, for example through working relatives, or through encouragement and information. Moreover, the financial resources of school-leavers are relatively limited, and both the length and quality of job search may be determined by family need or parental priorities. Professional advice from school or careers guidance would probably be helpful. However, some may have more information than others: perhaps they worry about unemployment, or have had direct experience of the workplace through part-time or voluntary work while at school. Thus, young people's knowledge and expectations are likely to be affected by external factors such as the home, school or peers. The socialization factors which influence their expectations are also likely to influence the information, contacts and resources available to them in their search for jobs, skilled or otherwise.

Gaining a Job: Empirical Work

Of the 1672 individuals who were considered at this stage, 1403 (84 per cent) gained work. Of the latter, there were 1223 (87 per cent) white, 121 (9 per cent) black and 26 (2 per cent) Asian; 630 (45 per cent) were female and 771 male; of those who responded to the question, 351 males (45 per cent) gained apprenticeships and 89 per cent of male apprentices were white.

The data-set provided specific details about how the school-leavers found work (see Table 4.2). The largest group, albeit a minority (40 per cent), claimed to have found work through a relative or friend. Only 12 per cent heard through a parent, though, unsurprisingly, for males relative to females, the father was significantly more likely to have been the means of finding work. The school was the second largest source of jobs for both males and females (34 per cent and 25 per cent, respectively). Employment agencies and advertisements were sources of jobs for only a minority. Part-time jobs while at school were significantly more important as a method of finding full-time work for females relative to males. For purposes of analysis, however, this information, though it can provide clues, is incomplete. This is because those who did not find work may have had access to similar assistance. Moreover, for this cohort type in the context of a time of rapidly increasing unemployment, any job decision was likely to have been a result of employer choice, perhaps based on other characteristics which must be taken into account in a model or set of theory. Consequently, a formal model must be set up to include variables apparent in the data-set.

Dependent Variable: JOB

During the summer holidays, in July and August 1979, the school-leavers were asked:

Have you been offered a job which you are planning to take by the end of summer 1979 or have already started?[5]

Table 4.2 *Job information. How did you hear about the job you were offered?*

Source	Males	Females	All
Family and friends			
Father	72 (10%)	13 (2%)	85 (7%)
Mother	32 (5%)	24 (4%)	56 (4%)
Either parent	5 (1%)	5 (1%)	10 (1%)
Other relative	66 (9%)	49 (9%)	115 (9%)
Friend	117 (17%)	87 (16%)	204 (16%)
Introduction	23 (3%)	9 (2%)	32 (3%)
Total	315 (45%)	187 (34%)	502 (40%)
Newspapers			
Local newspaper	30 (4%)	39 (7%)	69 (5%)
National newspaper	10 (1%)	10 (2%)	20 (2%)
Trade newspaper	0 (-)	1 (-)	1 (-)
Newspaper	17 (2%)	14 (2%)	31 (2%)
Total	57 (8%)	64 (11%)	121 (10%)
School			
Careers teachers	2 (-)	9 (2%)	11 (1%)
Careers Officer	36 (5%)	21 (4%)	57 (4%)
School	201 (28%)	113 (20%)	314 (25%)
Total	239 (34%)	143 (26%)	382 (30%)
Search institutions			
Job centre	22 (3%)	17 (3%)	39 (3%)
Employment agency	29 (4%)	29 (5%)	58 (5%)
Total	51 (7%)	46 (8%)	97 (8%)
Workplace			
Card at work	9 (1%)	14 (2%)	23 (2%)
Part-time job	13 (2%)	81 (14%)	94 (7%)
Total	22 (3%)	95 (16%)	117 (9%)
Other	22 (3%)	27 (5%)	49 (4%)
Total	706	562	1268

Dependent Variable: APPRENTICESHIP
They were also asked:

Are you/will you be an apprentice or are you/will you be on some other sort of training scheme that leads to a certificate or qualification?

This second enquiry was restricted to males because male apprenticeships are a clearly identifiable form of training in Britain with recognized qualifications. Further, by examining young men only, it was possible to see if some of Willis's results could be reproduced. Most important, though, in preliminary investigations it proved impossible to find meaningful results when females were included or examined separately. This was an interesting finding in itself, suggesting that female training is heterogeneous as it is less readily identifiable by common employee characteristics.

Explanatory Variables
The explanatory variables were proxies apparent in the data-set for the strands of argument outlined in the model.

1. *Job characteristics*
AREA OF RESIDENCE: Inner- or outer-city residence (+)

2. *Individual characteristics*
EXAMS: GCE examinations (+)

COMPREHENSION: The professional survey interviewers were asked to make an assessment of whether the young person displayed a good understanding of the questions or otherwise (+)

TAKE ANY JOB: Would you take a job that wasn't really what you wanted, just so you would have a job? (+ JOB, - APPRENTICESHIP)

RACE: White or non-white (+)

SEX: Male or female (+)

3. *Socialization processes*
OCCUPATION: Occupation of head of household: managerial/ professional or other (including those who did not state an occupation) (+)

HOUSEHOLD UNEMPLOYMENT: Is anyone in your household currently unemployed? (-)

4. *Matching process*
WORRIED: Are you worried about being unemployed? (+)

PREVIOUS WORK: Have you ever done any part-time or voluntary work? (+)

PARENTAL HELP: Have you (the parent), or has anyone else here (i.e. in the home), done anything to help the young person get a job when he/she leaves school? (+)

ADVICE: Have you been given advice by school, careers guidance or government agencies? (+)

IDEAL SKILL: Ideally, what kind of job would you like to do? Skilled manual or otherwise? (for the APPRENTICESHIP model only, to capture and control for search efforts specifically directed towards skilled work) (+)

Gaining a JOB

Results
Six of the coefficients were significant (see Table 4.3): non-whites (RACE); inner-city residents (AREA); those from households which had recent experience of unemployment (HOUSEHOLD UNEMP.); those who did not receive help from parents (PARENTAL HELP) in looking for work; those who were unworried about being unemployed (WORRIED); and those who would rather wait for a worthwhile job (TAKE ANY JOB). Persons in these categories were all less likely to find a job on leaving school than their respective counterparts, other things being equal. (For analysis of employment chances separately by gender, see Lynch, 1983, 1985, 1987.)

Discussion
The results replicated many previous findings and gave confidence about the validity and representativeness of the data-set. They support the existence of a conventional labour market of low-skill, undifferentiated work (segregated by gender). Racial disadvantage was

apparent; socialization influences were important via household unemployment; and youth seemed to be restricted to local labour markets. Also, there was strong evidence of some purposeful job search. Certainly, these jobs were not gained by mere chance.

Several interesting points emerge. First, the coefficients on the ability proxies, exams and comprehension, proved to be insignificant, probably indicating the low level of jobs most of these young people would take up. These results can be explained by other contemporary findings. Gordon (1984) reported that half the employers questioned in his survey thought academic qualifications irrelevant when choosing school-leaver recruits, demanding only basic literacy and numeracy. Hunt and Small (1981) found that, when filling lower-level manual and office jobs, employers looked for the 'right attitude'. Similarly, Livock

Table 4.3 *Logit model: gaining work. Dependent variable: JOB*

Variable	Coefficient	Coeff./S.E.
EXAMS	0.30	1.76
COMPREHENSION	0.11	0.76
TAKE ANY JOB	0.35	2.41*
RACE	0.84	4.76**
SEX	0.15	1.01
AREA	-0.51	-3.11**
WORRIED	0.48	3.17**
PREVIOUS WORK	0.13	0.84
PARENTAL HELP	0.43	2.91**
HOUSEHOLD UNEMP.	-0.56	-3.78**
ADVICE	-0.37	-0.98
OCCUPATION	-0.04	-0.19
Constant	0.78	1.67

Pearson chi-square 1578.33   p 0.46
Number of cases 595†.

 * Denotes significance at 5% level.
** Denotes significance at 1% level.

(1983) from a survey of young people recruited in Hull and Huddersfield in 1979, concluded that the employers' assessment of personal qualities was a stronger factor than any other screening criteria in relation to unskilled and semi-skilled jobs.

Second, the sex and race results were interesting. The sex coefficient was insignificant in a situation of largely segregated occupations, supporting the crude male and female unemployment statistics. The race result, however, suggests that some employers used the cheap screen of race to differentiate between applicants in the same labour markets. The significant result was expected and supports previous findings.[6] Policy-makers often suggest that it is the relatively poor performance of non-whites in exams which accounts for their labour market disadvantage. Certainly, contemporary surveys reported that non-whites gained fewer examination successes than whites. The Swann Committee of Enquiry found that West Indians were five times less likely to obtain five or more GCE passes than whites. Asians, though more successful in exams than West Indians, were less so than whites (Swann Report, 1985). Sillitoe and Meltzer (1985) concluded that inadequate qualifications were one of the major causes of West Indian disadvantage. However, preliminary investigations in this survey demonstrated that the exams coefficient was significant only until the race dummy was introduced. That is, exams was capturing in part the effects of race. It is possible to verify this assertion: the full equation, excluding the race variable, was constructed for whites and non-whites separately. In all cases, the exams coefficient remained insignificant, suggesting that for this ability range of school-leaver, examination entrance was not a determinant of initial employment status within racial groupings.

These results have serious implications regarding some of the remedies for black disadvantage that were proposed at the time. For example, Gibson (1985) maintained that examination failure comes about partly because black school-children speak a different form of English from their teachers and that English should be taught only as a second language. The point is that this investigation, which introduces race and an examinations variable in the same model, implies that examinations *per se* are not important regarding getting a job immediately after leaving school at the age of 16.

The probability, in fact, is that some employers of youths used race as a group discriminator. Sillitoe and Meltzer (1985) examined two annual cohorts of West Indian school-leavers of 1971 and 1972, in

Greater London and Birmingham. They concluded that 'there can be little doubt that discriminatory recruitment practices were the major reason West Indians encountered especial difficulty in obtaining suitable employment' (p. 99). Lee and Wrench (1983), in a 1979 study, found that discriminatory practices by employers were not necessarily deliberate but because of 'word of mouth' recruitment. If there is discrimination, then the proposed policies regarding examinations are unlikely to be effective and in fact may have a detrimental effect.

Third, in view of the strength of the socialization literature, most surprisingly, the parental occupation variable was unimportant, even though it was reconstructed in several forms (e.g. skilled or otherwise, unskilled or otherwise, manual/non-manual); so were several other variables that were tried to capture a similar influence: number of children in family, number of boys, number of girls, solo parent, solo mother, solo father, foster-parent, grandparents as head of household. Yet despite the findings, it is highly likely that socio-economic origins in the nation as a whole are an important determinant of occupational choice/destination, but it is less clear that the narrow and often marginal distinctions of this sample will be valuable predictors.[7] Moreover, though solo parents and large families may be disadvantaged, so well may be other sections of the population, thus helping to bring about the respective insignificance of those coefficients. However, there was also an attempt to capture a direct financial influence by setting up a crude replacement ratio. Young people were asked how much money they were likely to be in receipt of each week while they were out of work, and a variable was constructed based on the response; but once again, the results were statistically indiscernible. In itself, this is an important finding as some policy-makers believed that a withdrawal of benefit might make young people more avid in their search efforts, and non-insurance benefits were withdrawn from under-18-year-olds in 1988. The rationale was certainly not empirically sustained in this data-set.

However, in a time of growing unemployment, a different variable might more aptly capture socialization influences: household unemployment was significant. Other studies carried out at the same time also found this to be an important factor. A Manpower Services Commission report (MSC, 1977) produced correlations: *c.* 14 per cent of unemployed young people said their fathers were also unemployed, 22 per cent had brothers or sisters unemployed, while 19 per cent were living in households where no-one was in full-time employment. The findings of Pahl's contemporaneous, exhaustive five-year study of households on the Isle of Sheppey (Pahl, 1984) also identified head of household unemployment as an important influence whereby there were fewer contacts and information for jobs for the rest of the family. Certainly, those young people who lived in families with current experience of unemployment would, in general, have less money and information, and fewer contacts. They may have been aware of associated depression and anxiety associated with lack of work, and this may lower their own job expectations. Thus, they were likely to be less optimistic and assertive regarding their own job search.

Pahl (1984) also considered a different influence. He suggested that, in the case of wives whose partners were unemployed, social welfare benefits acted as a disincentive to job search for other family members. Thus the variable could also have been partly capturing this feature. Respondents in the London survey were not asked directly about social welfare benefits but it was possible to calculate which heads of household were currently unemployed and had been so for longer than twelve months. All of these would have been eligible for benefit, providing no other member of the household was in receipt of income, including wages. A dummy was constructed based on the employed and those unemployed and eligible for receipt of social welfare payments (SOCWEF). However, the coefficients were insignificant. Once again, the impact of availability of finance when unemployed was not apparent. There was no evidence that youth in general was work-shy.

Fourth, local labour market arguments were supported: the area coefficient was significant. However, the sign on the coefficient was the reverse of that implied. This finding reflects similar results noted earlier in the decade regarding the disadvantage of inner-city residents in finding work (Metcalf and Richardson, 1974; Smith, 1975). To investigate this issue further, separate models were constructed, using each borough as a reference category in turn: at some time, each of the inner-city coefficients was negatively significant and the Hounslow coefficient was positively significant; the Bromley coefficient was never significant. Thus, each of the inner-city boroughs seemed to be disadvantaged and only Hounslow of the outer areas enjoyed an advantage.

Information was available on job location (see Table 4.4). It demonstrates that the majority of young people worked in or near their

Table 4.4 *Job location and place of residence*

Full sample: 1138 respondents	
Work and residence in same borough:	
Inner-city residents	298 (26%)
Outer-city residents	380 (33%)
Sub-sample: 648 respondents (included in the above figures)	
Work and residence in same borough:	
Inner-city residents	200 (31%)
Outer-city residents	268 (41%)
Work in City/Camden/Hackney:	
Inner-city residents	72 (11%)
Outer-city residents	18 (3%)

borough of residence. Significantly more outer-London than inner-London residents did so, but this was counterbalanced by the greater amount of jobs taken up by inner-city residents in the nearby areas of Camden and Hackney. These findings support the argument that commuting and extended job search is expensive and difficult for young people who are confined to a limited part of the London labour market: in this case, the inner areas in entirety, Bromley and Hounslow respectively. Buck and Gordon (1986) also found that the labour mobility of young people in London was constrained by the high costs of commuting. Consequently, the findings suggest that relatively fewer jobs are available to youth in the inner areas, and relatively more in Hounslow. The likely reason is that the young face more competition for jobs in the inner city from unskilled adult workers, including those who are able to travel. There is some evidence to substantiate this viewpoint: a survey of five London boroughs by the Greater London Council (GLC) concluded that residents of other areas were obtaining jobs in east London (the inner city) at the expense of local people (GLC, 1980). Using the same argument, the positive Hounslow result suggests that youths in west London with its associated range of jobs did not face the same competition from local unskilled; that the area is not as easily accessible to commuters; and that job information may be more available to local residents.

Socialization arguments might also be considered in this case: the higher proportion of unemployed in the inner city may bring about a feeling of desperation and hopelessness regarding job chances. This is particularly likely to be the case where consequent poverty and deprivation give rise to a run-down in amenities, vandalism and crime.

Fifth, there was clear evidence of purposeful job search. Those who received help from parents in looking for a job and those who were worried about being unemployed were more likely to find work. Those who said they would take any job, rather than wait for a worthwhile one, were also more likely to gain work. Job search in the form of effort, encouragement and information was clearly important to newcomers to the labour market though its importance may have been a response to increasing levels of unemployment. Nevertheless, it implies that some early school-leavers had purposeful attitudes to work.

Finally, the last of the insignificant results provides interesting detail about the nature of this youth labour market. The coefficient on the previous work variable was insignificant, demonstrating that jobs carried out while at school led to few opportunities in the full-time youth labour market. The coefficient on the advice variable was also insignificant. This is contrary to the findings of Dex (1982), who suggested that, in particular, guidance institutions were very important regarding type of work sought, though this may well have been the case at the time of her study in the early 1970s.

From the viewpoint of the school-leavers, these were results with disturbing implications because although some youth efforts and attitudes were influential, personal ability coefficients proved to be insignificant while characteristics over which the young person had no control were important. Those who were non-white, resided in the inner city, came from households with current experience of unemployment, whose parents had given them no help in finding work, were disadvantaged in gaining work. Moreover, youngsters seemed unable to find valuable information from professional sources or from their own experience of part-time work.

Gaining an APPRENTICESHIP (Males)

Results

The male APPRENTICESHIP results (see Table 4.5) were similar to the JOB findings with some important differences which strongly indicate that there is a hierarchy of jobs for males with apprenticeships at the top and unemployment at the bottom. Some heterogeneity of skill level clearly exists for males for which there is a more careful selection process than for jobs in general.

Seven of the eleven coefficients were significant. There were strong similarities to the job results: race, household unemployment, worried about unemployment, and take any job were important again and, as predicted, the take any job coefficient had the opposite sign than previously. With regard to the race result, Lee and Wrench (1983) examined school-leavers in 1979, the same year as the survey, in 429 organizations in Birmingham, and also found West Indian males to be disadvantaged when seeking apprenticeships.[8]

There is also evidence in the results that points to greater employer care and objectivity in recruitment for apprenticeships relative to jobs in general because there are differences from the JOB results. In particular, the ability variables, exams and comprehension were important. This is supported by other results. Ashton *et al.* (1982) found that

Table 4.5 *Logit model: gaining an apprenticeship. Dependent variable: APPRENTICESHIP*

Variable	Coefficient	Coeff./S.E.
EXAMS	0.46	2.54*
COMPREHENSION	0.66	3.76**
TAKE ANY JOB	-0.40	-2.23*
RACE	0.52	2.03
AREA	0.10	0.56
WORRIED	0.43	2.12*
PREVIOUS WORK	-0.13	-0.66
PARENTAL HELP	0.17	0.93
HOUSEHOLD UNEMP.	-0.47	-2.25*
ADVICE	0.30	0.64
IDEAL SKILL	2.12	7.95**
Constant	-3.17	-5.12

Pearson chi-square   723.85   p205

(Pearson chi-square was significant, so a heterogeneity factor was used in the calculation of confidence limits.)

Number of cases 686

* Denotes significance at 5% level.   ** Denotes significance at 1% level.

for entry into skilled work, some employers asked for a minimum number of GCEs or CSEs, often at the request of local colleges, which demanded such qualifications for entry to their craft courses. Kerckhoff's (1990) analysis of 1970s' National Child Development Survey data also demonstrated that level of qualifications was the primary explanation for the prestige level of the first job that the cohort members held. Using logit analysis of National Child Development Study data for those born in early March 1958, Booth and Satchell (1996) found ability was an important predictor of obtaining an apprenticeship for their first job at age 16. All these results suggest that employers in jobs which offer formal training are concerned to recruit more able or suitable candidates than employers of youth in general. Moreover, the parental help variable, which had been important in the previous investigation, now had an insignificant coefficient, with the implication that just knowing someone was not important. Finally, the area coefficient was insignificant. It seems clear that the age regulations associated with apprenticeships meant that young people in the inner city did not face competition from older workers as they did for jobs in general. This is important and vindicates the previous interpretation of the area result.

Willis's study (Willis, 1977) was concerned with skilled and unskilled manual work for males. He suggested that school-leavers who were concerned with exams and took note of advice from school were more likely to gain work with skill opportunity. In fact, although the advice variable was unimportant, the examinations coefficient was significant. However, the examination result in this sample was part of a wider set of explanations and further investigation of the data provided no support for the basis of Willis's hypothesis. In particular, he suggested that effort in examinations was a proxy for a perception, while at school, that all manual work was boring. In fact, in their last year of school, most young people (90 per cent) were looking forward to work. Once again, this hardly demonstrated the lack of a work ethic. Moreover, when they started work (see Table 4.6), rather than being disillusioned, over half of those (62 per cent) said the job was better than they expected and hardly any thought it was worse. In particular, almost all male apprentices were looking forward to work and less than 2 per cent were disappointed. There seems to be little basis for either 'perceptions' or alienation. In his own analysis, Willis admitted that those who were uninterested in examinations were also likely to be the less able, and it

Table 4.6 *Male attitudes to job*

Males	Apprentice	Non-apprentice
Disliked job	9 (3%)	45 (11%)
Liked job	291 (97%)	366 (89%)
Total	300	411
Job better than expected	170 (59%)	247 (62%)
Job as expected	112 (39%)	127 (31%)
Job worse than expected	7 (2%)	30 (7%)
Total	289	404

may be that the simple explanation is just that this variable has captured some level of ability and/or effort. However, it might be that a context of high unemployment changed youth attitudes to the workplace, so in general work of any kind was deemed preferable to unemployment.

Wage Differences: The Model

There has been evidence of a range of individual and job characteristics, respectively, and of a matching process. The outcomes should be reflected in wage differences, as suggested by theory. They can be considered under four headings: employee, job, institutional differences and the effect of prejudiced decisions. First, they arise from employers' perceptions of productivity potential differences in terms of observable worker characteristics: examinations and level of comprehension are suitable proxies for this feature for school-leavers. Second, human capital theory (Becker, 1962) suggests that individual investment in general training in the form of lower wages (relative to unskilled work) in the early years brings about higher wages later and greater net present value returns (Pencavel, 1972). This is the price of an important occupational port of entry to a long-term career job which carries a transferable skill. Third, wage differences might result from institutional factors: for example, in the 1970s in Britain there was evidence of a union/non-union wage differential (Stewart, 1981). Finally, economic analysis of prejudice (Becker, 1971) suggested that in the short run, firms can pay a lower wage to women or non-whites relative to men or whites respectively, though the existence of anti-discriminatory legislation provides a constraint.

Wage Differences: Empirical Work

The financial characteristics of the jobs taken up by the 16-year-olds were investigated in the form of the determinants of weekly income level. The national mean starting wage for such males was £38 per week, the median £35 and the standard deviation £14.7; for females, the figures were £39, £38 and £12 respectively (New Earnings Survey, 1979).[9]

Dependent Variable: INCOME
How much are you earning/about to earn?
This variable was constructed according to the response, and ordinary least squares regression analysis was used with the resulting continuous variable.

Explanatory Variables
EXAMS (+)

COMPREHENSION (+)

GENERAL TRAINING: Are you/will you be an apprentice, or are you/will you be on some other sort of training scheme that leads to a certificate or qualification? (-)

UNION: Have you joined/do you intend to join a union in your job? (this is an imperfect proxy, but it was hoped to capture the union wage effect) (+)

SEX (?)

RACE (+)

Results

Four of the six coefficients were significant as expected (see Table 4.7): those receiving general training, who joined/intended to join a union, relatively more able at school and demonstrating a good level of

Table 4.7 *Regression: level of income (1). Dependent variable: INCOME*

Variable	Coefficient	T-statistic
EXAMS	3.05	3.87**
COMPREHENSION	1.86	2.39*
GENERAL TRAINING	-3.06	-3.77**
UNION	3.87	4.17**
SEX	-0.53	-0.66
RACE	-0.38	-0.32
Constant	37.37	28.71

F 9.56 R^2 0.45

Number of cases 1284

* Denotes significance at 5% level.   ** Denotes significance at 1% level.

comprehension received a higher wage initially. Wage differentials were not apparent either with regard to race or sex controlling for general skill acquisition. In the case of race in particular, this may point to the effectiveness of legislation and the importance of state intervention. These results concur with the analysis and it would have been surprising if they had been otherwise. In particular, there is verification of the existence of apprenticeships as important ports of entry to occupations offering transferable skill acquisition. Overall, the validity of the proxy nature of the independent variables is demonstrated and the integrity of the JOB and APPRENTICESHIP investigations reinforced.

Conclusions

The entire set of results has a pleasing internal consistency. The conventional low-skill character of the youth labour market, segregated by gender and with a disregard for personal ability, is clearly upheld. Nevertheless, the existence of jobs offering formal training, with associated lower wage levels, is apparent and there is a strong suggestion of a hierarchy, with unemployment at the bottom and, for males, apprenticeships further up. Moreover, there is also firm evidence of the importance of mature, purposeful job search in a situation of some heterogeneity. For jobs in general and training opportunities for males, influences outside the control of young people in the form particularly of race, inner-city residence and household unemployment were important. Analyses of the unemployed in the same sample (Lynch, 1985, 1987) demonstrated that initial unemployment had long-term effects in terms of the probability of later unemployment, leaving a long shadow. If major causes of initial employment type also lie outside the young people's control, then it is important to investigate whether there is a similar autonomous reinforcing effect of level of attainment.

Notes

1 There is an analytical work by Sexton *et al.* (1988), but it is concerned with Northern Ireland rather than Britain.
2 Occupational choice rested on the notion of the self-concept and, in particular, the centrality of the occupational self-concept within the overall self-concept. It was characterized as emerging from a sequence of stages of development as the child grew to adulthood. For example, Ginzberg *et al.* (1951) outlined the transition stage from 11 to 17 years of age, followed by exploration, crystallization, and specification as occupation was selected. In a similar approach, Super (1957) regarded the whole of life as comprising five major stages, including exploration from 15 to 25 years.
3 Of the five minor studies, two involved conformist groups, i.e. those who accepted and supported authority: one at the same school in the same year, and the other at a nearby mixed-sex 'rough' secondary modern. The three remaining groups were non-conformist in character: one at the town's boys' grammar school; one at a comprehensive in the same mixed-class area as the latter; and one, the only one of mixed gender, that attended a high-status grammar school in an exclusive residential area.
4 For a review of the conventional job search literature, see McKenna (1985) or Mortensen (1986). Most of these young workers took the first job offered (93 per cent), and there was no evidence that several wage offers were made and compared.
5 When questioned nearly a year later, seventeen of those who said they had no current job offer at the July/August 1979 interview, claimed to have started work by September 1979. This number may well have included those who had left school prior to the end of the school year and taken up work which they had left by the time of the interview. As there were no job details for either of these cases, and as the number is small relative to the size of the

sample, it was decided to exclude these individuals from the enquiry. There may still be inaccuracies due to the hindsight nature of this information, and as a result of the drop-out rate where retrospective checks could not be made. However, it was felt those who ceased to respond were more likely not to have received a job offer than otherwise. Finally, some may not have taken up their work as planned. Nevertheless, it was decided that the important factor was job offer and, in any case, intuitively, it seemed unlikely that those who had accepted a job would not reject it unless offered what they perceived as a better opportunity.

6 Asian and black dummy variables were constructed and introduced into a model using a white dummy as a reference category. Both coefficients were significant as expected, but the number of Asians was small.

7 This variable proved to be unimportant in all other explorations of the data-set and was omitted in subsequent investigations.

8 They did not find deliberate discrimination. The reasons they proposed were, first, lack of knowledge and awareness of how the market operates on the part of the job-seekers and, second, the approach of employers to selection for jobs offering formal training which was not necessarily deliberately discriminatory, but due to 'word of mouth' recruitment channels, family/school ties and subjective criteria when interviewing.

9 According to the *New Earnings Survey* (1979), the average gross weekly earnings of under-18-year-old males was £40.30; the corresponding female figure was £36.60. This included all 16- and 17-year-olds and took account of any returns on training.

5 Young People and Promotion: A Mutual Dependency Analysis

Introduction

The aim of this chapter is to investigate the existence of heterogeneity within the jobs available to young people that did not offer formal general training. If some young people exhibit mature behaviour and some employers view these youths as optimistic and eager to learn, then possibilities for responsibility and promotion might well exist in short-term jobs, providing vital experience and credentials for entry to later career work. Some very valuable investigations have been carried out regarding entry paths to long-term careers (Eyraud *et al.*, 1990; Marsden and Germe, 1990) but there have been few studies of opportunities for early school-leavers in youth jobs which did not offer general training opportunities. Marsden and Germe (1990) reported that 'certain industries . . . serve as staging posts for young workers on their way to longer term jobs in other industries' (p. 192); this chapter will investigate whether they may offer indirect entry ports to career work in other industries.

It is proposed that, in the post-war period, the existence of national institutions and traditions meant that there was a variety of job types available for youth, even amongst the kind of work undertaken by most early school-leavers. The argument put forward is that the wide range of ability apparent among the school-leaving cohort and the existence of the apprenticeship system in a situation of post-war boom, led employers to accept a level of maturity in some young people. This resulted in the availability of some jobs which offered promotion, responsibility and even a short form of on-the-job training in youth industries before the young people moved on to long-term careers. These jobs may be seen as entry paths to long-term careers in the following way. Young people may use their early years in the labour market as a 'practice pitch' for their adult careers. Thus, they acquire credentials in the form of a progressive work history which demonstrates loyalty, general aptitude, or a capacity to take responsibility, albeit in the short term, in the jobs traditionally available to them. In other words, although most youth may be barred from entry to long-term careers, they were not necessarily restricted to dead-end work. In fact, some studies reported that a few employers also viewed youths as possible future management, offering long-term prospects to them (Ashton *et al.*, 1982; Roberts *et al.*, 1987).

The chapter will be organized in the following way. First, relevant literature will be reviewed which helps explain the existence and character of promotion structures. Second, a mutual dependency theory of promotion will be applied to these structures in the kind of work which youths undertake. Finally, the theory will be tested by the use of appropriate material from the data-set.

Literature Review

In a recent US work, Hamilton (1990) remarked that 'Paul Osterman has provided the most convincing treatment of the floundering period' (p. 187). Osterman's work (Osterman, 1980) was a valuable pioneering study which continues to inform the basis of contemporary work, and many of the studies of young people in the last two decades have presented their findings within this perspective (e.g. Berger and Piore, 1980, Granovetter, 1981; Dex, 1982; Ashton, 1988; Marsden and Germe, 1990). Writing in the US context, essentially his work implies that entry ports to long-term careers do not exist in the youth labour market. His analysis relied fundamentally on the age-related immaturity interpretation of youth experience. He maintained that the main characteristic of high-school leavers with regard to promotion and training was their exclusion from them. In his US study, he argued that, in their first five years of work, most youths were restricted to participation in jobs which offered neither feature because of their age-related trait of instability. When they matured, many of them moved to career jobs in different occupations and industries where stable behaviour was a requirement.

Osterman's work rested on the Doeringer–Piore typology of career or 'primary' jobs, with either enterprise-specific or transferable skills, and 'secondary' work, which offered no training (Doeringer and Piore, 1971). He proposed that many, and probably most youths spend their initial years after school in the secondary segment of the labour market. He called this period the 'moratorium' stage (Osterman, 1980, p. 23). During this time, the central characteristic of youth labour is its marginality or exclusion from the stable portion or primary segment of the labour market. His assumption was that most youths spend a short time in secondary firms because their immaturity gives them a taste for instability. When they reach maturity, they wish to embark on a career which offers promotion and training. Therefore, for most youngsters the acquisition of a job in a primary firm marks the successful end to this period and a movement into the 'settling down' stage (Osterman, 1980, p. 25), which takes place when youths mature. From the demand side, Osterman claimed that primary employers are interested in attitude, which they feel is an important determinant of productivity in primary firms: they use age as a proxy for a mature approach and thus exclude young people from jobs which offer promotion. In summary, he claimed that young people were able to cross from secondary to primary jobs only when they matured, as employers used age as a proxy for maturity.

His results seemed to support such a proposition. He examined young people who left high school and did not proceed to tertiary education. His main sample consisted of mixed cohorts from National Longitudinal Survey data (1966–71). He also analysed US Department of Labor figures. Finally, he carried out interviews of male non-students, of firms, and of school officials, youth workers, manpower programme staff, etc., in the Boston area of the USA. He found that there were three major types of employment for youths: 'mom and pop' stores, 'under the table work' (including criminal activity), and large firms of a certain type – grocery stores, security firms, etc. All paid a very low wage, hiring youths for unskilled work offering no training or promotion. Not until the age of about 20 did most of the youths change their industries and occupations. At this point, their wages increased and their unemployment duration fell.

Nevertheless, in a context of much greater heterogeneity, some

British studies produced different findings. It was apparent that some employers regarded some youths as sufficiently mature to take on responsibility. Where explanations were provided, their inexperience and age were often regarded as assets with regard to training or loyalty issues. With regard to promotion in industries in which youth was highly represented, Roberts *et al.* (1987), in a study from the early 1980s, reported pre-existing patterns and found that internal promotion opportunities operated in firms of all types and all sizes: small firms were sensitive to the advantage of promoting and training existing staff. They claimed that 'some hotels prefer to start young people at the bottom, then promote. One fast-food chain obtains most managers from crew members who stick and display aptitude. Many clothing firms gain skilled machinists by training then upgrading unskilled recruits'. Some construction firms and hairdressers shared a preference for personnel without experience and 'bad habits' formed elsewhere.

However, there seemed to be only a few opportunities by the 1970s for young people to enter long-term careers directly. Ashton *et al.* (1982), in a study of 350 firms in three local labour markets in 1978–9, reported that some firms did recruit early school-leavers 'to be trained as potential supervisors each year' (p. 22) by a progression up the firm's internal labour market. They found it impossible to make simple generalizations, but claimed that such careers were only available to youth within certain industries, such as banking, where some young people could make a lifetime career within one organization, i.e. without moving on. Roberts *et al.* (1987) also found that some young people had the opportunity of promotion in banks, insurance companies, and building societies. They reported that young people were not being confined to the base of the job hierarchy in some firms. 'When senior positions are filled from within, young people are likely to be not only eligible but preferred for the junior posts that are advertised externally, and these entry jobs will open career prospects into primary segments of the companies' workforces' (Roberts *et al.*, 1987, p. 30). However, Ashton *et al.* (1982) found that such opportunities seemed to be declining in the 1970s and, in any case, the number of young people involved was extremely small.

With regard to training opportunities, Roberts *et al.* (1987) found that 'training was embedded in everyday work' (p. 48), that many skill requirements were 'particularistic' (p. 46), and that most firms were not interested in transferable skills but wanted trainees to acquire specialist skills for the job-at-hand. Nevertheless, they found that very few firms offered a separate programme of management training to 16- and 17-year-olds. These did exist, but many were restricted to older groups. However, they found several firms who saw their young intakes as potential managers but were only training them for this 'incidentally' (p. 49). They reported that extended, systematic on-the-job and off-the-job training was rare outside the professional, technician and craft apprentice grades. In general, training was short: it was expected to pay for itself within six months.

From the available evidence, it is apparent that some promotion and training opportunities were available within some enterprises to some young people. This aspect of heterogeneity has received little attention in the literature. In general, they existed in conventional 'youth' areas, that is, in the short term before young people moved on to different industries. In view of the enterprise-based training involved, the single tasks were clearly firm-specific. However, as a bundle developed over time, they were transferable in the sense that they indicated a level of commitment and responsibility in the young person. It may be that, in entirety, they also indicated a knowledge of general work routines, very important for the new entrant: it seems unlikely that a set of routines would be entirely firm-specific. Entry ports to long-term careers were only available to a small minority of young people and seemed to be declining in the 1970s. They were dependent on the industry in which work was gained and were confined largely to parts of the service sector.

It is argued, therefore, that Osterman's analysis is not applicable in entirety to the British context of the 1970s, where most young people left school at 16. Osterman's sample may well have consisted of a much smaller range of lower ability school-leavers than was apparent in the British case. Moreover, there was a richer mix of work for youth in Britain than was available for early school-leavers in the USA. In brief, if a range of both jobs and of school-leavers is apparent, this allows for an idiosyncratic match and some measure of maturity. The institutional and educational features of post-war Britain, at least until the end of the 1970s, made it possible for this situation to be apparent. First, early school-leaving was the norm and employers were faced with a wide range of characteristics, not just with a minority of youth who had left school early because they lacked ability or were rebellious or irresponsible. Second, the institution of apprenticeships meant that both employers and young people accepted the idea of skill acquisition among this group. Thus, because of the nature of the British youth labour market, some youths exhibited maturity and jobs were available to them which offered promotion even in the short term.

A Mutual Dependency Theory of Internal Promotion

It is necessary to introduce a theoretical framework which accounts for promotion and firm-specific training in the short-term jobs available to youth. Rubery and Wilkinson (1994) recently criticized 'the ideal-type models of segmentation theory which assume that forms can be divided or dichotomised into primary or secondary' (p. 13). Following their reasoning, it is proposed that the typologies which form the basis of early segmentation analysis are dysfunctional for purposes of analysing youth work because theoretically they are flawed and empirically they portray promotion structures in terms of lifetime-attachment internal labour markets from which most youth is clearly excluded. It is essential to consider analyses, first, which take account of tertiary industry as well as manufacturing and, second, which allow for stable jobs of short-term duration.

Osterman's work was based on the model of Doeringer Piore (1971). In their seminal work, the latter suggested that firms which employ complex plant and equipment are faced with a unique cost problem with regard to employee retention. That is, as capital is increasingly adapted to the needs of the organization, over time it becomes firm-specific so workers who learn to operate and mend such machinery acquire skills which cannot be transferred to other organizations. Non-transferable training only increases the marginal productivity of workers in firms which endow the skill (Becker, 1962, 1975). Employers must therefore incur some expenses of training and this investment must be safeguarded in the most cost-effective way available. One method used is the setting up of the internal labour market for such workers, in which recruitment is based on traits denoting stability. Skill acquisition is by informal on-the-job training by fellow workers, and promotion is made largely on the basis of seniority in terms of long-term career ladders. These jobs form the enterprise part of the primary sector. In such a situation it seems unlikely that employers will recruit many early school-leavers on initial entry to the workplace, with no credentials of work history.

Despite numerous attempts to build on the initial dichotomous typology by presenting empirical studies categorizing subsystems, including secondary sector internal labour markets (ILMs) (Carter and Carter, 1975), closed and open ILMs (Dalton and Snelling, 1983), extended ILMs (Mainwaring, 1984), firm discrete subsystems (Osterman, 1984), white-collar ILMs (Osterman, 1984), craft subsystems (Osterman, 1987), occupational ILMs (Althauser, 1989), most work has not offered an alternative theoretical base to Doeringer and Piore. Thus, the internal labour market with its specific skills/on-the-job training basis has remained the centrepiece of the enterprise primary segment from which most youth is said to be excluded and therefore restricted to the secondary labour market with its disregard for stability and its lack of training or promotion structures. This is surprising. First, there are empirical problems. The work refers to capital-intensive enterprises and manufacturing industry, while internal labour markets are clearly apparent in British service organizations (e.g. Metcalf, 1988; Marsden, 1990; Thompson *et al.*, 1993). Moreover, in a comprehensive review of the empirical literature, Althauser (1989) found that, although there was hardly any evidence to suggest that informal on-the-job training was a progenitor of internal labour markets.

Second, there are theoretical problems. Why build up a promotions structure to retain workers whose non-transferability lies in the nature of the skill itself? In fact, Williamson (1975) had demonstrated that a situation of skill specificity was merely an example of bilateral monopoly whereby the internalization of labour can be explained using transaction costs analysis for both parties. It occurs when the costs arising from lengthy written contracts to take account of all contingencies in a situation of bounded rationality make it more efficient to internalize resources than resort to lengthy written contracts. 'Where asset specificity is great, buyer and seller will make special efforts to design an exchange relation that has good continuity properties' (Williamson, 1981, p. 1546). This reasoning has implications for the character of the firm's wage structure. Doeringer and Piore (1971) suggested that the job ladder itself was the means by which internalization was brought about; it was the instrument of employee retention via promotion by seniority. But no such tool is needed in a situation where the asset specificity of labour means it is effectively 'locked into' the organization (Williamson, 1981, p. 1546). In response to this 'closure', most arguments have been concerned with the use of wage as an incentive or effort-motivating mechanism. For example, Kreckel (1980) suggested that effort would need to be encouraged from workers who were secure in their jobs. Williamson *et al.* (1975) also used this line of argument. They claimed that, under certain conditions, workers may behave opportunistically and thus need a system which will motivate them. This is especially the case where consummate co-operation, or an affirmative job attitude, is required from them. This comes about, for example, where there is asymmetry of information and employees can hoard information in the form, say, of on-the-job specific training. In such a situation, employers can facilitate an 'idiosyncratic exchange' by setting up an internal promotion system where wages are attached to jobs (Williamson *et al.*, 1975, p. 236). In this way, the firm can reward co-operative behaviour. The resulting wage structure thus reflects long-term objectives rather than current individual bargaining strengths.

From the viewpoint of an analysis of youth, Williamson's arguments are interesting in that specific skills in manufacturing industry are only one example of such bilateral monopoly. Thus, it allows a transaction costs approach to be applied to non-production workers (Williamson *et al.*, 1975) where, say, a knowledge of firm-specific routines might be important. This is important for young people and promotion structures in the tertiary industries. However, there are two major problems which remain. First, the analysis still assumes some kind of long-term internalization process with on-the-job training and job ladders and thus takes no account of short-term promotion that might be more appropriate in the case of young people. Second, it fails to take into account the different levels of power apparent in the employment relationship. Labour is relatively immobile and depends on capital for its employment. Consequently, there can never be a situation of equal bilateral monopoly, except in a specific context and therefore an ephemeral sense. This has important implications both for the respective strengths of the agencies which provoke internalization (employer and employee in the context of legislation) and the type of motivating wage structure that emerges from that process. For example, it may be that exogenously determined influences, say, in the form of unemployment, motivate individual workers to pass on information without the necessity of a hierarchical wage structure. This is empirical support for such an argument. Baker and Holmstrom (1995) concluded from their study of internal labour markets that 'despite rigid policies, there is scope for rewarding individual performance, much more so than we initially had imagined' (p. 259). Moreover, competitive pressures may bring about a redesign of jobs (Kelly, 1982), making it difficult to maintain a structure of job ladders.

It is possible, however, to deal with these issues. With regard to short-term promotion, a recent work builds on the notion of Williamson *et al.* of a workforce 'locked into' the organization and thereby makes it possible to examine internal promotion structures in which lifetime career attachment and ongoing bilateral monopoly are not essential ingredients. Further, it provides a framework in which different levels of power and optional organizational outcomes can be considered. A situation of bilateral monopoly implies mutual commitment to the employment relationship, and Wachter and Wright (1990), in an important paper, suggest how such mutual dependency can arise. They analyse this situation from two different perspectives. First, it comes about whenever there is a 'lock-in' effect. This occurs when the sunk costs of investment by both parties (in the firm by the worker, and in the worker by the employer) make it more advantageous for each to remain with the other than to resort to other opportunities by means of quits and lay-offs, respectively. Where sunk costs of any kind are not portable, immobility results.

The second way they analyse the situation is in terms of mutual benefits. They argue in terms of match-specificity, whereby the combination of a particular job and worker brings about a 'coalition's surplus' above what each could gain in a combination elsewhere. This is clearly a quasi-rent situation. It need not be a result of skill acquisition, but merely where a given worker and job/firm 'fit together' or match each other: the idiosyncratic nature of the match is the source of the surplus and discourages rent-seeking activity by either party. In fact, it renders it superfluous.

This analysis makes it possible to allow for heterogeneity in the youth labour market in a situation where stability and internal promotion might be short term and not part of a lifetime attachment. If there are jobs which require a level of responsibility and ability, and where familiarity with the firm's procedures are important, then, initially, there are joint sunk costs of investment perhaps followed by mutual benefits of a job/individual 'fit'. Employers incur recruitment and training costs above and beyond firms who require no skill or aptitude. For their part, employees invest in a knowledge of firm-specific routines which are not portable across organizations. Mutual dependency does not necessarily imply infinite duration and it is possible, therefore, to investigate heterogeneity in the youth labour market without making assumptions about entry to lifetime careers. Furthermore, skill is not an essential ingredient (though it may be in evidence) as mutual search costs may be sufficient for a short-term dependency to be apparent even before the investment is recouped in terms of mutual benefits. In fact, a short-term work record leading to another job may be the main benefit for the young person. Thus, the dependency may be particularly strong for young people in a situation where it may be difficult to gain other work easily, especially career jobs, without the credentials of a progressive work history. In other words, the mutual fit is apparent just for a short time, reflecting the small costs of employer investment and the time needed by the employee to build up workplace credentials before moving on. Wachter and Wright's analysis, of course, only applied to long-term career jobs, in which a 'coalition's surplus' becomes apparent: the availability of such work was only apparent, however, for a minority of early school-leavers.

The theory also has interesting implications for the internalization process and the structure of the organization because match specificity does not necessarily imply a situation of equal dependency. Under the assumption of purposeful behaviour, an inexperienced young person, facing decreasing opportunities and competition from substitute workers, is likely to experience a greater need to stay in a meaningful job than that of the employer to retain the worker. This was the context in Britain from the mid-1970s onwards. Moreover, motivation for work effort is likely to emerge from fear of dismissal from an important entry port or of unemployment with its long shadow. Even where the unfair dismissal legislation of 1975 was in operation, the need to build up a track record in the early years as credentials to gain career work should have provided sufficient stimulant for consummate co-operation. A hierarchy, in which wages are attached to jobs, might be in evidence but it is just one of several outcomes and is likely to depend on the respective strengths of the firm, its employees and their agents, and existing legislation.

These optional wage outcomes, which are not necessarily linked to long-term career hierarchies, can be accommodated by efficiency wage theory (e.g. see Krueger and Summers, 1988). This analyses the same problems that arise from asymmetry of information and opportunism, not precisely in terms of unequal power, but of 'principal–agent' relationships where one party, in this case the employer, hires the agent, the worker. Employees invest in the relationship in the form of acquiring specific knowledge and in this way attain some decision-making authority which they can use to pursue their own goals. To prevent this, the prediction is that firms will pay internalized workers more than the market clearing wage to present them with the incentive to 'work rather than shirk'. It does not, therefore, necessarily imply the attachment of wage to job and, once account is taken of the costs of any training, there may be a 'true' internal market without any need for a long-term career structure. Consequently, efficiency wage analysis can be used in a situation of unequal bilateral monopoly and where there is no long-term career structure with formal on-the-job training at each level.

Hence, while accepting the features of the youth labour market apparent in the literature, it is possible to investigate a heterogeneity which departs from the typology of unskilled work and a disregard for stability that exclusion from internal and occupational labour markets generally implies. A mutual dependency approach with efficiency wage outcomes dependent on context provides an alternative theoretical basis for market failure of this type.

Investigations

One of the problems which had bedevilled empirical investigation of promotion structures is the difficulty of establishing their existence. The aim of these investigations is to identify the existence and character of these jobs and the young people who take them up. This can be carried out in this survey in several ways.

First, Osterman questioned individuals about expectations of promotion but admitted that answers might have reflected workers' self-perceptions rather than institutional structures. During the summer holidays, in July and August 1979, in this survey, those young people who had been offered a job which they were planning to take or had already started, were asked 'Do people who do your job normally get promotion?' The response differentiates the jobs themselves, and should capture promotion structures. It is important to note that this is not an arbitrary division of a continuum or selection of occupations or industries. Moreover, the question was phrased so as to avoid trapping personal expectations and therefore should identify jobs *per se*.

The findings for this sample did not support Osterman's results that most of the young people entered jobs without any kind of promotion structures. A third (456) of the 1401 who gained work attained jobs which offered promotion prospects. Of these, 285 (63 per cent) were females and there were 47 (10 per cent) non-whites. It is unsurprising that females should form a majority as they did not participate in the traditional male apprenticeship scheme.

Second, it was possible to identify precise details about the nature of

Table 5.1 *Job progressions (1). Which of these things is most likely to happen while you are in that job?*

Response	Number of responses		p
	No promotion	Promotion	
Either			
I will keep doing the same work*	58 (20%)†	12 (2%)	<0.0001
I will keep doing the same work but will get more money*	99 (35%)	77 (14%)	<0.001
Or			
I will change to different work	76 (27%)	208 (37%)	<0.01
I will do more difficult work	46 (16%)	171 (30%)	<0.001
I will supervise other people's work	6 (2%)	100 (22%)	<0.001
	285	568	

* Respondents were allowed to give more than one response. Several said they would be doing the same work but also that it would be more difficult and/or would involve supervising other work. These were excluded from the two 'same work' categories as the aim was to capture those whose situation was not changing at all.

† Percentages refer to the number of responses.

the promotion (see Table 5.1). There are significant differences in the kinds of responses made between those who gained jobs which led to promotion and those with no promotion prospects. Only 3 per cent of

those with promotion jobs said they would be doing the same work
(p < 0.001), while only 2 per cent of those in non-promotion jobs said
their work would involve supervision (p < 0.001). The job distinctions
are not clear cut in the two middle categories and this seems to signify
the existence of a continuum rather than polar types, as suggested by
Rubery and Wilkinson (1994). Furthermore, there may have been lack
of information on the part of the young people.

Third, a more rigorous examination is needed to establish whether
the characteristics which determine the existence or absence of a
promotion structure are meaningful. The apprenticeship model (see
Chapter 4) was employed again, but substituting promotion as the
dependent variable, omitting the desire for skilled work variable (ideal
skill), of course, and including both males and females. Otherwise, the
same independent variables were used and the same analysis and
predictions are possible as the assumption is that, leaving aside formal
training opportunities, jobs offering promotion are more desirable/
more difficult to acquire then those which do not. From this viewpoint,
it was the intention to exclude those who were receiving general
training, but, interestingly, none of them made a response to the
question, clearly feeling it was not relevant. This is important as the
answers demonstrate accuracy in the young people's responses: jobs
which offer transferable skill acquisition do not lead to internal promotion and vice versa.

Results

The results (see Table 5.2) clearly indicate that the promotions variable
has meaning: the coefficients of the examinations, comprehension,
household unemployment, worried and the take any job variables were
all significant as predicted. More important, these results were very
similar to the apprenticeship model (see Table 4.5). The only result
which was different in an important respect was for the race variable
where the coefficient in the promotion model was insignificant.[1] The
findings, therefore, demonstrate that the determinants of gaining a job
which offers promotion prospects are similar to those for a job which
offers male apprenticeships.

Fourth, after a year, those who stayed in the same job were asked if
they had been promoted or did different work (see Table 5.3). By
March 1980, although most in each category were still doing the same

kind of work, significantly more of those in jobs which led to promotion were doing different work ($p < 0.001$). By December 1980/January

Table 5.2 *Logit model: gaining a job with prospects. Dependent variable: PROMOTION*

Independent variable	Coefficient	Coeff./S.E.
EXAMS	0.53	2.86**
COMPREHENSION	0.44	2.57*
TAKE ANY JOB	-0.36	-2.10*
RACE	0.15	0.56
SEX	-0.08	-0.49
AREA	0.24	1.43
WORRIED	0.40	2.21*
PREVIOUS WORK	0.22	1.21
PARENTAL HELP	0.01	0.08
HOUSEHOLD UNEMP.	-0.48	-2.65**
ADVICE	0.04	0.14
Constant	-0.25	-0.52

Pearson chi-square 693.46   p 0.36
Number of cases 682

* Denotes significance at 5% level.   ** Denotes significance at 1% level.

Table 5.3 *Job progressions (2). Those who remained in the same job: is your work different work or have you been promoted?*

	Same work	Different work	Total
By Mar/Apr 1980:			
Job with promotion	180 (69%)	79 (31%)	259
Job with no promotion	108 (89%)	14 (11%)	122

	Not promoted	Promoted	Total
By Dec 1980/Jan 1981:			
Job with promotion	114 (64%)	65 (36%)	179
Job with no promotion	70 (81%)	16 (19%)	86

1981 (i.e. about 18 months after they started the job) significantly more of those in promotion jobs had been promoted, although unsurprisingly they still formed a minority in such a short time ($p < 0.01$).[2]

The young people were also asked if they had received any training

Table 5.4 *Formal training. To those who remained in the same job:*

(a) Have you undertaken any formal training?

	Yes	No	All
Job with promotion	116 (45%)	142 (55%)	258
Job with no promotion	26 (22%)	92 (78%)	118

(b) If yes, what kind of training have you received?

	On-the-job	Off-the-job	Both	All
Job with promotion	96 (83%)	17 (15%)	3 (2%)	116
Job with no promotion	23 (88%)	3 (12%)	(–)	26

(see Table 5.4). Of those who replied, significantly more employees in promotion jobs had received training, though it was still a minority of the total. Nevertheless, all of those who said they had received training were able to provide details and the vast majority of it was on-the-job training. This was an interesting finding which strongly suggests that promotion and enterprise-specific training for youth should not be overlooked, even within their traditional short-term areas of work.

Overall, therefore, the results strongly suggest that the promotion variable has internal coherence and that, leaving aside apprenticeships, the British youth market, even for early school-leavers, was heterogeneous with regard to training and promotion. The likelihood, however, is that by the end of the 1970s most of these were in short-term jobs.

Finally, the income regression was run again (see Chapter 4), substituting the promotion variable for general training with the same predictions for the other variables. However, unlike jobs which offered general training opportunities, it was expected that jobs which led to promotion would offer a higher starting wage than those which did not. This is because, following efficiency wage theory, a wage higher than the market level would be needed to give young people the incentive to work rather than shirk in a situation of short-term 'lock-in', until their singly endowed specific skills or information became a transferable bundle. The promotion coefficient was positively significant as expected (see Table 5.5).[4]

Table 5.5 *Regression: level of income (2). Dependent variable: INCOME*

Variable	Coefficient	T-statistic
EXAMS	2.66	2.77**
COMPREHENSION	1.02	1.11
PROMOTION	3.00	3.27**
UNION	5.76	4.98**
SEX	-1.10	-1.20
RACE	0.97	0.70
Constant	34.76	22.31

F 10.71 R^2 0.08

Number of cases 711

* Denotes significance at 5% level.   ** Denotes significance at 1% level.

Conclusions and Discussion

The findings demonstrated the existence of some heterogeneity among jobs which did not offer general training. There were jobs which offered promotion prospects which were associated with training and varied work. However, there was an overlap and evidence of a continuum rather than a polarization. Jobs with promotion prospects were more formally identified by producing findings which showed the variable was coherent in itself and by comparing these findings to characteristics which were found to be important regarding attainment or not of male apprenticeships. Moreover, the wage effect confirmed the existence of heterogeneity.

The likelihood is that British educational and training regulations accounted for the experiences of some of these young people, which explains some differences between these results and findings from US studies. Many early school-leavers in the USA did not graduate from high school: some were the 'drop-outs', the minority of youth whose

British counterparts might well be Willis's 'lads'. Consequently, much of the instability of the US early school-leaver may well have been a characteristic of such a group, perhaps linked with absenteeism at school, but it was not necessarily an age-linked immaturity variable. This conclusion receives support from Blanchflower and Lynch (1992) who compared training opportunities for US and British youths and found considerable differences.[3] The authors summarized their general findings thus: 'non-college graduates in Britain received much more post-school training than similar youths in the US' (Blanchflower and Lynch, 1992, p. 20). Thus, the strong evidence which suggests that young people of this age are unlikely to embark on career jobs, does not mean that all of them in Britain undertook unskilled work without responsibilities.

Notes

1 Non-whites seem to be disadvantaged only with regard to gaining apprenticeships and not to jobs offering promotion or work in general. Lee and Wrench (1983) found that they lacked information/contacts in such a traditional area.
2 The numbers of responses at the end of the survey were too small to make any kind of conclusive analysis worthwhile.
3 The British data from National Child Development Survey tapes referred to 16-year-olds in 1974, while the US National Longitudinal Survey data referred to 18-year-olds in 1981.
4 The low explanatory power of the model is unsurprising in view of Roberts *et al.*'s findings (1987) that, leaving aside apprenticeships, similar youth jobs in different firms paid different wages.

6 THE FREE RIDER PROBLEM: A NEW THEORY OF TRADE UNION MEMBERSHIP

Introduction

This chapter and the following one are concerned with youth and trade union membership. The main argument put forward is that, given a sufficiently wide range of young people and the availability of some jobs with training or prospects, many youngsters will have a mature approach to the workplace which will be manifest in the form of their attitude to trade unions. Young people have lower unionization rates than adults (Metcalf and Richards, 1983). This is not questioned. It was generally thought that this was because they had a low demand for union services. But in fact more recent work claims that their lower rate of unionization is a result not of an uncommitted outlook but of lack of union recognition or availability in the jobs in which they work (Spilsbury *et al.*, 1987; Payne, 1989). Spilsbury *et al.* (1987) claimed that if young people were represented in the same kinds of jobs as adults, their density rates would be no different from older workers. However, both sets of findings are challenged in these chapters because, it is argued, they emerge from a fundamentally flawed tradition of union membership theory. Consequently, to examine the issue of youth attitudes, a new model must be constructed which overcomes these problems.

This chapter will deal with theoretical issues, and the following one with the empirical work. The aims of this chapter are two-fold. First, by an appraisal of the literature, it will be suggested that the traditional approach to union membership is flawed because it is based on an individual instrumental framework from which problems arise concerning endogeneity and the free rider paradox. Second, in order to provide a theoretical basis from which to investigate the character of youth behaviour, a model of union membership will be built up to solve these problems. It will be developed from an interdisciplinary approach which abandons the assumption of employee homogeneity and takes account of several sources of motivation and action. Although this model is constructed for the purposes of an investigation of young people, it provides a foundation for a general theory of union membership.

Literature Review: Theory

There is major controversy in the theoretical arena which is directly relevant to youth. The pioneering work based on the Ashenfelter–Pencavel model (Ashenfelter and Pencavel, 1969; Sharpe, 1971) considered density to be wholly the result of a demand for union services. But more recent empirical work on young people suggests that the availability of unions is more important. Payne (1989), producing evidence indicating lower UK membership rates of young employees relative to older workers, contended that her findings for youth support British results for other age groups (Bain and Elias, 1985; Booth, 1986), i.e. that personal characteristics are largely unimportant in determining union membership. She found that union recognition at the workplace seemed to be the most important determinant of membership, and argued that the opportunity factor is a crucial explanation of age differences in membership rates. Another British study of young people demonstrated the same viewpoint, suggesting that a major reason why few of them join unions is that many of them do not work in occupations or industries where unions are available (Spilsbury *et al.*, 1987).

Both Payne and Spilsbury *et al.* acknowledge that it is the theoretical basis of the Bain and Elsheikh model (1976, 1979) which provides the focus for their investigations. Bain and Elsheikh introduced a dual framework in which they hypothesized that young workers have both less propensity and opportunity to unionize than do older employees. Opportunity has been interpreted by Spilsbury *et al.* and Payne as union availability at the workplace. It is this latter feature which their research suggests is the more important item. In fact, Payne's conclusion seems to be that propensity is largely unimportant and that younger and older workers do not differ greatly in their respective attitudes to union membership.

However, although at the time of publication the Bain and Elsheikh work marked a major advance in trade union theory and has been the basis of most empirical work for over two decades, several writers have pointed out that it contained fundamental problems in relation to endogeneity (Richardson, 1977; Booth, 1983) and the free rider dilemma (Richardson, 1977). In fact, these were also apparent in earlier works but the detailed exposition in the Bain and Elsheikh model made them more apparent. It may be, therefore, that the more recent studies are also employing a flawed model as a framework for their empirical analyses of youth experience.

The early work on union membership was based on a conventional consumer services approach (Hines, 1964; Ashenfelter and Pencavel, 1969; Sharpe, 1971) whereby unions were regarded as firms and employees as customers, 'operating in a market where union services are the commodity being bought and sold' (Bain and Elsheikh, 1976). Analysis tended to focus on demand issues, implicitly assuming that unit cost is exogenous and constant in the form of membership subscription, and concentrating on union density *per se* where density can be defined as the proportion of potential union members in the workforce who are unionized. Density was considered to be wholly the result of a demand for union services, and for Ashenfelter and Pencavel (1969) these arose from a stock of grievances on the part of the employee. Within this framework, it can be assumed that many school-leavers are unlikely to join a trade union because they have unsettled attitudes and/or work in jobs which do not provide long-term careers. Consequently, the union services, particularly those related to tenure or age, are not considered worth the price they have to pay.

This model, however, is weakened because it takes no account of the constraints imposed by a lack of union presence, and the work of Bain and Elsheikh was important because it attempted to remedy this limitation by introducing a dual framework. The authors adapted the arguments of Shishter (1953), which suggested that workers need both the propensity or inclination, and also the opportunity to unionize via employer attitudes to union existence. Thus, they introduced two sets of explanations for most variables, linking the latter to both propensity and opportunity features by means of a sequence of effects. For example, via a 'credit effect', workers may be prompted to join a union because they feel that wage rises are a result of union activity: workers 'rightly or wrongly credit rises to unions and thus by starting/ continuing to support them, hope to continue into the future' (Bain and Elsheikh, 1976, p. 64). In the same way, to ward off the 'threat effect' of unemployment, they are likely to join a union. These arguments, however, merely seem to indicate that propensity replicates the demand for union services.

Moreover, although for Shishter opportunity referred to union existence (and both Payne and Spilsbury *et al.* have made this interpretation) the Bain–Elsheikh work employed arguments which referred not to union availability in terms, say, of the existence of a closed shop, but to employer ability to resist or concede to union demands. For example, opportunity is said to be greater when employers can pass costs on to the consumer, the 'prosperity effect'. Yet, if there is any element of an inverse relationship between union and employer power, then these arguments merely mirror the propensity explanations and reinforce the traditional demand approach.

In fact, Bain and Elsheikh did produce arguments which can be accommodated within an opportunity analysis. They appended an extra section to their work, set apart from the dual framework and introduced a level of union density variable by which they hoped to capture two conflicting trends. First, there was the 'saturation effect' whereby they suggested that those who were the last to join a union are likely to be least prone to union membership. Second, there was the 'enforcement effect' whereby heavily unionized workplaces are more likely to bring social coercion to bear on other workers and to provide union security provisions. These arguments refer to union recruitment and attraction power rather than the employer-based opportunity arguments of their model. Nevertheless, they will be considered later as, with reference to the kind of workplaces in which many young people are represented, they may be very important.

For the most part, however, the model lies firmly within the consumer services tradition[1] and therefore the two major weaknesses of the earlier work are still apparent. First, Richardson (1977) and Booth (1983) have remarked that endogeneity is a feature of the Bain–Elsheikh work. There is a strong intuitive explanation. If the basis of the argument is that individuals join unions precisely because collective action brings about a supply of the services demanded, in aggregate terms, union density is likely to be an important method of achieving that end through the strength of collective action. Therefore, to some extent density proxies both demand and supply so there is a problem of simultaneous causation. Moreover, the opportunity factor is also linked to this relationship because it may well be that the non-existence of union organization at a workplace may not merely result in lack of opportunity to join for the youngsters represented there, but may also be a result of their low inclination or propensity to collectivize due to age-related traits. This point can be explained in a different way. Those young people who have an uncommitted attitude to the workplace are likely to have the same kind of response to union membership. Thus, some of those who take jobs where union organization is weak or non-existent may not be interested either in steady work or in joining unions. The same arguments in reverse are likely to apply to those who gain work where, say, closed shop regulations apply. In other words, it is difficult to disentangle the two features because collective strength (or opportunity) may be in part determined endogenously by collectivization impulses (or propensity).

The second problem is a direct result of the demand character of the models, with arguments based on the premise that the rewards from union membership are confined to union members in the form of private goods. In fact, increased wages, say, may be reaped by non-members (Richardson, 1977). Over three decades ago Olson (1965) claimed that individuals would not join large groups to obtain a good available to them without their participation. If employees make a decision based on what amounts to voluntary payment for a workplace public good, no rational individual will join – the free rider paradox.

There have been several attempts to challenge Olson. Gamson (1975) and Schwartz (1976) argued that individuals would participate in collective activities because they are aware that if no-one did, the good would not be produced. The problem is, though, that they have not produced a reason why any given individual should join a union: the whole point of the free rider dilemma. Oberschall (1973) suggested that two elements were important: first, the value of the good (in this case, union service), and second, the contribution of the individual's participation to success in its achievement. This work was seized upon by Klandermans (1984, 1986a, b), who developed it into a most interesting expectancy-value analysis which deserves serious consideration as a basis for an individual, instrumental model. He maintained that the uniqueness of his theory is that it takes into account the fact that at the time of the membership decision individuals do not know whether others will participate. Consequently, provided that they value the goal to be achieved, in this case the rewards of membership, they will make their decision based on their estimate of the probable success of its attainment. An important factor in bringing this about is how many other people they expect to join. Klandermans summarized his case: 'If many people think that few people will participate, many people will have doubts about the efficacy of their own participation' (Klandermans, 1984, p. 588). In short, low participation makes success improbable and, therefore, their own membership ineffective. Consequently, the implication for youth is that those who work in industries or jobs where there are only a few union members are less likely to join than those who work where union organization is strong. This is an interesting argument and adds to an understanding of non-membership decisions.

The problem is that the reverse of his argument, which is the part of the analysis that tackles the free rider dilemma, is difficult to sustain. If individuals believe there will be high participation then it certainly seems plausible for them to think that their own effort will be worthwhile, in the sense that it will not be wasted, in view of the probability of success. But this is not to say it will be effective. This is because the value of their own membership is likely to be inversely related to the size of the membership, other things being equal. This means that the higher the participation of others, the more likely is the reward attainable without any given individual's membership. Thus, a rational person will benefit from union gains without joining and incurring the costs of membership, in the manner predicted by Olson. In other words, there does not seem to be any situation in which a youngster would choose to join.

Klandermans' expectancy-value theory also has limitations for the purposes of this study because new entrants to the workforce are unlikely to have sufficient information on which to build up expectations of others' membership decisions. It is also improbable that they will all be immediately faced with a crisis situation. So, in the normal course of events, it is difficult to know how to determine individuals' goals and their values, because they may well be under a continuous process of negotiation.

Thus, a selective instrumental approach with regard to wage gains does not satisfactorily explain the trade union membership behaviour of young people, and the basis of much of the work carried out over the last decade in the UK on union growth and density patterns, though interesting, is insufficient to investigate the proposed argument: that young people, by mere virtue of their age, are not necessarily immature in their attitude to union membership. Nevertheless, an individual or selective instrumental approach will be employed within a wider framework which takes into account ideology, collectivism, social identity, grievance release, dissatisfaction and utility models of membership and the norms and pressures at the workplace.

The Free Rider Overthrown: A New Theory of Union Membership

It is contended that this interdisciplinary model of union membership solves the problem of the free rider paradox and endogeneity by abandoning the use of a single discipline with its underlying selective instrumental approach and thus the assumption of homogeneity. Consequently, it allows the argument to be empirically verified. The theory will be built up by providing a comprehensive definition of unions which extends their character beyond that of mere instrumentality and by linking its different facets to formally derived and tested analyses from several disciplines, often not previously related to unions *per se*.[2] It is contended that the model can be built up into a general theory of union membership to embrace all age groups and therefore to explain youth–adult differences.

A trade union is rarely defined explicitly in studies of union membership. The assumed reasons for its existence are instrumental and therefore determine its purpose, namely that collective strength can achieve more than the sum of separate individual actions. However, if a more complete definition is produced, then wider motives of young people may be more fully investigated. A union can be seen as a group of people with common interests or aims – as an institution, i.e. a group which exists regardless of composition of membership, but more so, as a social movement. This can be defined only in dynamic terms, as a group or institution whose goal is the attainment of a collective good or goods to be achieved in the future by means of growth and pressure. Some sociologists have suggested that social movements have a lifecycle in terms of membership. For example, with particular respect to unions, Oliver *et al.* (1985) proposed that this cycle is brought about by resource mobility. By this they meant that some members deliberately recruit others. They asserted that those who undertake the recruitment are core members who have quite different characteristics from the remainder. The suggestion made here is slightly different: that some members of a union join the movement via different sources of motivation than others, or acquire those characteristics once they have joined. These members are more active in mobilizing non-members who join for different reasons. However, there is no insistence on a strict dual basis to the analysis: first, there is likely to be a wide range of characteristics and, second, individual workers may change their characteristics according to influences and circumstances. Nevertheless, for purposes of clarity the argument is presented in terms of core and non-core features.

Core Union Members: Reasons for Joining

Those young people who join a union for the following reasons may be said to display core characteristics.

Values

The first explanation for core union membership applicable to young people is that individuals decide to become part of groups because they share the interests, values or beliefs of other members of the group or institution. Ideological theories of union-joining are clearly apparent in the literature (e.g. Wheeler and McClendon, 1991; Newton and Shore, 1992; Gallagher, 1998). This motivation may arise from external influences, but locality, workgroup, occupation and industry may also be important. These values may imply that an expectation must also be met about the level of democracy apparent within the union's organizational structure. Cartwright (1968) put forward a formally derived theoretical analysis in more general terms, which implies that association with union members at the workplace brings about attraction to the union. From a slightly different viewpoint, a similar analysis can be employed to explain a moral obligations viewpoint of union membership, whose roots may well lie in a shared set of values.

Collective Instrumental

Second, there are those who employ a collective instrumental approach based on identification of their own interests with those of a social movement: that is, they recognize that only by collective action can they achieve their ends. The effect of group solidarity and class consciousness on union membership decisions has been given due consideration in the British literature (e.g. Goldthorpe *et al.*, 1968). The strength of a worker's identification with the group, be it workgroup, skill level, class, etc., is likely to account for the strength of this source of motivation. For some young people, this impulse is likely to develop as tenure in a given occupation or industry increases, other things being equal. It may well be, however, that a perception of group identity has become apparent to them prior to labour market participation via family (Huszczo, 1983), culture (Klandermans, 1986a), or the influence of the prevailing political ideology. Clearly, collective instrumentality is the rationale for the existence of trade unions because the strength of collectivity is greater than that of mere aggregation. Nevertheless, individual action which stems from this approach falls prey to the free-rider dilemma unless it is presented within an ideological framework whereby altruism forms part of the reasoning. Solidarity and an 'all-for-one, one-for-all' attitude mean that altruism brings about individual instrumentality. Consequently, without a normative approach, the rational individual will not be a union member from this viewpoint.

Social Identity

Third, a cognitive model was developed by Tajfel (1982) which suggests that group participation, in this case membership, takes place to enhance self-esteem. That is, young people wish to belong to a group which they perceive to be distinct from other groups, and this perception forms the basis of an individual's social identity.[3] The existence of a union as a social movement dedicated to ideals may well attract some youngsters in this way.

Individual Instrumental

Fourth, some union gains are private goods, not available to non-members, and some people may join because they place a high value on them. For example, there may be some individuals who, by paying the membership fee, perceive that they will gain benefits from a club or institution above the cost of joining; some may enjoy the camaraderie of its social club. Some youths may have a penchant for power or organization: those individuals who are in jobs which give them little access to managerial positions may well find the union institution a channel for their ambitions. Some young people may have a personality which enjoys conflict or excitement. Skilled unions may pass on knowledge about jobs in other areas to members only. This may be particularly important in a time of recession. However, if some school-leavers job-swap, the costs of membership on an annual basis may exceed any selective benefits apparent during shorter tenure.

Release of Grievances

Fifth, as a group, institution, or social movement, the union acts as a symbol of opposition to the supervisor, manager or organization, and grievances may cause a youngster to join. Frustration-aggression theory (following the pioneering work of Dollard *et al.*, 1939) has become a major strand of contemporary social movement thought. This source of motivation for union membership is quite different from the rational responses that have formed the respective bases of the previous arguments. That is, in simple terms, the grievance leads employees to join in an uncalculating way, and the act of joining is a form of personal tension release. There is an alternative form of grievance release in the form of individual action (Kelly, 1987) which may be particularly applicable to many youngsters. Those who feel that they have little to lose by quitting, being late or absent, or committing acts of vandalism, may be less likely to join unions to remedy their grievance.

These themes can be underpinned by psychological theories of union membership. A tentative approach can be briefly outlined. Following Gordon *et al.*'s seminal work (1980), a separate branch of the literature has dealt with union commitment and, more recently, dual commitment to union and company (Angle and Perry, 1986; Barling *et al.*, 1990). Nevertheless, it lends itself to an interdisciplinary analysis and, unsurprisingly, several industrial relations' studies have utilized some psychological explanations (Guest and Dewe, 1988; Cregan and Johnston, 1990; Cregan, 1992). In particular, the perception of union efficacy in achieving desired outcomes is an important consideration in membership decisions in terms of their general image (Kochan *et al.*,

1986) or specific impact at the local workplace (Deshpande and Fiorito, 1989). Moreover, expected outcomes in terms of the probabilities of the likelihood of an outcome, may be particularly important (Klandermans, 1986a; Gallagher, 1998). However, apart from a private goods approach, union efficacy, general and specific, is important in ways other than financial instrumental, otherwise it falls prey to free-rider problems. For both values and collective approaches – and they are closely allied – viewpoints based on egalitarianism and social justice may imply that an expectation must be met about the level of democracy and consultation apparent within the union's organizational structure. Moreover, workers are unlikely to seek social identification with a movement not dedicated to consultation or one experiencing failure, while the impetuous aggrieved are likely to seek a social movement associated with justice.

It may be that dissatisfaction-utility models of union membership can provide a basis to some of the themes such as collective or selective instrumental approaches, or values, say where there is outrage at inequity. In these cases, dissatisfied workers seek mechanisms to resolve the dissonance of which the voice option is one. Indeed, the pioneering work of Ashenfelter and Pencavel (1969) was based on a 'stock of grievances' argument and this approach is still embedded in much of the econometric work (e.g. Borland and Ouliaris, 1994). However, all rational approaches, even those which are normative, can lead to a utility approach to membership by means of an instrumental calculation of items which may or may not be subject to financial analysis in terms of either motivation and/or union efficacy.

Core Non-members

Interestingly, there may well be a group of core non-members for similar but opposite reasons. There is, however, unlikely to be total symmetry between these groups. That is, unions emerge as a response to collectivization impulses of employees, i.e. from within the workforce. However, some young people may feel that they can negotiate an individual contract as a result of their monopoly talents which would not be represented by collective demands. Others may not enjoy the social club camaraderie; some may dislike power, lack organizational drive, dislike clubs, hate conflict and/or its associated excitement. The values of some may lie in loyalty to the company, plant, individual manager, or they may hold an individualistic ideology. They may prefer to be associated, in terms of esteem, with their supervisors or managers. Some youngsters, particularly those who hope for long tenure with a firm and/or recipients of firm-specific training, may well have a corporate identity, ideology and commitment, and see the union as transgressing or betraying this. Finally, some may have a grievance against unions, for example, perceiving them as causing unemployment.

The Remainder

The final strand of the analysis concerns those who are not motivated in the ways that have been described. The suggestion is that these youngsters, the remainder, are subject to influences at the workplace which result in decisions to join/not join/stay in/leave the union. The decision to join is likely to be determined by the youths' perceptions of the respective strengths of employer and union and by their opportunities to take individual and perhaps alternative action, for example, in the form of quits. In other words, they employ a cost–benefit analysis in relation to two interdependent and often inversely related forces,[3] but taking into account exit options.

The first set of influences can be seen as pressures. These are exerted by both union and the employer. In social movement theory, the core forms the basis of union organization which is responsible for the recruitment of the remainder. Recruitment takes place for evangelical purposes, to gain more power and/or finance and to attain legitimacy in the eyes of management. Moreover, the theft of efforts via free riders is particularly apparent at the workplace and provides an impulse for members to pressurize fellow workers into sharing their costs. However, the policies and finance of the national organization are likely to be important as well as other issues such as the personal charisma and intrinsic abilities of leaders' personalities. If youngsters who would otherwise be susceptible to union recruitment are in industries or occupations where organization is weak, or if unions think they are unstable, then there will be less pressure on them to join.

However, employers may put pressure on employees not to join unions, or offer, say, the option of a staff association. Human resource management techniques may be very important as an alternative to union services. Yet perhaps more important is employee perception of the effects of their joining a union on, say, promotion and redundancy prospects, perhaps via a policy of capital substitution or shut-down. It may be, however, that some young people care little about job security or advancement at this stage of their lives, while others are very concerned.

The second set of influences can be categorized as the norms or customary practices of the workplace. It may merely, for example, be the norm of the industry, occupation, or workgroup to be a union member (or otherwise). The willingness of a young person to join a union is likely to be influenced by the norms of any group to which he/she belongs. Montgomery (1989) proposed that behaviour (in relation to union elections) was influenced by what other people think the individual should do and how much importance that individual attached to their opinion. Family and friends might be significant influences outside the business organization, but at the workplace co-workers are important referents. Moreover, in terms of objective norms, it is generally thought that young people are highly represented in workplaces where density is low, i.e. where most co-workers are not union members: this will be explored in the next chapter. The norms are likely to be the result of a number of features: the existing density of union membership; the extent of a legitimizing process of, say, an apparently co-operative employer, particularly where check-off arrangements exist; and the legislative framework set by the state.

The most important point about norms is that the previous analysis has concerned those who use a rational cost–benefit approach: however, there may be no conscious act of calculation at all. Moreover, once in the union by this method, a desire to leave implies costs of arranging exit and therefore increases the prospect of union victimization. Furthermore, on becoming a union member, values may be assimilated and social and collective identities become important. If many young people work in jobs where it is the norm not to be in a union, then their lack of knowledge or interest may make them particularly susceptible to follow the norm and take on the values of the employer or firm.

Conclusions and Implications

Once the urge to collectivize via the sources outlined has been taken account of, it is asserted that the free rider dilemma is resolved. This comes about in the following way. Olson is correct in his major proposition. If all employees make a decision based on what amounts to voluntary payment for a public good, no rational individual will join. However, individuals will join not only for selective reasons as he suggested, because alone these cannot explain membership of unions whose major goals are in the form of workplace public goods. The crucial point is that motivations other than selective financial instrumentality inspire some employees to join a union. Attempts to recruit other workers then take place either from a sense of the union as a social movement for the better attainment of goals, or from a sense of injustice at would-be free riders. Consequently, one would expect the urge to recruit to be largely determined and carried out at the workplace itself, the site of the union's inspiration and effectiveness on a day-to-day basis. Thus, the remaining employees are subject to the influences of union and employer alike and are likely to make their membership decision based on a selective financial instrumental analysis which is unrelated to wage gains, taking into account the costs/benefits of joining the union and those of staying out.

In other words, there is no free ride.[4] If wage rises accrue to everyone regardless of union status, members pay in the conventional ways and non-members by a resistance to pressures. Moreover, for some of the remainder, a conscious analysis may not occur, for employees may merely behave according to their reaction to norms which are likely to reflect the existing state of union–employee relationships. Therefore, the existence of any union-induced wage increases and wage effects on non-members is not an essential feature of individual membership decisions, which may be based on the perceived costs and benefits of membership *per se* rather than the collective rewards it may offer.

This analysis is highly significant for an understanding of the character of youth membership decisions and of differences between young people. By abandoning the basis of homogeneity, it resolves the issue of endogeneity and the free rider problem. In this way, by providing a new framework, it sheds light on some of the reasons why few young people join trade unions. In the next chapter, it will be investigated empirically by a critical appraisal of recent work and several investigations of the data-set to determine more accurately the level of maturity of young people in their attitudes to union membership.

Notes

1 This is surprising as they explicitly rejected the consumer services approach: a market analysis, they claimed, cannot cope with psychic factors (Bain and Elsheikh, 1976).
2 This theory is an extension of the industrial relations model of union membership (Cregan and Johnston, 1990; Cregan, 1991).
3 In some situations, there may be dual commitment to union and organization.
4 Theoretically, there may be a 'cheap ride' (Albanese and Van Fleet, 1985). Non-members may not pay, or at least not in full, if recruitment pressures are low. Outrage at the 'theft' means this situation is unlikely to persist.

7 Trade Unions: An Empirical Account

Introduction

The aim of this chapter is to investigate empirically the proposition that many young people are mature with regard to their union membership decision. It will be argued that many of them share adult motivations in terms of the core themes outlined in the last chapter. It is expected, however, that because of their inexperience in and unfamiliarity with the workplace, only a minority will be union members because most young people will not display these core characteristics. Moreover, as remainder will not have been recruited or will have yet to make up their minds because of their newcomer status. Nevertheless, immaturity is expected to be apparent for some of them. In carrying out the investigation, it is hoped to substantiate both the theoretical critique and the trade union model presented in the last chapter.

First, relevant empirical work will be appraised. Spilsbury *et al.* (1987) demonstrated that young people had the same inclination as adults to join unions. However, it is proposed that the theoretical basis of their study might render inaccurate the findings. Consequently, their analysis will be reappraised. Second, a different approach, exemplified by the new trade union model, will be used to investigate the main proposition.

Review of Empirical Work: A Critical Appraisal of the Propensity-Opportunity Approach of the Conventional Models

Bain and Elsheikh (1976; 1979) claimed that union membership decisions could be explained by propensity and opportunity factors, but in the last chapter it was argued that it is difficult to disentangle these features empirically due to the problem of endogeneity. This is because, for example, if groups with a low propensity to unionize are over-represented at a given workplace, union organization, i.e. the opportunity factor, will also be low (other things being equal). At first sight, however, it does seem possible to identify these factors by the use of disaggregated data, and thus the findings of the individual-based studies of Spilsbury *et al.* (1987) and Payne (1989), respectively, are interesting.

The Spilsbury *et al.* conclusions of regarding the importance of opportunity relative to propensity factors were based on the following method of investigation. Their raw figures demonstrated that 21–24 per cent of their sample were in unions. However, there was no union presence in some of the workplaces. Thus, they made a recalculation based on the premise that, if they changed job, those young people from such workplaces would unionize in the same ratio as that of youths in establishments where unions were available. On the basis of their findings, they concluded that if unions were available to the whole sample, 61–64 per cent of youngsters would join. Nevertheless, endogeneity has not been avoided because, as a basis for their calculations, the authors have made the assumption that propensity (i.e. the joining ratio) is constant across establishments. However, it might be that some establishments have low union membership precisely because the people who work there do not want to join. Others might have closed-shop-type arrangements. In the same way, Payne's remarks carry the implication that the trade union recognition variable employed in her work might capture not just union availability but also the willingness of employees to collectivize: 'employers are more likely to grant recognition where union density is already high, and conversely employees are more likely to join a union if it is already recognized' (p. 113). Propensity and opportunity cannot be disentangled in these investigations. Consequently, the implication of the results, i.e. that youth has mature attitudes, must be re-examined empirically.

In fact, it is possible to compare the findings of Spilsbury *et al.* with those from a similar investigation in the London survey. In July 1979, the London young people were on the point of leaving or had just left school. Some had a firm job arranged about which they were able to provide details of union membership: they had either just started work or were on the point of doing so. In March 1980, the only group who were asked to provide information about union membership were those who had a job arranged in July 1979 and who had taken up and remained in the same job.

In July 1979, respondents were asked whether they intended to join a union or not and to provide up to three reasons for their decision. Thus, sole and multiple reasons for membership status could be identified. There were 1340 individuals who made responses about whether they had or intended to join a union or otherwise. Of these, 1328 gave

Table 7.1 *Reasons for union membership (1). Respondents with a job arranged who provided reasons for union membership in July 1979*

Total number of respondents	1328 (100%)
Had joined/intended to join a union	281 (21%)
Had not joined/did not intend to join/did not know	1047 (79%)
Positive respondents (total)	281 (100%)
Sole reason given: membership compulsory	98 (35%)
Other reason given	183 (65%)
Negative respondents (total)	1047 (100%)
Sole reason given: non-availability	345 (33%)
Other reason given	702 (67%)
Total number with decision based on reasons other than compulsion/ non-availability (1328 − 98 − 345)	885 (100%)
Positive respondents	183 (21%)
Negative respondents	702 (79%)

reasons for their reply (see Table 7.1) and 281 (21 per cent) said they had or were about to join a union. However, 119 (9 per cent) also said the reason they joined was because membership was compulsory. Because interviewers explicitly asked youngsters if they had any further reasons for their decision it seems clear that the 21 youngsters who provided at least one more explanation would have joined anyway and therefore it is sensible to conclude that 98 (119 − 21) of the 281 who had joined/intended to join a union did so because membership was compulsory. This figure is 7 per cent of the total of 1328.

One thousand and forty-seven (79 per cent) said they had not joined/did not intend to join/or did not know at the current time whether they would join.[1] Of these 411 (31 per cent) said none was available, but 66 also gave another reason. Thus, it can be concluded that 345 of those who did not join a union were non-members because of lack of availability. This figure is 26 per cent of the total of 1328.

If one excludes those whose membership status was solely due to the fact that they said it was because they had no choice (i.e. compulsory or not available), then 885 are left. Of these, 183 (21 per cent) were or intended to be union members, while 702 (79 per cent) were negative or unsure. They are very similar to the original percentage figures, but very different from the results of the recalculation of Spilsbury *et al.*, which suggested that most youngsters (61–64 per cent) would join a union given the opportunity; these figures suggest the reverse.[2]

A convincing solution seems to lie in the fact that, compared to this survey, in the Spilsbury data there is a large figure denoting non-availability of a union which was subject to their recalculation. It was not presented but can be derived to be 40–45 per cent. The reason may well lie in the character of the respective samples: the sample of Spilsbury *et al.* explicitly concerned the unstable while this sample contained at least 97 per cent who were to stay in the same job till March 1980 at the earliest (i.e. 1303 of the 1328 of July 1979 replied that they were in the same job). The difference in result, therefore, may indicate that the unstable are more likely than the stable to work in establishments where unions are unavailable. It may be that their instability attracts them to such work and/or is an effect of it. Thus, the assumption may be erroneous that those to whom unions are not available will unionize in the same ratio as the rest.[3]

In summary, the findings of Spilsbury *et al.* have not been reproduced and it is concluded that this is largely because opportunity and propensity elements are inextricably linked in both investigations. Thus, recent results which purport to demonstrate that most youngsters find work in jobs in which there are no unions may also suggest that some young people and other participants in such jobs have a low propensity to collectivize. Any findings regarding comparative youth–adult union-ization rates must also be interpreted with regard to this issue. Even with the use of disaggregated data, the application of this simple approach means that endogeneity is unavoidable and therefore the propensity-opportunity approach is empirically intractable. Thus, it is impossible from this theoretical stance to determine the level of maturity of youth attitudes to union membership.

A New Model of Trade Union Membership: Empirical Investigations

The main argument of this chapter concerns the labour market matu-rity of young people. In the empirical work it is expected that though few young people joined/intended to join a trade union, those who did so will have attitudes that can be ascribed to people in general. Specifi-cally, it is expected that though most did not join, they will display neutral rather than immature views, while positive attitudes in the form of core themes will be apparent among the joiners. Two separate investigations will be made to enquire into the existence of heteroge-neous motives.

Investigation 1

These data make it possible to make a direct enquiry because sources of motivations are clearly identifiable in the form of reasons given for union membership decisions other than non-availability or compul-sion, at two points in time: July 1979 and March 1980. These results strongly indicate that for this sample core traits were clearly apparent in the minority who wished to join while remainder traits were evident in the rest. Moreover, they demonstrate that a selective instrumental approach with regard to wages is an inappropriate explanation of union membership decisions, and therefore they negate the basis of the theoretical framework employed by many previous writers.

Core Members

Most of the young people who joined a union did so for positive reasons. An examination of reasons for pro-union membership attitudes disclosed the following information, and core motivations were clearly apparent (see Table 7.2).

Table 7.2 *Reasons for union membership (2). Reasons for union membership decision, July 1979: Why have you/do you intend to join a union?*

Reason	Had job arranged			No job arranged
	Males	Females	All	All
I am expected to by workmates/ friends/people I know	20 (16%)	11 (12%)	31 (14%)	14 (21%)
I want to support it	69 (56%)	54 (61%)	123 (53%)	33 (50%)
The union can get me higher wages	21 (16%)	7 (8%)	28 (13%)	2 (2%)
For strikes	3 (2%)	5 (6%)	8 (4%)	2 (2%)
For family reasons	4 (3%)	5 (6%)	9 (4%)	1 (2%)
For reasons of job mobility	3 (2%)	0 (0%)	3 (1%)	5 (8%)
Other	4 (3%)	2 (2%)	6 (2%)	0 (0%)
Don't know	5 (4%)	5 (6%)	10 (5%)	9 (14%)
Total no. of responses	129	89	218	66

First, the use of values could clearly be discerned from the responses of those who said they wanted to *support* the union. In fact, most responses demonstrated that youngsters maintained they joined (or intended to) for this reason, and this response was significantly greater than any other single category.[4] The other reasons, when given, were of much lesser importance.

Second, those who offered the reason of *higher wages* seemed to be expressing a collective instrumental approach on perceiving their lack of individual bargaining power. It may be, however, that school-leavers were just ignorant of the bargaining system and thought they had to join the union to gain the benefits of a negotiated wage rise. In fact, Chaison and Dhavale (1992) proposed that some employees who preferred to join a union might do so because they thought that, by doing so, the union would provide them with higher wages and benefits.

Each of these two reasons was displayed in July 1979 amongst both employed and those with no job arranged (see Table 7.2), and in March

Table 7.3 *Reasons for union membership (3). Reasons for joining union, March 1980: Why have you joined a union since the last time we spoke to you (i.e. July 1979)?*

Reason	Males	Females	All
Expected to	9 (14%)	11 (14%)	20 (14%)
To support it	33 (52%)	36 (46%)	69 (49%)
For higher wages	5 (8%)	4 (5%)	9 (6%)
For strikes	1 (2%)	3 (4%)	4 (3%)
For family reasons	3 (4%)	3 (4%)	6 (4%)
For job mobility	2 (3%)	1 (1%)	3 (2%)
For social reasons	1 (2%)	4 (5%)	5 (4%)
Everyone else is in it	6 (9%)	9 (12%)	15 (11%)
Other	2 (3%)	5 (6%)	7 (5%)
Don't know	2 (3%)	2 (3%)	4 (3%)
Total	64	78	142

1980 for those who had remained in the same job (see Table 7.3). The March 1980 responses included some of those who were positive about membership in July 1979 and those who were negative at the time but had since joined a union (see Table 7.4).

Third, selective instrumental reasons in the form of *for job mobility* and *for strikes* were of the least importance for all groups. In March 1980, after some time in the workplace, *social reasons* demonstrates a selective approach but is also of little relative importance.

Fourth, some of the decisions were shaped by external influences. For example, family influences were apparent as a reason for joining unions but not for the reverse: this is unsurprising in a data-set where most heads of household held manual occupations. There was also evidence for the existence of workplace influences. *Expected to* refers to workplace or peer group forces. Furthermore, there were additional reasons in the March 1980 categories after the youngsters had been exposed to the workplace for some time: *everyone else is in it* points to an

Table 7.4 *Reasons for union membership (4). Reasons for joining union, March 1980: Why have you joined a union since the last time we spoke to you (i.e. July 1979)?*

Reason	Positive about membership in July 1979	Negative about membership in July 1979
Expected to	9 (16%)	9 (15%)
To support it	34 (59%)	28 (45%)
For higher wages	2 (3%)	7 (11%)
For strikes	1 (2%)	2 (3%)
For family reasons	1 (2%)	3 (5%)
For job mobility	1 (2%)	1 (2%)
For social reasons	2 (3%)	3 (5%)
Everyone else is in it	6 (10%)	5 (8%)
Other	2 (3%)	4 (6%)
Total	58	62

exposure to norms, customary practices, or to a desire to identify with the union.

In general, therefore, for those who were or wanted to be union members, attitudes tended to be positive and there was a variety of distinct sources of motivation which upheld the core themes of the model. Moreover, attitudes demonstrated maturity: *strikes* was of minor importance. Those who wanted to join a union did so because they were committed to the workplace, not to undermine it. They were not 'troublemakers'.

Core Non-members

Very few young people showed a distinctly negative attitude to trade unions (see Table 7.5). In particular, no pro-employer interests or values were apparent. This is unsurprising from a sample which consisted of those who either had not yet or only recently started work and thus had no time to develop, say, loyalty or firm-specific skills. Explicit cost–benefit approaches in the form of *they do not help* and *because of strikes* (clearly from those who disliked conflict and disruption) were also of least importance to non-members. Moreover, there were no

Table 7.5 *Reasons for union non-membership (1). Reasons for union membership decision, July 1979: Why haven't you/do you not intend to join a union?*

| Reason | Had job arranged | | | No job arranged |
	Males	Females	All	All
Not decided	52 (16%)	45 (10%)	97 (13%)	2 (3%)
They do not help	6 (2%)	11 (2%)	17 (2%)	2 (3%)
Had not thought	33 (10%)	49 (11%)	82 (11%)	10 (15%)
Not asked	99 (31%)	193 (43%)	292 (32%)	N/A
Not interested	42 (13%)	53 (12%)	95 (12%)	33 (49%)
Because of strikes	5 (2%)	17 (4%)	22 (3%)	9 (13%)
Other	46 (15%)	38 (9%)	84 (11%)	10 (15%)
Don't know	34 (11%)	40 (9%)	74 (10%)	2 (3%)
Total	317	446	763	68

responses which indicated that youngsters felt that unions did not act in the interests of their age group, that they could negotiate better individual contracts, or that the subscription fee was too high relative to their wage. Most interesting, there was no clear evidence in the responses given for a perceived and deliberate instrumental free rider approach. Chaison and Dhavale (1992) argued that some people who joined unions did so because they were ignorant of the fact they could free-ride. For young workers, perhaps it only becomes apparent through experience in the workforce that membership costs can be avoided. However, perhaps those who intend to benefit from union gains do not care to admit openly to such an attitude: Chaison and Dhavale (1992) also claimed that some would not free-ride because they did not want such a stigma on their reputation.

The Remainder

Most young people did not join a union because they were neutral. An examination of reasons for negative or undecided attitudes to union membership clearly demonstrated that, for this sample, there was little symmetry between types of reasons given for joining and not joining.

But most interestingly, from the viewpoint of the main argument, was that the largest response was from those who were *not asked*, which was significantly higher (at the 1 per cent level) than any other single category. This is important because it implies that unions could gain more members by recruiting young people, though the data does not allow for youth–adult comparisons. A comparison between genders can be made and, most interestingly, this was the only response in which there was a significant difference (at the 1 per cent level) between males and females whereby young women offered it more as a reason for lack of membership than did young men. This may be because these young females were less assertive than their male counterparts and needed to be asked. On the other hand, unions might feel it is cost-ineffective to recruit those with the likely impending interruption to their career of the females in this sample. Endogeneity is clearly an issue again for it may also be that young females are crowded in jobs where union organization is poor, partly as a result of lack of assertive collectivization impulses. Overall, the difference between young men and women points to the existence of union organization and recruitment at the workplace that is less effective, at least in this sample, for females.

Most responses, in fact, seemed to demonstrate lack of knowledge, unassertiveness, indecision, or disinterest, in the forms of *don't know, not decided, not interested*, or *not thought*. It is difficult to identify an immature attitude, rather than just inexperience or unfamiliarity with the workplace, but *not thought* may well be a suitable proxy as the others imply some level of consideration. This was only 11 per cent of the sample who found work. An analysis of the *other* responses might have been helpful, but this was not possible.

Don't know was a significantly larger proportion than in the pro-union responses, though it was apparent there also, and could be the result of workplace norms, like the absence of check-off arrangements. This was not caused by those whose non-membership was also a result of a 'don't know' response (see Table 7.6). In general, the similarity of the character of the respective lists of reasons and their largely passive character[5] seems to demonstrate that the split is between those who wanted to join and those who were neutral or undecided rather than pro-employer or even anti-union.

It was possible to discern differences in attitudes to unions and employers by an examination of the respective responses of employed and unemployed; there was some hostility apparent to trade unions

Table 7.6 *Reasons for union non-membership (2). Reasons for not joining union, July 1979*

Reason	No	Don't know
Not decided	36 (7%)	61 (28%)
Do not help	17 (3%)	0 (-)
Had not thought	51 (9%)	31 (14%)
Not asked	218 (40%)	74 (34%)
Not interested	87 (16%)	8 (4%)
Because of strikes	21 (4%)	1 (-)
Other	60 (11%)	22 (10%)
Don't know	51 (9%)	23 (10%)
Total	541	220

though not to employers or firms (see Table 7.5). Although numbers were small, there were several significantly different reasons offered by the respective groups (all at the 1 per cent level). In general the unemployed demonstrated considerably less passivity. For example, they were more likely to be *not interested* and less likely to be *not decided*. Most interestingly, they were more likely to offer *because of strikes* as a reason. These differences suggest a sentiment of antipathy towards unions, and it may be that those without work feel less committed to the workplace and therefore to union organization.

In summary, an examination of responses to open-ended questions regarding reasons for union membership decisions demonstrates that a heterogeneity of reasons exists which can be broadly categorized into 'core' and 'remainder' types. However, the data analysis of reasons for joining or not joining a union demonstrated a symmetry only with regard to the low importance of selective instrumental motivation. For those who wished to join, personal values were identified as highly significant whilst collective and selective instrumental approaches, the influence of cultural and workplace norms and pressures were also evident alongside a recognition of differences in the efficacy of union recruitment.

For those who did not intend to join or were undecided there were no overt pro-employer sentiments and very few anti-union sentiments.

In fact, most responses suggested a neutral or passive attitude. Furthermore, if differences in total responses are examined regardless of union membership status or intent, the neutral replies remain of greatest importance.[6] The general impression gained from all the results is that while a minority of youngsters positively wanted to join unions for what has been termed 'core' reasons, most were passive and, as a consequence, did not join.[7] Of these, the largest group gave non-recruitment as the main reason. A clear lack of consideration was apparent in a small minority, which may have identified the immature. This may be an underestimate as the passive and other responses were very general. Consequently, the main argument has been supported, and the elements of the new trade union model have been validated.

Investigation 2

Two separate examinations of the data were undertaken, from two stages: at the start of the survey in July 1979, and nearly one year later in March/April 1980. Formal models were constructed based on the theoretical framework constructed in the last chapter. The purpose was to ascertain further that the core/remainder motivations, based on purposeful behaviour, can be applied to young people with regard to their union membership decision. This was carried out by statistically identifying those more or less likely to join a union via the several sources of motivation that have been outlined. This will enable identification of the employee and job characteristics of those more or less likely to join a union.

The End of the School Year: July 1979

Dependent Variable: UNION
School-leavers were asked in July 1979 if they intended to or had joined a union. Young people provided reasons and it was possible to identify those who had a free choice because those who made the responses *had to* or *none was available* were excluded. Of the 885 who exercised choice, 183 (21 per cent) said they had joined, or intended to.

Explanatory Variables

At the start of the job, before the operation of workplace norms and pressures, all those who joined or intended to join are said to have core characteristics because of the positive nature of the motivations already identified. Proxies were set up to capture these characteristics as they related to the young people.

1. Values. The likelihood is that the values of young people, not yet formed by direct experience, are assimilated from family and cultural background. Those whose parents held manual work might be more strongly in favour of unions than, say, clerical or shop workers or managers because manual workers might belong to a more enduring union tradition whose values they had passed on to the inexperienced school-leaver as a set of beliefs. In the same way, those who lived in the inner-city areas which, relative to the suburbs, contain densely populated working-class districts, seemed more likely to have more pro-union values in the sense of representing a culture, than those who lived in the suburbs.

OCCUPATION OF HEAD OF HOUSEHOLD (+)

AREA OF RESIDENCE (+)

2. Selective instrumental reasons. Some individuals were more likely than others to be prompted by instrumental motives. For example, it seemed probable that those who did not intend to stay in the job would not benefit from the rewards of membership as much as others because they can be seen as largely pertaining to stability. A financial cost–benefit analysis in terms of services relative to annual subscription fee would dissuade them from taking up membership in a job of short tenure. Moreover, the male camaraderie evident in some unions and related social clubs seemed unlikely to offer many attractions to females. Certainly, for early school-leaving young women at this stage of their careers, the likelihood of an interruption to full-time work might make any attraction based on the selective rewards of long-term participation less enticing in terms of initial costs. In the same way, it seemed that Afro-Caribbeans and Asians would feel they had less to gain socially and culturally from an Anglo-Saxon tradition often steeped in nineteenth century custom and lore. The survey took place at the time of the Brixton Riots when black youngsters might be expected to express anti-

white institution sentiments. Finally, it was felt that those youngsters who were judged by the trained interviewer to have exhibited a relatively good level of understanding were more likely to appreciate the rewards offered by union membership. This was thought to be particularly the case in the range of jobs available to these youngsters where their own negotiating talents were unlikely to be useful.

DURATION (+)

SEX (+)

RACE (+)

COMPREHENSION LEVEL (+)

3. Grievances. Although school-leavers had no direct full-time experience or perception of their vulnerability at the workplace, they may well have suffered indirectly. In particular, if unemployment engenders a perception of the lack of power of the individual, then those from such households may want to join unions as a response.

HOUSEHOLD UNEMPLOYMENT (+)

Results

The coefficients on the level of comprehension, area of residence, and sex variables were significant as predicted (see Table 7.7). The level of comprehension result implies that perceptive youngsters did understand the power of collective action. It might be a result of the occupation range of this group and might also be context-related as the perceived selective services of unions could relate to lay-off terms or redundancy agreements.

The area of residence coefficient was significant, suggesting that those from inner-city areas were more likely to have a positive attitude to unions than those from the suburbs. It may well be, however, that this variable is capturing job location rather than cultural values. Accordingly, a job location (JOB LOCATION) variable was substituted for area of residence: its coefficient proved to be insignificant, though the location information was available only for part of this sample.

Because the sex coefficient was significant, suggesting that young females were less likely to join/want to join unions than young males, it was decided to investigate further. Separate models were set up for the sexes. The pattern of each was very similar to the joint findings. The only major difference concerned the race result. For males, the race coefficient was insignificant, as it had been in the joint male-female result, but for females, it was significant, suggesting that non-white females were more likely to have a negative attitude to unions than their white female counterparts. Interestingly, Sillitoe and Meltzer (1981) also found that West Indian female school-leavers, controlling for job type, were more unlikely than whites or West Indian males to want to

Table 7.7 *Logit model: joining a trade union (1). Dependent variable: UNION (July 1979)*

Variable	Males and females		Males	Females
	Coefficent Coeff./S.E.	Coefficent Coeff./S.E.	Coefficent Coeff./S.E.	Coefficent Coeff./S.E.
OCCUPATION	0.01	−0.02	−0.01	0.01
	(0.04)	(−0.61)	(−0.44)	(0.41)
AREA	0.37		0.39	0.39
	(3.71)**		(2.97)**	(2.45)*
JOB LOCATION		0.08		
		(0.70)		
DURATION	−0.51	−0.48	−0.80	−0.43
	(−1.88)	(−1.53)	(−1.51)	(−1.31)
SEX	0.31	0.28		
	(3.23)**	(2.36)*		
RACE	−0.08	−0.24	0.12	−0.54
	(−0.56)	(−1.43)	(0.73)	(−2.30)*
COMPREHENSION	0.44	0.35	0.35	0.59
	(4.44)**	(2.87)**	(2.78)**	(3.30)**
HOUSEHOLD	−0.09	0.01	−0.20	0.01
UNEMP.	(−0.83)	(0.04)	(−1.34)	(0.01)
Constant	3.78	4.15	4.03	4.03
	(19.73)	(16.73)	(18.00)	(13.28)
Pearson chi-square	532.67	516.43	352.18	420.26
p	0.57	0.57	0.34	0.47
Number of cases	773	528	399	377

* Denotes significance at 5% level.   ** Denotes significance at 1% level.

join unions. The non-white female response, however, may partly indicate an unassertive attitude rather than a negative selective instrumental approach. The findings of Dex (1982) regarding the unassertiveness and even lack of interest of black women regarding job satisfaction seems to corroborate this supply-side interpretation if these sentiments are applicable to the general area of labour market participation.

The variables with insignificant coefficients are also interesting. In particular, one result has implications for union recruitment policies: the length of expected stay in the current job. It had been predicted that attitude to union membership was likely to be closely linked to this variable and this was not the case. This means that if unions do not target school-leavers because they expect them to be unstable, they may be losing potential membership.

The insignificance of the household unemployment coefficient was a surprising result which merited further investigation. A model was set up including the unemployed, who were also asked to provide their attitude to union membership if they had a job. This variable was replaced with one which identified employment status (job/no job dummy). This coefficient also proved to be insignificant. Thus, the likelihood is that unemployment is neither blamed on unions by new entrants to the labour market, nor are unions seen as a symbol of a source of relief in that situation. It may be that union membership as a response to grievance is a result of personal workplace experience and does not affect new entrants.

Finally, the insignificance of the parental occupation coefficient may well indicate that white-collar union values are similar to those of the traditional values of manual workers or that, once again, the variable was too crude a socio-economic indicator.

March/April 1980

The second part of the investigation concerned a sub-sample of those who were examined in July 1979, i.e. those who had a job then and remained in it. In March 1980, the only individuals who were asked to provide information about union membership were those who had a job arranged in July 1979 and who had taken up and remained in the same job. Thus, this enquiry in March 1980 concerned many stable youth employees: 70 per cent of both young men and young women who had arranged jobs in July 1979 had not changed jobs by March 1980. However, the very purpose of this part of the study was to capture the effects of continuous workplace experience: such a focus necessitated a selection of a stable group, which in fact formed the majority of the sample.

By this stage of the investigation, there was a drop-out rate of 10.4 per cent of the relevant respondents from the first interview. This seemed likely to be largely comprised of the unstable employees. Eight hundred and fifteen young people replied that they had remained in the same job; of these, 241 responded that the reason for union membership or non-membership was compulsion or non-availability. Accordingly, they were excluded from the analysis. Of the remaining 574 who exercised choice, 132 (23 per cent) were union members. Thus, it was possible to examine the same individuals after nearly a year in the same job and examine the effects of workplace influences on union membership. Furthermore, the data gave us the opportunity to explore what may be alternatives to union membership which Kelly (1987) claimed are often overlooked: lateness, absenteeism and other job opportunities.

Dependent Variable: UNION2
Respondents were asked whether they were members of a union as at March/April 1980 and a dummy was set up in the usual way excluding those who had suggested that membership or non-membership was compulsory.

Explanatory variables
1. The core. The core variables of the coefficients which had proved to be significant in the previous investigation were included in this model:

AREA OF RESIDENCE (+)

LEVEL OF COMPREHENSION (+)

SEX (+)

RACE (?) was also included as its coefficient had been significant for females.

2. The effect of workplace experience on the remainder. Those who had received training, particularly in the form of trade apprenticeships,

seemed more likely to have been subject to the recruitment pressures of well-organized unions. It is also generally thought that the larger the size of the plant, the easier it is for unions to recruit and maintain union membership, perhaps just through workplace norms. Respondents were asked how many people there were at their place of work and it was hoped to capture the feature of workplace size more accurately than data usually permits.

GENERAL TRAINING (+)

NUMBER OF PEOPLE AT THE WORKPLACE (+)
Specific numbers given ranged from 2 to 450. A few (26) said 'over five hundred' or (49) 'over a thousand' and the corresponding variables were allocated values of 1000 and 1500 respectively.

3. Individual options. Individual exit options are a method of helping to alleviate dissatisfaction: absenteeism, lateness, and quit behaviour are examples and may be alternatives to union membership (Hirschman, 1970). More important, with regard to the argument, it was hoped to capture the immature by use of these proxies.

LATENESS: Are you late for work: very often; often; occasionally; never? (using Labovitz's (1977) justification, and coded 1,2,3,4) (-)

ABSENTEEISM: Are you absent from work for reasons other than sickness? (-)

Results
The results are reported in Table 7.8. The core motivations retained their importance. The level of comprehension, area of residence and sex coefficients were all statistically significant again and reinforce the earlier results. However, in an unreported separate gender model, non-white females were not disadvantaged. The likelihood is that so few non-white young women remained in the sample that it is most difficult to generalize from their experience as they may be uncharacteristic: only 36 (8.7 per cent) of the 410 females were non-white, compared to 77 (19 per cent) of the 405 males, a significant difference at the 1 per cent level. The general training coefficient was highly significant, suggesting the existence of union recruitment pressures or norms for skilled workers, central to the theme of workplace influences, or the dissemination of union values. This is important as the survey took

Table 7.8 *Logit model: joining a trade union (2). Dependent variable: UNION (March 1980)*

Variable	Males and females	
	Coefficient	Coeff./S.E.
AREA	0.29	(2.44)*
SEX	0.28	(2.19)*
RACE	0.29	(1.47)
COMPREHENSION	0.30	(2.43)*
GENERAL TRAINING	-0.55	-(4.37)**
NUMBER OF PEOPLE	0.01	(0.08)
LATENESS	0.07	(0.79)
ABSENTEEISM	0.26	(1.46)
DURATION	0.13	(1.17)
Constant	4.33	7.23

Pearson chi-square 463.27   p 0.51

Number of cases 498

* Denotes significance at 5% level.   ** Denotes significance at 1% level.

place at a time of decreasing union power and density levels (Booth, 1983).

Finally, the individual option coefficients were both insignificant. The size of the workplace also seemed to be unimportant. This is interesting as it was possible to directly identify the number at the workplace rather than using the oft-employed imperfect proxies of plant or firm size.

The results offer support to the new theory of union membership and imply that young people display several sources of mature, purposeful motivation with regard to union membership. Core attributes are apparent at both stages of the survey in the form of an instrumental approach to selective rewards, of collective attitudes, and of values. Workplace influences became apparent after exposure to the labour market. Some immature attitudes were identified, but could not be linked to identifiable characteristics. It is contended that this model can be applied not just to youth but in general, and further testing needs to be carried out with other age groups and in different contexts.

Conclusions and Implications

The Bain-Elsheikh propensity-opportunity model of trade union membership, commonly used as a basis for investigations in the UK over the last decade, is interesting and provided a basis for rigorous investigation. Nevertheless, it proved to be empirically intractable because of the feature of endogeneity. Moreover, the selective instrumental approach that informs its theoretical framework is insufficient as a sole explanatory basis because it is flawed by the free rider paradox and, consequently, not upheld by these findings. However, the main proposition has been upheld empirically by the use of a different theoretical model. Although a minority of young people joined a union, purposeful attitudes were apparent. It proved difficult to identify precisely those with immature attitudes.

Two distinct features are apparent in the results. A minority of youngsters displayed core characteristics while the remainder were usually not in unions though they were generally neutral about them. These results refute the findings of studies which suggest that the propensity factor is not important for young people because, in this sample, passivity of attitude was the key determinant of the low level of union membership. As these were new entrants to the job market (at least at the first stage of survey) attitudes could not have been occupationally determined. Moreover, it is possible to include the results of the first investigation in this summary. Although it was suggested that it had little meaning in terms of a simple propensity-opportunity approach, the notion of availability can be redefined to include not merely union presence but also recruitment power, since each measures strength of union organisation to a different degree.[8] Using this definition, half (49 per cent) of the sample of new entrants to the workplace who did not join suggested that union organization was too weak to reach them. Consequently, this result offers some support to the opportunity arguments of previous writers, suggesting that more young people would join unions if they were recruited. In general, they do not remain non-members because they are immature.

Clearly, these findings have important implications for union policy in relation to youth, particularly as this sample is stable and union membership is likely to be correspondingly valuable. Moreover, even though the survey was conducted shortly after the 'Winter of Discontent' when unions were unpopular, little antagonism to them was apparent and there were no pro-employer sympathies. Nevertheless, this analysis throws new light on methods to be used in relation to these young people because recruitment is seen to be most effective at the workplace itself. However, the low proportion of pro-union respondents and the non-membership of the remainder is likely to be a result of the character of the youthful age of the sample itself. These individuals lack experience and information. If many are in workplaces where young people are in the majority or where many other workers have a low propensity to collectivize, then the mechanisms for union recruitment will remain weak, other things being equal. The lowering of subscription fees is unlikely to make a difference to youths who are unaware of the existence or value of unions. Consequently, apart from targeting youth in workplaces where union organization is already apparent, the greatest weapon for unions might lie in education at school, so those young people with positive reasons for joining become members when joining the workforce, regardless of union presence or power at any particular workplace. Through the mechanisms outlined, some of the other employees could be recruited before the benefits of loyalty to the employer become apparent.

Notes

1 Those responding 'Don't know' numbered 234, of whom 220 gave reason(s). They were included in the negative figure for purposes of analysis because of the similar character of their reasons to those who responded 'No' (see Table 7.6).

2 Unfortunately, only brief comparisons can be made with the situation in March 1980 because young people were not asked then about reasons for not joining. There was no significant difference between the proportions who joined/did not join on each occasion. In March 1980; 259, (20 per cent) of the 1303 who responded were in the union. Of the 184 who gave reasons for their membership, 75 said it was compulsory but 10 of these gave another reason(s). Thus, 35.3 per cent of those who joined a union did so for the sole reason that it was compulsory. This is not significantly different from July 1979.

3 This argument causes problems for this work for more of those who claimed they had to join a union have been excluded than those who said no union was available. If endogeneity means that these responses also capture in part propensity then this may mean that more of the stable than the unstable

have been excluded, making this figure an underestimate and certainly as unreliable as that of Spilsbury *et al.*

4 Significance testing is based on number of responses and not respondents though in fact in July 1979 only 52 positive respondents offered two reasons and only three offered three reasons, while of the corresponding negative respondents only 87 offered two reasons and three offered three reasons. However, it is assumed that equal weight is given to each response and it may be that the first response is considered the most important. Thus, the same tests were used on first reasons offered only, producing similar levels of significance.

5 There are significant differences for most other responses between 'Don't knows' and 'No's for the most part indicating a greater level of passivity on the part of the 'Don't knows'. In particular, the only two anti-union reasons (they do not help, strikes) were expressed almost entirely by the 'No's.

6 Total responses excluded those concerned with compulsion or non-availability. These youngsters' attitudes to union membership are not known but as they only form a minority of total responses their omission seems unlikely to distort the conclusions.

7 This means that the vexed question of whether reasons given by individuals denotes union presence or otherwise is unimportant, for the interesting feature is the recognition of union presence by the youths. This variable provides the measure of the effectiveness of union influence on them.

8 This figure is not completely accurate as youngsters were not asked at the second stage for reasons why they did not join a union. Thus the figure used is probably an overestimate of free choice. The likelihood is, however, that the stable are more likely to be in workplaces where there is union representation. However, the lack of a complete non-availability figure meant that it proved to be impossible to examine those who had joined, left, stayed in or out since the first stage.

8 YOUNG PEOPLE AND INSTABILITY: JOB-SWAPPING AND QUITS

Introduction

It is generally accepted that young people experience high separation rates as part of the job-swapping phenomenon (Hirschleifer, 1973) said to be apparent during the early years in the labour market. The aim of this chapter is to investigate the extent of instability in young people and to enquire into its character. That is, to examine whether youth that is unstable demonstrates this trait because it is immature and feckless, or whether the instability is a result of purposeful information-gathering about jobs and/or the workplace in general. Following the main arguments of this book, it is proposed that the context of the survey allowed for the exercise of some rent-seeking behaviour. First, the relevant literature will be reviewed. Second, there will be investigations of the data relating to the extent of the job-swapping process. Third, an interdisciplinary model of quits will be constructed and empirically investigated.

Metcalf and Richards (1983) claimed that, although it is well known that young people have a higher rate of turnover than adults, there is virtually no cross-section empirical work to explain differences in turnover rates among youth with the same levels of education. The investigations in this chapter will help remedy that situation.

Literature Review

One of the major characteristics of young people is said to be their indulgence in a period of job-swapping as part of their transition into the labour market. Job-swapping can be defined as a process of job changing by means of a series of quits and/or lay-offs. In general, it is accepted that young people, by virtue of their inexperience, have high separation rates. They need time in which to become accustomed to the new experience of jobs and the labour market. They are said to need a period of adjustment (Ashton, 1975; Smith, 1975; Springhall, 1986); they struggle with the acquisition of the social roles required in the work setting (Von Maanen, 1977); they suffer disorientation in the absence of social and ritual events marking an important change of status (Glickman,1975). Because they have few responsibilities and a low replacement ratio and may also be relatively risk-prone, they can indulge in quit behaviour. Moreover, employers may find it easy to sack youngsters who are unsatisfactory because they are less likely to seek, say, union assistance, or to have the confidence and knowledge to allege unfair dismissal. In any job, young people are more likely to be made redundant on a 'last in, first out' basis. Dex (1982) proposed that some employers use quit propensity for youngsters as a substitute for recruitment procedure costs, but it may be that they also directly employ sackings for the same reason. Not all sackings may be employer-initiated: some young people may engineer a sacking in order to be eligible for the benefit payments which were payable during the next six weeks of a subsequent period of unemployment,[1] rather than directly quit. From a different stance, evidence in Europe, the UK and USA suggests that some industries and occupations have a high proportion of youth workers (e.g. Osterman, 1980; Ashton *et al.*, 1982; Marsden and Ryan, 1986). Thus, the jobs in which many youths are represented may engender traits of instability (Doeringer and Piore, 1971) for purposes of respite. Furthermore, these industries may well offer unsteady or seasonal work, or may be subject to recessionary forces and experience high redundancy or closure rates.

Within this broad framework, which suggests that youth will experience high separation rates, there are nevertheless two distinct viewpoints. The first stresses the age-related immaturity of school-leavers, for whom labour market entry therefore is a 'moratorium stage' (Osterman, 1980) or a 'floundering period' (Hamilton, 1990). It may be that many young people deliberately choose a range of occupations and industries in which they can take on casual work because they want an initial period of instability. They could also be restricted there by some employers who perceive that they are insufficiently mature to cope with career jobs (Osterman, 1980). Thus, there is an underlying assumption that most young people and/or the jobs in which they work, are relatively homogeneous: their age-based immaturity, reinforced by the kinds of work in which they are represented, leads them into a pattern of aimless job-swapping on entry to the labour market which persists until they get older. From this viewpoint, most young people, therefore, are quit-prone. Moreover, they are particularly susceptible to lay-offs because they are easily replaceable and mainly represented in jobs which do not offer stable employment.

However, there is a different viewpoint with regard to youth mobility which implicitly assumes that there is heterogeneity apparent amongst young people with regard to their individual characteristics and/or the places in which they work. This results in differing mobility patterns so that only some youth are unstable. The general instability of youth is explained from a different stance, making an assumption of purposeful behaviour. The main argument put forward is that because young people have no experience or work history, both they and employers lack information, so the youth labour market is said to be characterized by initial job–worker mismatches (Elias and Blanchflower, 1989) which result in a sequence of separations for purposes of information-gathering by both parties. For example, search theory in economics applied to young people suggests that they indulge in a special kind of rent-seeking behaviour which accounts for their high mobility. They can gain information by 'shopping around' (Johnson, 1978). They move from job to job to gain knowledge, which they had not obtained at school, in order to calculate which position might offer the best returns by direct experience. This is because they have little knowledge about the labour market generally, and about any job they may be offered. For Jovanovic (1984) workers move from job to job, and in and out of employment, as a part of continual job search. From this viewpoint also, young people are said to be prone to involuntary separations. These can be seen as rent-seeking activity on the part of employers who have no work histories to consider.

In summary, both viewpoints predict high separation rates in terms of both quits and lay-offs. However, there is an important difference based round the respective assumptions of youth characteristics. The first viewpoint assumes that many young people are immature and will be represented in low-skill work. The second viewpoint implicitly assumes that most are purposeful and, consequently, will be represented in a wider range of jobs. Predicted separation rates reflect these differences. The first set of arguments proposes that the extent will be greater than that implied by the second set, and that the period merely serves as a 'growing up' time until youths mature. The second set of arguments proposes that, for most youth, it is a necessary purposeful period. It involves a process of information-gathering whereby resources are allocated more efficiently from a position where initial job–individual mismatches were likely to occur through lack of knowledge.

There are several empirical studies which deal with the extent of youth instability. Carter (1962) investigated 200 15-year-old school-leavers in Sheffield, who left school in 1959/60. One third had left their first job by the end of the first year of work. Maizels (1970), in a study of 330 London 15/16-year-olds who left school in 1964/5, found that by the spring of the following year, 6 per cent of the sample had recorded four or more jobs since leaving school. Sawdon *et al.* (1981) examined 250 early school-leavers in 1977. They maintained contact with 90 per cent of the original sample; 6 per cent of them had experienced four or more jobs just over two years later. Dex (1982) examined two British panel data-sets, both very similar to the survey examined in this book, which also included both male and female school-leavers and was carried out in London (1972–6) and Birmingham (1973–7). She reported that only a minority of young people experienced high quit rates.

It is difficult to make any generalizations from these findings. However, although a sizeable proportion leave their first job in a short space of time, they still form a minority and only a small proportion seem to be involved in job-swapping. Osterman (1980), however, in a famous US work, produced different results. He demonstrated that over half of the young white people in the sample he observed were unstable during the ages 16 to 18 (for blacks, 16 to 19).

There are very few empirical investigations of the determinants of youth instability. The results of Osterman's logit analyses of National Longitudinal Data, 1966–71, for 16–24-year-old youths, demonstrated that out of twelve explanatory variables, only wage rates had a significant relationship to quits into unemployment (for blacks and whites separately). Blau and Kahn (1981) analysed National Longitudinal Survey data (1969–71 for males; 1970–2 for females) for 16–24-year-olds. They demonstrated that when personal and job characteristics were held constant as far as possible there was no significant difference between gender quit rates, young blacks seemed less likely to quit than their white counterparts; low wages, lack of availability of training opportunities, and collective bargaining wage arrangements also seemed likely to lead to higher quit rates. Both of these investigations produced very interesting findings in a new area, but age and skill cohorts were mixed and experiences resulting from differing lengths of tenure make it difficult to satisfactorily examine mobility. However, Dex (1982) examined the quit behaviour of two cohorts and her results demonstrated that young women had higher quit rates than young males, and blacks seemed to have higher quit rates than whites.

In summary, very little work has been conducted from which to draw firm conclusions. It is generally accepted that young people are separation-prone as a group. However, there are two broad views with regard to this instability: one regards most young people as immature, the other regards them as purposeful. Empirical work is also inconclusive. Studies carried out in the UK suggest that only a minority was unstable; Osterman (1980) in the USA, found that the majority was unstable. The likelihood is that the extent and character of any job-swapping period are, at least in part, related to context. There was a much wider range of school-leavers and jobs in the UK than in the US data of Osterman (1980). The maturity level of some of the British early school-leavers was recognized by employers, for example, in the institution of apprenticeship and the availability of opportunities. The respective sets of results seem to reflect these different levels of heterogeneity in the labour market.

Investigations

Based on these conclusions, and following the main argument of the book, it is proposed that patterns of stability are, in part, context-based. In Britain in the late 1970s, where a heterogeneity both of school-leavers and of the kinds of jobs available to them was apparent, it is expected that many separations will be purposeful. Consequently, because of the constraints imposed on the efficacy of rational job-swapping in the context of increasing unemployment, it is expected that instability will be restricted to a minority. Nevertheless, among this group, the 'immature' should be apparent.

The Extent of Youth Instability

The job-swapping process involves a series of separations in an attempt to find a job–individual match by direct experience, or merely to come to terms with the reality of the workplace. In a context of increasing unemployment, where separations are likely to lead to unemployment with its associated negative effect on re-employment, it seems unlikely that a general purposeful sequence will be apparent for many young people. Nevertheless, there may be some who job-shop in the traditional way, perhaps through initial difficulty in finding meaningful work, or perhaps after a lay-off. There may be job-engendered quit behaviour for purposes of respite. Finally, there may be a group which is transient in attitude and displays 'immature' behaviour. Overall, it is expected that only a minority will indulge in the process because there is a wide range of young people, not merely a minority of high-school drop-outs. Moreover, purposeful shopping behaviour is likely to be constrained by a rational response to unemployment and lack of opportunity.

The majority of the sample, both males and females, was stable throughout the period of the survey (see Table 8.1). To some extent, this might have been accounted for by the inclusion of apprentices in the sample, but when they were excluded the majority of the rest was stable. Moreover, only a small minority of youngsters experienced repeated turnover: only 7 per cent with three separations or more in eighteen months (see Table 8.2). This figure may be low because increasing unemployment had affected quit rates, either directly in a demonstration of labour market maturity, or by a process whereby many of those who quit remained unemployed, so the sub-sample over-represents the stable. In fact, both sets of results from this investigation may well underestimate the numbers who experienced turnover because those who dropped out at any stage of the survey were excluded from the total separation figures in all the investigations as there was incomplete information:[2] it may well be that these represent the immature.

In conclusion, only a small minority demonstrated unstable behaviour in the first two years after leaving school, supporting results from other British studies.

Determinants of Instability: An Incentive–Opportunity Model of Quit Behaviour

This model is based on the interdisciplinary approach of Cregan (1991) and Cregan and Johnson (1993).

In order more precisely to isolate employee motivation, quit behaviour from the first job will be identified and examined. This is because the period 1979–81 marked a sharp increase in youth unemployment

Table 8.1

(a) Stability patterns: July 1979–December 1981

	Stable throughout period of survey	Held more than one job	All
Females	284 (59%)	200 (41%)	484
Males	340 (60%)	227 (40%)	567
All	624 (59%)	427 (41%)	1051

(b) Separation frequency: July 1979–December 1981

Number of separations	Females	Males	All
0	283 (59%)	340 (61%)	623 (60%)
1	123 (26%)	124 (22%)	247 (24%)
2	39 (8%)	57 (10%)	96 (9%)
3	19 (4%)	26 (5%)	45 (4%)
4	11 (2%)	8 (1%)	19 (2%)
5	5 (1%)	2 (-%)	7 (1%)
6	1 (-%)	1 (-%)	2 (-%)
7	1 (-%)	1 (-%)	2 (-%)
11	- (-%)	1 (-%)	1 (-%)
Total	482	560	1042

Table 8.2 *Separation frequency (excluding those with general training opportunities)*

Number of separations	Females	Males	All
0	199 (60%)	90 (50%)	289 (57%)
1	81 (25%)	44 (25%)	125 (25%)
2	24 (7)	27 (15)	51 (10)
3	13 (4)	13 (7)	26 (5)
4	8 (2)	3 (2)	11 (2)
5	5 (2)	1 (1)	6 (1)
6	- (-)	- (-)	- (-)
7	- (-)	1 (-)	1 (-)

when some young people could have been laid off because of their representation in recession-prone industries, such as manufacturing, rather than through their own misdemeanours or the rent-seeking activities of employers.

A multidisciplinary theory of quit behaviour will be constructed which allows for both purposeful and transient behaviour. This will be carried out by analysing existing themes in the literature and building them into a cohesive explanation which allows for both motivations.

Purposeful Behaviour

In the pioneering work of March and Simon (1958), voluntary separations acted as a means of restoring balance to the individual psyche,[3] and such a theory lends itself easily to an analysis of youth behaviour. The authors defined quits as direct job-to-job changes and essentially saw motivation for voluntary separation as arising from a personal imbalance which resulted from both financial and psychic circumstances of the present job. A return to equilibrium might be achieved by finding a new job, hence quitting, or by attempts to ameliorate current circumstances or to come to terms with them.

For the economist, however, quits are seen as part of the clearing mechanisms of the labour market: part of an on-going individual utility-maximization process whereby wages are continually being matched to marginal productivity levels. Initially, the mechanism in this approach also was seen as a series of direct job-to-job swaps, and Stoikov and

Ramon (1968) were thus able to adapt the March–Simon model to introduce a simple economic cost–benefit analysis whereby net dissatisfaction provides the incentive to leave while a better job elsewhere constitutes the opportunity.

For the purposes of this investigation, incentive and opportunity can provide a framework in which separately developed theories can be usefully discussed in relation to quit behaviour. For example, if the model includes a lifetime theory of employment, then human capital analysis must be considered. The suggestion is that a worker will allocate employment between jobs, via the mechanism of quits, so as to maximize the rate of returns over costs over his/her lifetime. If this is so, a youngster will quit one job to move to another if offered higher discounted real net returns (Pencavel, 1970). However, lifetime returns involve the issue of skill acquisition. Theory proposes that transferable skills are paid for by employees during the training period in the form of low wages, the investment being recouped in later stages of the career (Becker, 1962). Thus, an approach based on net present returns means that, for some of this age group, a response to training opportunities, rather than a higher wage, may indicate maximizing behaviour.

Job search and information theory has also been used to explain quit behaviour. Job search was seen by Stigler (1962) as a cost of gaining information about jobs. For economists it is, therefore, the central mechanism with regard to quit behaviour and is the focus of enquiry for more recent work (Holmlund and Lang, 1985; Ito, 1988). It is a particularly important issue for school-leavers who have little information about the labour market. This feature can be comfortably integrated into the March–Simon model, providing the measurable link between incentive and opportunity, thereby playing a large part in the determination of voluntary separation by adding to the financial and psychic costs of leaving an employment situation. Parsons (1973), applying search theory directly to quits, maintained that the higher the search costs, the lower the propensity to quit, and economists who have used this approach to explain quit propensity (Pencavel 1972; Parsons 1973) have calculated the ability of different groups to bear costs of search for the next job. From the viewpoint of youngsters who employed the same cheap methods of job search (newspapers, job centres, personal contacts), lived with their parents and applied within the area of Greater London with its efficient transport system, the cost is likely to be in terms of effort and time rather than finance. Thus, differences in these costs are likely to be determined by levels of initial ignorance of the labour market and the amount of information needed to overcome this lack of knowledge.

The main problem, however, for any model based on the March–Simon framework and which employs quit propensity as a dependent variable, is that the authors asserted that the *coincidence* of dissatisfaction and job availability is essential for the occurrence of a quit. Stoikov and Ramon's work listed hypotheses and variables under incentive and opportunity headings separately, implying that there are two clearly identifiable sources of quit behaviour emanating from within and outside the organization, respectively. But this does not solve the problem because, say, incentive alone cannot always lead to a quit whose sole destiny was defined as an alternative job, particularly in the context of high and rising youth unemployment.

Nevertheless, it is possible to overcome this dilemma in a number of ways. First, incentive and opportunity, though analytically distinct, are unlikely to be autonomous elements. In particular, the awareness of the availability of a better job elsewhere is likely to lead to dissatisfaction with the current position; in the context of deepening recession, perception of decreasing opportunities may well have the reverse effect.

Second, information, brought about by the mechanism of job search, may be more efficiently pursued while unemployed and later writers argued that direct job-to-job changes were not the only manner of utility maximization. For example, Gronau (1971) asserted that workers may undertake unemployed search to minimize costs. Mattila (1969) hypothesized that a worker will only line up a job before quitting when the expected costs of unemployed search exceed the additional pay-off of a more intensive search while unemployed. Consequently, unemployment and even exit from the labour market[4] can be seen as opportunity factors, or at least as mechanisms for their attainment. The immediate cost of entry to unemployment is cheap for young people because they have few domestic responsibilities, a low replacement ratio, and may receive a subsidy from parents in terms, say, of rent-free accommodation. If this is the case, then opportunity is always available when dissatisfaction arises. In a similar way, a return to school may be an option, though only for a short while after leaving.

Finally, utility maximization may be seen in terms of a combination of work and leisure. For some school-leavers, entry to the labour market might bring about quits into unemployment for leisure over a period of adjustment. Thus, analysis can be employed in terms of incentive and opportunity without assuming exclusivity of either because these arguments ensure that such an approach is empirically tractable.

Immaturity and Transience

The previous theories have all been concerned with mature, purposeful behaviour. However, as a result of their age, it is said that some young people are immature and risk-prone. Osterman (1980) felt this was an age-related feature of most young people. Thus, a casual and temporary attitude to work might be expected. Their quit behaviour could be a result of a premeditated short-term approach, but frustration-aggression theory has a long pedigree (from Dollard, 1939) and suggests that it could also be an impetuous, spur-of-the-moment decision. In this case, the quit itself may provide the relief from imbalance and therefore acts simultaneously as incentive and opportunity.

The new model, therefore, can be couched in incentive-opportunity terminology, but the analysis must also be more complex than that offered by some earlier writers in order to accommodate developments in human capital, search and information, and frustration-aggression theories. It will allow account to be taken of job-to-job quits, and voluntary separations into unemployment and out of the labour market.

Empirical Work

Two separate types of empirical study were undertaken. First, the existence of incentive and opportunity features was investigated by an examination of youngsters' stated motivations for quitting work. Second, there was statistical modelling. Most empirical work has suffered because the data have made it difficult to disentangle quits and lay-offs. This data-set makes it possible to carry this out but the information used in these particular enquiries was gained in the first three stages only, for it was impossible to isolate quits from other separations in the last two.

In July 1979, 1403 of the 1922 sample had obtained work. By April 1980, 1190 of the 1401 had replied to the survey;[5] of these 815 (68 per cent) had remained in the job and 375 (32 per cent) had quit. By

January 1981, 1064 relevant replies were received. Those remaining in the job numbered 638 (60 per cent) while 426 (40 per cent) had left voluntarily. At the first stage, 54 others replied who said they had been sacked or made redundant; at the second stage there were nine in this category. These were excluded from the quit analysis on the grounds that they formed a different group than those under comparison, namely who remained in the job or who had left involuntarily.

Investigation 1

Reasons for Quitting Job

On two separate occasions, March/April 1980 and December 1980/January 1981, young people who had taken up a job which they had been offered and had accepted by the time they left school were asked whether they had remained in it or had left during the respective previous period. Those who had quit were asked, in an open-ended question, to provide a reason and, overall, 326 (77 per cent) of the 426 provided a response. The results are presented in Table 8.3 and clearly demonstrate the usefulness of the framework for they can be easily categorized under incentive and opportunity headings. Certainly, evidence of purposeful job search was very apparent under both headings.

The incentive groups can be subdivided as follows:

1. *Not like* denotes general dissatisfaction with the job or workplace.

2. Some responses refer to dissatisfaction with specific characteristics, namely *boring, hours, conditions, colleagues, journey*[6] and *inside work*. Dissatisfaction with wages is an unsurprising result from those whose major reward from work is likely to be financial.

3. A mismatch between job and individual abilities or ambitions was apparent: *too hard*.

4. Some remarks were clearly characteristic of school-leavers: *not learn, no prospects, parents* and *holidays*.

Opportunity in the form of alternative employment is demonstrated clearly in *better job* and *this job*. However, the quitters were asked if they had a job arranged before they left their current position. Of the 375, 275 (73 per cent) replied, and it is interesting to note that, of these, 123 (48 per cent) of them had no job arranged; moreover, there were no significant differences in types of reasons offered from those who had a job arranged. Clearly, nearly half of those who provided a response viewed unemployment as an opportunity or the means to achieve it. Furthermore, this seemed to be a generally held view, i.e. not particular to any group, for there were no significant differences in reasons offered for leaving, nor between genders.

Moreover, there were no significant differences between males and females regarding reasons for quitting except for the response *better job*, whereby males were more likely ($p < 0.01$) to give this reason. This is likely to relate to the differences in training opportunities.

Table 8.3 *Reasons given for leaving first full-time job*

Reason	By Mar/Apr 1980			Mar 1980 to Dec 1980/Jan 1981				
	F	M	All	F	M	All	Total	%
I did not like it	14	24	38	1	3	4	42	13
It was boring/I was fed up	30	20	50	1	0	1	51	16
The money wasn't enough	24	24	48	2	1	3	51	16
I was not learning anything	4	6	10				10	3
I got a better job/this job	10	25	35	4	3	7	42	13
I did not like my colleagues	24	20	44	2	2	4	48	15
I did not like the journey	14	8	22	1	0	1	23	7
The work was too difficult	3	4	7	2	0	2	9	3
There weren't enough holidays	1	1	2				2	1
I do not like inside work	0	1	1					1
I was pregnant	3	0	3				3	1
I only took it up temporarily till I found something better	4	11	15	3	1	4	19	6
There were no prospects	1	4	5				5	2
The conditions were poor	2	2	4	0	1	1	5	2
My parents advised me to give it up	0	1	1					1
My health was poor	0	1	1					1
I went back to school	0	3	3					1
Other	4	3	7	0	3	3	10	3
Totals	138	158	296	16	14	30	326	

The ranking order of the responses provides some interesting information about this sample of early school-leavers. Overall, *money* was offered most frequently, followed by *boredom, colleagues, not like* and *better job*. Each of these was offered significantly more frequently ($p < 0.01$) than any other reason outside this group. It may well be, for example, that jobs with low wages or unsatisfying work cause youngsters to be relatively quit-prone or attract the unstable. However, care must be taken when interpreting these responses as, say, some school-leavers may earn a low wage and decide not to quit: no information is given regarding reasons for decisions to remain in the job. That is, the reasons refer to individual perceptions and not to objective personal, job, or workplace characteristics. It is essential, therefore, to set up a formal model in which to investigate the importance of the factors implied by these responses. As they stand, the responses indicate some individual reasons for quit behaviour, including a purposeful approach, and as such are a valuable demonstration of the validity of the incentive-opportunity framework.

Investigation 2

Determinants of Quit Behaviour

Dependent variables: a QUIT or otherwise from the job gained immediately after leaving school as at March/April 1980 and December 1980/January 1981, respectively. Dummy variables were set up according to whether youngsters remained in the first job or had left it voluntarily by the time of each interview.[7]

There were two equations, referring to the overlapping periods July 1979 to March/April 1980 and July 1979 to December 1980/January 1981, that is to the first nine and eighteen months respectively after leaving school. In other words, this was a specific investigation into quit propensity from the first full-time job gained after leaving school because many of the variables used refer specifically to that job. It might be interesting to see if relationships which were apparent in the time immediately after leaving school were sustained over a longer period.[8]

Explanatory variables: A simple incentive-opportunity framework is established initially, followed by human capital analysis, search and information theory, and a consideration of 'immature' behaviour.

1. Incentive-opportunity. Incentives/opportunities can be identified within the data-set. Although mirror images, they can be discussed most clearly from a single viewpoint. Consequently, in terms of incentive to leave, subsequent dissatisfaction, might be averted before entry to the market: where the employer interviewed or examined a candidate, there would be less likelihood of a mismatch between job and individual which might result in dissatisfaction expressed in the kind of responses such as *not like, boring, fed up, too hard.* Once in the workplace, a relatively low income for those in jobs which may provide few other rewards seems likely to provide a major source of incentive to leave and means that replacement ratios are likely to be low. Certainly, the majority of studies by economists of quit behaviour in general have found that income seems to be an important determinant of quit behaviour and the response *money* was given most frequently as a reason in Table 8.3. Finally, problems that might bring about an incentive to leave could be averted by a remedy of problems within the current situation. It might be possible to capture this feature to some extent, for example Hirschman (1970) proposed that unions can provide a collective voice for workers' dissatisfaction thus ameliorating conditions of work. Quits can be seen as an alternative response to such a situation in the absence of a union: the exit option.

Opportunities in the form of a better job seemed likely to be available to the more able, or at least those whom teachers had judged capable of sitting external examinations. Perceptions of unemployment as opportunity or trap are also important (Ragan, 1984; Hall and Lazear, 1984). Those who were new to the labour market might wish for intermittent periods of unemployment for job search or for leisure purposes in a time of transition or adjustment. However, if they were worried about being out of work, particularly in the context of decreasing vacancies and lengthening average duration of youth unemployment, unemployment might not be seen as an option.

INCOME (-)

INTEX: Were you interviewed or given an exam by your employer? (-)

UNION (-)

EXAMS (-)

WORRIED (-)

2. Human capital. *Not learning, no prospects, better job* were some of the responses offered by these young people for their quit decision. It does seem unlikely that those who were in the process of receiving general training would sacrifice their chances of later bargaining power or at least other job opportunities, in order to take up work which offered no formal training.

Gender is a controversial factor with regard to quit behaviour and can be investigated from a human capital viewpoint. Findings from the investigation of a similar data-set by Dex (1982), suggested that young women had a higher quit propensity than their male equivalents. The explanation that she offered is that their jobs provide little training or few prospects and that they are more dissatisfied and leave for better opportunities. However, Blau and Kahn (1981), in a US study, found that when other factors were controlled for, there was no significant difference in gender quit propensity.

GENERAL TRAINING (-)

SEX (?)

3. Job search and information. Experience prior to leaving school might have provided information leading to a realistic view of the labour market. For example, those who had worked in a part-time or voluntary capacity while still at school would have more information and experience of the workplace than others. Economies of scale of unemployed search may explain quit propensities of some youths, and those school-leavers with a low income were likely to have a relatively lower replacement ratio.

With regard to race, conventional theory holds that non-whites are likely to have poor information: Richardson *et al.* (1977) suggested that immigrants in London may only have good information in that part of the labour market in which they are crowded. They are also likely to be informed that they may be discriminated against.

Finally, some young people might have deliberately decided on a period of window-shopping, perhaps some of those who had given the reason *temporary.*

PREVIOUS WORK (-)

INCOME (-)

RACE (+)

DURATION (-)

4. The immature or transients. Those who were unworried about unemployment, particularly in the context of decreasing vacancies and decreasing opportunity, were likely to have a casual attitude. Those who had a part-time job at school were less likely to be shocked at the workplace and engage in impetuous quits.

WORRIED (-)

PREVIOUS WORK (-)

Results

The apparent validation of the framework, and the significance of most of the variables within it is particularly pleasing and suggests that the model may provide a useful platform for further theoretical developments. The results also provide some interesting new evidence about the determinants of youth quit behaviour. In the first set of results, (see Table 8.4), of the ten independent variables, seven proved to have significant coefficients at the March/April 1980 stage, and five of these remained so at the December 1980/January 1981 stage. It is important to note, however, that any interpretation must take into account several factors concerning the representativeness of the sample. First, 21 per cent of the respondents who left their first job by March/April 1980 and 23 per cent who left during the entire period did not give a reason so some of them may have left involuntarily. Second, between the two stages, there was a drop-out rate of 7 per cent of those who had initially gained a job. It is difficult to assess their status but the likelihood is that they had not remained in the same job: quitters may therefore be under-represented to a small extent.

In general, the findings demonstrate that amongst the unstable, purposeful quit behaviour[9] was apparent. First, the income, general training, union, exams, and length of duration coefficients were all significant ($p < 0.01$) and, more important, at both stages of the survey. However, there is always difficulty in dissociating individual from job-related characteristics when discussing findings from this kind of study, and four of these results can be interpreted from both of these viewpoints.

The income result seems to reflect previous findings, with the caveat that the variable that was used referred to income level at the start of the job. In Britain, a contemporary Manpower Services Commission report (MSC, 1980) found that pay was a most important reason given for why young people left their jobs. In the USA, Osterman (1980) and Blau and Kahn (1981) also found that income was an important predictor. However, rather than increasing incentive to leave, it may be that youngsters who gained low-income jobs offered signals which employers felt indicated lack of stability, and they subsequently performed in this way. There is a strong implication that those who started in low-income jobs are likely to remain with lower incomes in the first eighteen months or so.

The general training result also reflects the findings of Blau and Kahn (1981), that training opportunities were a most important determinant of quit behaviour for young people. The result suggests that those with few skill acquisition opportunities have more incentive to leave.

The union result may also refer to attitudes to work. Those prepared to pay a union fee and think in terms of commitment to a workplace

Table 8.4 *Logit model: quit behaviour. Dependent variable: QUIT*

Variable	Mar/Apr 1980		Dec 1980/Jan 1981	
	Coefficient	Coeff./S.E.	Coefficient	Coeff./S.E.
INCOME	-0.01	-2.43**	-0.02	-4.12**
INTEX	0.06	0.53	0.06	0.49
UNION	-0.39	-3.90**	-0.29	-3.04**
EXAMS	-0.46	-3.63**	-0.48	-3.32**
WORRIED	-0.37	-2.70**	-0.09	-1.00
GENERAL TRAINING	-0.35	-4.20**	-0.26	-3.14**
SEX	0.09	1.19	-0.06	-0.71
PREVIOUS WORK	0.02	0.27	-0.01	-0.12
DURATION	-0.51	-4.17**	-0.51	-3.65**
RACE	-0.37	-3.36**	-0.20	-1.53
Constant	5.38	23.72	5.64	23.12

Pearson chi-square 562.51   p 0.39   498.78   p 0.32
Number of cases 1052   917

* Denotes significance at 5% level.   ** Denotes significance at 1% level.

institution are less likely to quit their first job than those who do not, other things being equal, confirming the general argument of Chapters 6 and 7. This is because, while instability does not necessarily imply fecklessness, nevertheless, stability, especially in a time of increasing unemployment, does imply maturity. Positive attitudes to union membership are one reflection of such an approach. However, in July 1979, 42 per cent of those who had joined/intended to join a union, and gave a reason for their decision said they *had to*, while of those who had not joined and gave a reason, 39 per cent said *none was available*. Consequently, the result may reflect, at least in part, rewards of organizations where unions are present, leaving less incentive to leave, according to the Hirschman thesis. Finally, it may be that unions are stronger in larger establishments. It may be, therefore, that this variable has captured a size factor, leading to the possibility of intra-organization transfer, a major feature of the March and Simon work.

The exams result is the only significant finding contrary to that which was predicted, suggesting that those perceived by teachers to have no chance of success in examinations, are more likely to quit over each period surveyed. A Manpower Services Commission report (MSC, 1980) also found that workers with few or no qualifications had experienced more jobs than the better qualified, though it was a mixed-age cohort. It may be that these individuals also find it difficult to find satisfaction in work and are more likely to be unstable when entering the workforce. However, it could be that this feature places individuals low in the job queue because employers of school-leavers, in the absence of full-time work experience records, are likely to use examinations as a signal. Consequently, exams could proxy, to some extent, jobs with relatively poor rewards giving occupants more incentive to leave, either by calculation or from frustration, and perhaps more opportunity in terms of unemployment just for leisure or relief. The duration result was important and remained so even after the twelve-month period. It was clear that some young people took up work temporarily while they looked for a job they wanted, once again belying the view of youth as workshy and signifying their mature appreciation of the context of unemployment.

Second, two variables had coefficients which were highly significant originally, but lost their discernibility by the second stage, suggesting that their respective influence lost its importance over time: race and worried. These may be characteristics of the changing economic context over the period. The race result is particularly interesting as it is contrary to the findings of Blau and Kahn (1981) that the quit propensity of non-whites was less than that of whites. Instead it suggests that young non-whites were initially more likely to quit and thus offers some support for Zax's more recent findings that the black effect was positive (Zax, 1989). It may well be that non-whites lacked labour market information and were more optimistic about alternative opportunities than non-whites in the first nine months, but during the course of the eighteen-month period they may well have acquired sufficient knowledge of increasing youth unemployment to regard the holding of a job as sufficient incentive to stay. In the same way, longer exposure to the labour market was likely to inform those who initially claimed to be unworried about unemployment. In other words, race results may be context-specific.

Third, three coefficients proved to be insignificant at both stages. The result for the employer's interview/examination (INTEX) implies that organizations are not using screens/signals which efficiently match stability to the firm's requirements. The previous work result suggests that jobs undertaken by school-children give no valuable information about the labour market in general and perhaps are in a separate category from full-time jobs. The importance of a temporary approach did seem to be incontrovertibly apparent in the unworried attitude to unemployment result. Interestingly, this lost its significance in the second study. The likelihood is that this variable captured the immature, but that exposure to the labour market rendered initial attitudes superfluous. In other words, they grew up quickly (or remained numbered among the unemployed).

Finally, the insignificance of the sex coefficient is interesting. There have been conflicting views on female turnover. It is popularly assumed that women quit to follow their partners and to have children and/or do not invest in firm-specific skills. In this study, the young women have no family commitments or responsibilities: school-leaver behaviour provides a unique opportunity to test gender attitudes to the respective type of work undertaken and controlling for domestic obligations. These findings are in contrast to those of Dex (1982) and of a survey in the *Department of Employment Gazette* (1982b), which reported that 16/17-year-old females experienced higher turnover rates than males. Both of these studies used methods of analysis that were not able to control for other influences. However, they support the results of the regression analysis of Blau and Kahn (1981), suggesting that there is no significant difference between young male and female quit propensities, despite the broadly different types of occupations in which they were represented. This interpretation, of course, assumes that opportunities, or lack of them, are perceived to be broadly similar for each of the sexes. In the light of respective unemployment chances,[10] it seems likely that this assumption can be made.

Conclusions

The first empirical finding is that the experience of job-swapping, even during increasing recession, was apparent only for a minority of males and females, respectively. Indeed, the majority of both genders were stable throughout the entire period. This is likely to be context-related, but it does support the findings of similar British studies of working-class early school-leavers. The second finding is that the temporary attitude, said to be typical of youth, was identified only among the minority who quit their first job. Quit behaviour resulted from both purposeful job-shopping and immature behaviour. That is, the results point to the existence of heterogeneity among this range of school-leavers which included the deliberate transients. Although the findings of any study are likely, in part, to be peculiar to context because of the importance of opportunity factors, it is interesting that the results offer support for recent work regarding the importance of income, training opportunities, union presence, gender, and race. This interdisciplinary model of quits, which integrated separate developments in turnover theory from different disciplines within a revised incentive-opportunity framework, has been specifically adapted to the case of young school-leavers but it might be interesting to compare these results to those of different age groups.[11]

Notes

1 This was the regulation in 1979–81 when 16–17-year-olds were entitled to benefits in their own right.
2 Moreover, some of those who left work became unemployed so it is likely, therefore, that the job-swapping tendencies may be understated for it is necessary to gain a job in order to leave it. This investigation, however, is concerned with the actuality.

3 Their quit model was part of a larger decision-making conflict model based round an inducements contribution balance with regard to job participation.

4 Quits which result in departure from the labour market can also be explained by failed unemployed job search leading to 'despair' (Gronau, 1971).

5 This demonstrates a drop-out rate of 15 per cent by the second stage.

6 'Journey' is an interesting result as Zax (1991) reported an inverse relationship between moves and quits. Young people, therefore, if restricted to the parental home, would find it more difficult to move than adults.

7 All youngsters who had quit their jobs voluntarily were included in this analysis, not merely those who had given reasons. Interviews took place over a number of days so there is likely to be a very small margin of error as some who had not quit when interviewed may have done so when the last of the cohort was approached.

8 There were insufficient quitters in the second part of the eighteen-month period to make a separate investigation worthwhile.

9 The data-set allowed a test of Willis's assertion (Willis, 1977) that, for a sample of mainly working-class 'lads', the diversions they learned at school, including absenteeism, prepared them for the shock of the workplace, where they were likely to be initially the more stable. Ashton (1975) supported this viewpoint so it seemed worthwhile making a separate investigation. These early school-leavers were asked if they were regularly absent from school for reasons other than sickness: it was thought that a positive response might identify the 'lads'. The dummy was constructed in the usual way, and models were constructed which included both genders, males only, then white males only, to more closely correspond to Willis's sample. In all cases, the coefficient was insignificant, but it may be that the differing context of increasing recession changed some behaviour, both at school and at the workplace.

10 Eighty-three per cent of females and 89 per cent of males from this sample found work immediately on leaving school.

11 The theory can easily be developed into a general model which must also include the features of transfer costs, levels and types of skills, and loyalty to the organization: issues irrelevant to the new entrant to the workforce.

9 THE END OF THE 1979–81 SURVEY: THEMES AND PATTERNS

Introduction

The aim of this chapter is to draw together the themes of the 1979–81 survey. First, this will be carried out empirically by examining the effect of each of the issues investigated on the change in the young persons' incomes by the end of the survey. If mature, purposeful behaviour is apparent in many of the cohort in a situation of heterogeneity, then the rent-seeking mechanisms of the market and institutional devices in the form of unions should operate. However, where homogeneity and casual or impetuous transience prevail, predictable increases in income will not be apparent. Second, an overall summary will be made of the entire set of findings of the survey and conclusions will be presented.

The End of the Survey: Changes in Income

The London survey covered two years so this is not an investigation into the effect of youth experience on adult life. Instead, it is an attempt to examine the characteristics of the labour market in which youth gained jobs by investigating the effects of individual characteristics, initial job types, union membership, and mobility patterns on a change in income over the period. In this way, entry ports to long-term careers might be identified in a situation of heterogeneity.

Literature Review

There is little empirical work in this area but, nevertheless, both results and explanations of them are conflicting. Several studies are concerned specifically with the short-term earnings effect of youth mobility patterns.[1] Over a five-year term Osterman (1980) claimed to find no effect. This is because, he argued, most young people only took up unskilled work in the early years in the labour market. However, some studies suggest a heterogeneity of available job types in which, say, skill acquisition or tenure might be important. Blau and Kahn (1981) found that quitting had a positive effect both on current earnings and on long-term prospects, implying that some quits involved a move to jobs with training opportunities. Dex (1982), in a survey very similar to the London enquiry, reported that those young people who experienced high quit rates had relatively low earnings and occupational status after four years. Elias and Blanchflower (1989), in a 1981 British study of the National Child Development Survey birth cohort of those born in 1958 (but including some 17- and 18-year-old leavers), also found that 'young people who switch jobs appear to put themselves at a disadvantage' (p. 8).

Determinants of Change in Income over the Two-year Period

If there is some heterogeneity amongst individuals and jobs, then a change in income over the period should result from predictable factors: productivity changes, rent-seeking behaviour, discrimination and the effect of institutions.

Productivity Changes: Ability, Effort and Training

Economic theory suggests that a change in income over the period is the result of change in productivity. In the case of school-leavers with no previous skill label, this can only be manifest in terms of productivity increases (as opposed to the redundancy of an existing skill). First, individual ability and effort would be likely to lead to greater acquisition of skill. For example, those who had been considered more able by teachers, provided they were able to express it in the job(s) they were doing, would more easily acquire expertise of many types; those who said they intended to stay in their job after the end of the survey were likely to be making greater efforts and be rewarded accordingly.

Second, skill acquisition is a major source of increased productivity: those who initially took up jobs which offered general training opportunities would be likely to acquire skill. Finally, it is generally accepted that, overall, males as a group receive more in-depth training than females and thus would be more productive by the end of the period.

Rent-seeking Behaviour: Separations

The arguments that have been put forward suggest that young people are unstable, i.e. they job-swap for different reasons, both instrumental and otherwise. For example, they quit or behave badly and are sacked because they can (or think they can) find better returns, because they need a respite from their current situation even by a period of unemployment, or as a result of an unthinking shock reaction to new entry to the workforce; they may be sacked because they are 'last in', do not have union protection, or because they are in jobs especially subject to recessionary forces. Thus, it is expected that there will be no overall earnings effect because although the process includes rent-seeking on the part of different parties, it is not merely one of the purposeful acquisition of information about greater rewards.

Discrimination

One would expect non-whites to develop expertise at the same rate as whites, but if there is a taste for prejudice (Becker, 1962) then whites may receive a greater reward than non-whites for their increase in productivity, because some employers may prefer to promote inferior whites, thus exercising these tastes.

Institutions

There is manifold evidence to suggest the existence of a union/non-union differential (see Stewart, 1981, for a contemporary estimate). It is expected that those young people who had joined a union would, in general, receive a greater increase in wages than those who had not.

Empirical Work

Change in income (per week) was employed as the most pertinent measure of this investigation.[2] Individuals included in the samples were those who said they had accepted a job, and knew wage details, by July 1979, and could supply the same details at the end of the period. Consequently, it was possible to control for real and nominal wage changes over time. The young people included in this investigation numbered 877. Of these, 382 (44 per cent) were females; 798 (91 per cent) were white, 53 (6 per cent) black and 7 (1 per cent) Asian, 19 (2 per cent) other.

Dependent Variable

CHANGE IN INCOME : A simple calculation was made, subtracting weekly income at the beginning of the survey from weekly income at the end and the dependent variable was constructed accordingly.

Explanatory Variables

SEPARATIONS: Number of job separations experienced over the period July 1979–January 1981 (?) (Separation frequency over the entire period was used and drop-outs excluded.)

INTENTION TO LEAVE JOB: Are you seriously considering changing your job at the moment? (-)

EXAMS (+)

SEX (+)

RACE (?)

UNION (+)

GENERAL TRAINING (+)

Results

In the first equation, all of the coefficients were significant (see Table 9.1). The sex coefficient was positive as expected and, as it was significant, it was decided to set up separate models for each of the sexes.

Most findings clearly support the arguments and demonstrate the validity of the model and the proxies. They strongly support the notion that there is heterogeneity within a conventional youth labour market. Males and females with no initial access to skill acquisition were

Table 9.1 *Regression: change in income (1). Dependent variable: change in income over period (CHANGE IN INCOME)*

Independent variables	Females and males	
	Coefficient	T-statistic
SEPARATIONS	2.38	2.59**
INTENT TO LEAVE	4.94	2.12*
EXAMS	9.96	2.69**
SEX	4.46	2.50*
RACE	5.04	1.55*
UNION	6.97	3.66**
GENERAL TRAINING	4.87	2.71**

F 8.26 R^2 0.26

Number of cases   715

* Denotes significance at 5% level.   ** Denotes significance at 1% level.

disadvantaged financially by the end of the survey. Returns to general training were becoming apparent even within two years. In some respects, this is a disturbing finding as the results in Chapter 4 demonstrated that major determinants of gaining skilled work lay outside the young people's control. It is a parallel finding to that of Lynch (1985; 1987) who explored this London data-set to examine the experiences of the unemployed, as opposed to those in work, and concluded that initial unemployment had long-term effects in terms of the later probability of gaining a job. The strong implication is that 'ports of entry' are very important on immediate entrance to the labour market. Unsurprisingly, both males and females who lacked the care of a union received less of an increase in income than those who did/had intended to join.

The results also point to interesting differences in the characteristics of the gender-based market structure not evident in the mere difference in occupations that have already been noted (see Table 9.2). First, separations frequency was unimportant for females though not for males. This suggests that job-swapping 'paid off' financially for male school-leavers even during recession, provided they held a job at the

Table 9.2 *Regression: change in income (2). Dependent variable: change in income over period* (*CHANGE IN INCOME*)

Independent variables	Females		Males	
	Coefficient	T-statistic	Coefficient	T-statistic
SEPARATIONS	0.99	0.95	3.85	2.56*
INTENT TO LEAVE	5.60	2.17*	4.69	1.21
EXAMS	9.80	2.31*	10.81	1.82
RACE	10.20	2.06*	3.13	0.71
UNION	5.44	2.21*	8.00	2.87**
GENERAL TRAINING	4.67	2.11*	5.58	2.02*
F		3.90		3.59
R^2		0.67		0.53
Number of cases		321		393

* Denotes significance at 5% level.   ** Denotes significance at 1% level.

end of the survey. This is an important result and must be interpreted carefully. Because separate gender market structures were identified, this difference is likely to be accounted for by the respective characters of job types. The young males took up a narrower range of jobs in which, however, the training opportunities offered skill acquisition suitable for a long-term career, and in some cases probably faced a formal progressive wage structure. Their job-swapping process was likely to be motivated by this situation, and the effects seem to reflect its success because a (series of) separation(s) can lead to a job which offers better rewards. Providing they were in work at the end of the survey, this seems to be the effect of the phenomenon for the male school-leavers of this study. Young females, however, faced a wider range of job opportunities, which nevertheless provided less overall training. Thus, job-swapping for them had no significant effects on a change in earnings (though it did not worsen their situation). There was no significant difference in separation frequency between genders so some female quit behaviour might have been motivated by a search for psychic rather than financial rewards, in terms, say, of a more appropriate occupation type.

Second, for females the coefficients of the individual variables exams and the proxy for effort made in current job (INTENT TO LEAVE), were significant.[4] For males, they were insignificant. The likelihood is that the wider range of jobs types and the informality of wage structures available to females (relative to males) meant that personal characteristics and endeavours could be rewarded. More males, mainly in manual work, could well have been paid the 'rate for the job'.

Finally, the race coefficient was significant only for females. It may be that a more formal male wage structure prevents employer discrimination and/or that this sample of non-white women was disadvantaged in 'female' jobs which offer training because customers discriminate against them, or employers think they do (for example, sales and reception work). However, it must be noted that 94 per cent of these females were white and there were only ten black and four Asian women in this part of the analysis. It may be unwise to make generalizations from such small numbers, though the proportion is representative of non-whites in Britain.

In summary, the results suggest that heterogeneity exists within a conventional labour market, that initially gaining a job with general training opportunities and an intention to join a union is important for both genders. But it also points to very different gender-based markets in which, for males, more rewards for training and the likely existence of formal wage structures make job-swapping efficacious. While the reverse case for females, and the wider range of job types, allows scope for the effect of individual attributes, the existence of non-white disadvantage was apparent. There is a caveat. It may be that the unstable were under-represented in this part of the sample and were represented in the unemployed.

Overall Summary and Conclusion of the 1979–81 Survey Findings

It has been argued that, during the post-war period in Britain, idiosyncratic features meant that some heterogeneity existed within the youth labour market in Britain, with an associated general labour market maturity of many of the participants. These features were apparent in the survey findings. However, there was no challenge to the conventional view of the youth labour market. Most of the young people gained work in typical youth areas while males and females demonstrated preferences for traditional gender-based occupations which were the kind they gained. Ability had no importance in gaining work in general.

Nevertheless, within this context, the proposition was strongly upheld. First, there was evidence of heterogeneity of jobs and of individuals, with associated purposeful job search and a matching process. There were jobs which offered formal general training, including apprenticeships, and jobs which offered promotion (albeit short term), some with on-the-job training. A hierarchy was apparent, particularly for males. There was a range of young people with different examinations, levels of comprehension and group characteristics. Many jobs were not gained by accident: job-search variables were influential and there was a matching process. Ability was important in gaining the skill and promotion opportunities: the most able at school and the more articulate were advantaged in finding work with promotion, and, for males, gaining an apprenticeship. Socialization and group influences were also influential: inner-city residents and non-whites were disadvantaged. However, traditional occupational choice variables were usurped by an important influence more appropriate to an era of persisting unemployment: the importance of household unemployment. Nevertheless, it must be stressed that this was a working-class sample and it might not have been possible to capture adequately the nuances of class divisions within such a group.

Second, there was evidence also of a general labour market maturity. As expected, a transient attitude was identified in some youth. However, only a minority of the young people who gained work quit their first job; even fewer indulged in a period of job-swapping and there was evidence of much purposeful behaviour with regard to quit behaviour. Moreover, although a small proportion joined a union, this was mainly the result of non-recruitment rather than the non-inclination of youth to join. It is important to note that a positive attitude to union membership demonstrated maturity and commitment to the workplace. Young people who wanted to join a union did so not because they were rebellious. For example, very few joined because of strike activity and they were matched in number by those who would not join for the same reason. In fact, union membership and job-swapping options in general paid off in terms of an increase in income by the end of the period.

Within this framework of heterogeneity, it was possible to discern some sources of disadvantage in a situation of job scarcity where matching, for the most part, was made by employer decisions. Most disturbing for youth was the importance of those characteristics over which they had no influence, in the form of the group variables: non-white ethnicity, inner city residence; and the presence of household unemployment. Moreover, there was a 'long shadow' effect of initial job type on wage gains at the end of the period, which paralleled Lynch's studies of the unemployed in this data-set which suggested that initial unemployment adversely affected the probability of gaining a job (Lynch 1985, 1987). There was also gender disadvantage, but of a different type. Females did not find it more difficult to get a job but received less of a financial increase than males over the period; moreover, for females, job-swapping did not help in gaining an increase in income. This is probably because females took up different kinds of occupations than males, some of which offered skill acquisition that was rewarded less well than that offered to males.

In summary, the main implication of these findings is that, given a range of opportunities and of individual characteristics, respectively, a matching process can occur. Although in general, the young people lacked control over their own destiny, nevertheless, the idiosyncratic features of the market improved the lot of the group as a whole. For some young people, it was possible to initially search for jobs, use ability to gain those with skill and promotion, job-swap purposefully, and join unions, even within traditional youth jobs.

Moreover, the main argument has been upheld which linked labour market maturity to this situation of heterogeneity and the existence of a matching process. It can be explained, at least in part, by the legal, institutional, and traditional influences apparent in Britain, which gave its youth labour market a distinctive character. Osterman's analysis (Osterman, 1980) has dominated studies of the youth labour market, yet its findings may well be context-specific. Kerckhoff (1990) analysed National Child Development Study data for comparison with US figures and concluded that there are national differences resulting from the fact that 'in the 1970s, the majority of young Britons entered the labour force at 16 or 17'. Heterogeneity in the post-war decades in Britain provided important ports of entry to youth in several ways. The 1979–81 survey marked the end of such an era as radical changes took place which were to affect the situation dramatically.

Notes

1 Some studies are concerned with the earnings/occupation effect of youth mobility patterns for a wide range of youth, not just early school-leavers, and over quite a long period of time. The Department of Employment (*Department of Employment Gazette*, 1982b) published findings from longitudinal analysis which suggested that a lot of job changing in the initial occupation did not result in disadvantage with regard to occupations in later life relative to stable youth. Metcalf and Richards (1983), in a longitudinal analysis of National Training Survey data, 1930–75, demonstrated that early turnover had no impact on later occupational status. Cherry (1976) reached the same conclusions, but with a sample of only 73 cases.

2 Absolute income at the end of the period (November/December 1981) was considered to be an inadequate measure as it was likely to be highly correlated to initial income. Percentage change in income would clearly augment this problem. Moreover, Roberts *et al.* (1987) reported that there were wide disparities between the starting rates for similarly qualified young people entering similar occupations in the same areas but in different firms.

3 In exploratory investigations, the COMPREHENSION variable was introduced. The coefficient was never significant, though it had been important when gaining work. This may have implications for recruitment policies.

10 THE YOUTH LABOUR MARKET IN BRITAIN AT THE END OF THE CENTURY

Introduction

By the mid-1990s the character of the youth labour market in Britain had changed dramatically from the context in which the London survey took place. Until the later years of the 1970s, fewer than one in five 16-year-olds in Britain stayed on in education. The vast majority left school and gained work. By the mid-1990s, however, the situation was reversed. Most stayed in education and less than 10 per cent started work.[1] Payne and Payne (1994) concluded that 'the youth labour market is in the process of disappearing' (p. 94). By an analysis of empirical work that took place during the Conservative era, this chapter will attempt to analyse and explain this revolutionary change in terms of the changing context of the 1980s and 1990s.

The main aim is to demonstrate that the British youth market for early school-leavers apparently converged towards the conventional model of homogeneous, dead-end work (Osterman, 1980) by the partial loss of idiosyncratic features which had been a product of the contextual and institutional factors apparent in the post-war decades. It will be argued, however, that the outcome is a hybrid. Rather than providing 'youth jobs' as a transitional stage before entry to the adult world of work, the labour market offered increasingly low-skill jobs from which entry to career work became more difficult. Moreover, job-swapping for purposes of information or respite became more difficult in an era of persisting high youth unemployment, especially when state benefits were withdrawn. In such a situation, youth responded by turning to education or training schemes. There have been several major on-going studies of young people conducted in Britain during the 1980s and 1990s,[2] and for clarity of presentation the cohort years referred to by each study of the England and Wales Youth Cohort Series are described in Appendix 3.

The Changing Pattern: Economic Activity Rates of Early School-leavers

Available figures suggest that during the Conservative era, there were two distinct patterns of early school-leaver economic activity rates:

Table 10.1 *Participation rates (per cent) of early school-leavers*

Year	Out of work	YT/YTS	Full-time job	Full-time education	Other	Reference
1984	8	28	17	42	4	Sime (1991)
1985	7	30	19	40	3	"
1986	7	30	20	40	4	"
1988	2	25	22	47	3	"
1989		24	23	48	5	Payne (1995a)
1991		16	16	58	10	"
1992		15	11	66	8	"

before 1988, and thereafter (see Table 10.1). About 45 per cent of 16-year-old pupils stayed on in full-time education during the early/mid-1980s compared to less than 20 per cent for most of the 1970s. By the mid-1980s, most 16-year-olds were delaying entry to jobs by staying on at school, taking up government training, or experiencing long periods of unemployment (Brown, 1987). However, there was a further rising trend beginning in 1988/9 so that by 1991/2, nearly two-thirds of 16-year-olds stayed on (*Department of Education Statistical Bulletin*, 1992). These results are supported by Byford (1983)[3] and by estimates from the England and Wales Youth Cohort Series (Sime, 1991; Payne, 1995a) which give other important details (see Table 10.1). This new pattern persisted and by the end of the Conservative era only 8 per cent of 16-year-olds were in full-time employment[4] (Yates, 1996).

These changes can be explained in terms of 'push' and 'pull' factors (Raffe, 1992). In the post-war decades, growth in the UK economy combined with certain demographic trends had led to a situation where there was an identifiable youth labour market in Britain in which customs and traditions were apparent. By the 1970s, however, changes were occurring which were portents of further transformation. These changes accelerated in the 1980s, as radical departures in political style resulted in decreased government spending and a deregulation of markets, including that for labour. In combination with the effects of the impact of international economic influences, these policies resulted in major changes in the labour market, manifested, for example, in persisting high levels of youth unemployment, a shift in the industries and job types available to young people, changes in work organization, particularly with reference to the introduction of new technology, and a further decrease in the number of traditional training opportunities. These changes acted as 'push' factors, while educational reform and the expansion of Youth Training 'pulled' young people into the quest for more qualifications. It will be argued that the dramatic decline in the proportions of 16-year-olds in the labour market can be explained in this context.

'Push' Factors

Job Opportunities

There were major changes in the amount and types of opportunities available to young people. First, unemployment did not go down again to pre-1979 levels. Overall, despite fluctuations, there were persistently higher rates than in the post-war era. After an average level of just under 4 per cent in the 1970s, between 1979 and 1983, the unemployment rate rose from 5 per cent to 12 per cent and remained higher than 11 per cent until 1986 after which it fell somewhat, but not to previous levels (Waddington and Whitston, 1995). Official estimates put unemployment at about 7.5 per cent during 1996, the last complete year of Conservative rule. By spring 1997, at the end of that political era, it was 7.2 per cent (Labour Market Trends, December 1997). This figure was double that of the 1970s' average. Moreover, based on estimates of actual hours of jobs, Casey (1991) calculated that there was a job deficit relative to that of 1979 of close to 2.5 million full-time jobs.

In the 1990s, most 16- and 17-year-olds were ineligible to register as unemployed, so it is difficult to find a meaningful figure to compare to pre-1979 measures. Nevertheless, using Labour Force Survey (LFS) estimates, there was an even higher plateau of youth unemployment which was over double that of the overall rate: for 16–19-year-olds in spring 1997, at the end of the Conservative era, it was 20 per cent (Labour Market Trends, December 1997). Maguire (1991), in fact, reported that opportunities for youth deteriorated more in the 1980s than in the 1979–82 period. This was in large part a result of a fall in recruitment, which had a severe impact on first entrants: employers were hiring less youth labour. Biggart and Furlong (1996) analysed the results of 160 in-depth interviews which took place in 1994 in four Scottish labour markets and identified a group who stayed at school just because there was no work available. They had originally expected to enter the labour market at an early stage 'following an established working-class tradition', but were worried by high unemployment rates and the difficulties faced by friends and relatives in local labour markets: 'often scared [because] YT was seen as the only option' (p. 262). Consequently, although the overall trend of the British economy after 1982 was one of expansion, this growth was failing to create jobs for young people (Roberts, 1995). In such a context, job-swapping by new entrants was severely constrained.

Second, structural change greatly affected young people. In particular, there was a slump in manufacturing[5] (which had been the largest employer of both young males and young females in 1979: see Table 3.1). Employment in manufacturing as a percentage of the civilian population decreased by 25 per cent between 1980 and 1990 (OECD, 1991). Conversely, since the mid-1950s the service sector had been expanding in terms of numbers employed, reaching a plateau during 1980–3, then experiencing a sharper expansionary trend. From 1979, there was a net increase of two million jobs , mainly in the private sector (Nolan and Walsh, 1995) and by 1993 there were over 3.6 jobs in services for every one in manufacturing (*Department of Employment Gazette*, 1994). Payne (1995a) reported that practices of youth recruitment had changed to accommodate this structural shift.

This shift was reflected in changes in the industrial and occupational patterns of school-leavers. Some simple themes can be derived from the relevant tables presented in the Youth Cohort Series (Courtenay and McAleese, 1993a; 1993b; Payne, 1995b). Although there is a strong continuity whereby young people continue to work in the same set of industries and occupations throughout the second half of the century, there were some important changes. With regard to industrial distribution, the overall proportions of both male and female youths employed in manufacturing had declined, with a concomitant rise in the percentage of those employed in the service industries. Of those who found work, most young people of either gender found jobs in the service industry. Nevertheless, manufacturing remains an important employer of young people, responsible for more than a quarter of their jobs. Thompson *et al.* (1993) produced similar results showing falls in school-leaver recruitment by manufacturing firms at the same time as the growth of the service sector in the 1980s and its recruitment of 16–18-year-olds. Maguire (1991) found evidence of specific decline in areas which had formerly recruited school-leavers – in labour-intensive industries such as textiles, hosiery, and footwear. These had been amongst the most important employers of young people (Marsden and Ryan, 1986).

Continuity and change were also apparent in the Youth Cohort Series' occupational tables (Courtenay and McAleese, 1993a; 1993b). Young people participated in the same cluster of occupations as in the pre-Thatcher era. Clerical work was still the most important job for females and material processing for males. The changes, however, reflected the structural shift: for both genders there were smaller proportions represented in material processing, etc. This meant that, compared to 1979, by the end of the 1980s a lower proportion of young males (just over a third) held that type of job. For females, the effect was to increase the already high proportions in clerical and related jobs. By the end of the 1980s, nearly half of female youth held that kind of occupation.

Third, structural change also affected training opportunities, especially in the manufacturing area, so this naturally greatly affected young people. Unsurprisingly, the trends led to a greater decline in apprenticeships and a shift in the industries in which they were offered. From 1983 they were part-funded by government under the Youth Training Scheme.[6] By 1992, two-thirds of apprenticeship places were funded under Youth Training (YT), in the first year at least, and were less heavily concentrated in the traditional craft areas (Payne, 1995a). Even so, the decline was not halted. In 1980 apprentices accounted for nearly 2.3 per cent of the workforce but by 1990 this figure had dropped to 1 per cent (Keep and Rainbird, 1995). Between 1970 and 1983, the number of apprenticeships available halved from 218,000 to 102,000 and by 1990, at 53,600, was only a quarter of the 1970 total (Keep and Rainbird, 1995). Between 1989 and 1995 the total number of apprentices[7] in the UK fell by nearly half to 191,000 (*Social Trends*, 1996). The effect of the government's Modern Apprenticeships scheme, launched nationally in September 1995, for skill acquisition in technical, craft, and junior management, covering job-specific and core skills[8] (*Department of Employment Gazette*, 1995, December), was not apparent by the end of Conservative rule.

Fourth, there were important work-organization changes in the form of the introduction of flexible practices. In the 1980s and 1990s there were several major changes that affected young people.

1. There was a substitution of full-time jobs for part-time, contract, and casual work.[9] Horrell and Rubery (1991) found evidence of increased importance attached by employers in both the public and private sectors to extended and flexible hours, largely in the form of overtime and part-time work. Nolan and Walsh (1995) reported that in 1971, only one in six employees worked part-time; by 1995, it was one in three. They found there had been a dramatic move from 'standard' to 'non-standard' employment in the form of approximately 1.5 million part-time jobs created since 1979, mainly in the private sector of the service industry and within that, in banking, finance, insurance, retail, hotel, and catering; and that while public service employment had not expanded, part-time work there had increased its share of the total. Maguire (1991) also found evidence of the replacement of full-time by part-time work in clerical jobs, and the hotel, catering, and retail industries. Many of these areas were traditional employers of young people. In terms of rewards for this work, there is evidence that part-time jobs were worse than full-time jobs with respect to hourly pay, training opportunities, fringe benefits, and statutory rights (Rubery, 1995). Nolan and Walsh (1995) found that the part-time jobs in the private sector 'are often poorly paid, unstable and commonly fail to attract such benefits as redundancy and sick pay' (p. 57).

2. There was also a move towards new technology generally, and the production of quality goods in manufacturing industry, especially through the application of computer-aided design techniques. Geary (1995) claimed 'although changes in work organisation have been widespread, this effect has been modest so that they do not amount to

a transformation' (p. 369). Nevertheless, youths and other low-skill workers were amongst those affected most profoundly in an adverse manner by the changes. In particular, new technology led to the replacement of traditional work practices, including some craft apprenticeships, with high-skill, specialist jobs from which youth was excluded because of its lack of expertise. Roberts *et al.* (1987) observed in the 1980s that training had shifted from craft apprenticeships towards training which led to the requirement of workers with higher qualifications and occupational levels. Maguire (1991) concluded that, in the 1980s the introduction of new technology in clerical work and manufacturing, especially engineering, meant that 16- and 17-year-olds were excluded from some jobs because they were insufficiently qualified. Thompson *et al.* (1993) found that some service companies in the 1980s, assisted by information technology, had introduced high-skill jobs which needed better qualifications and therefore older workers. Finally, Hart (1988) reported limited evidence of the replacement of youth labour, especially in manufacturing, not by other workers, but by the capital equipment itself.

Youth, therefore, was increasingly restricted to opportunities in low-level work. Roberts *et al.* (1987) reported a polarization whereby high-skill workers existed alongside low-skill workers. There is evidence that some jobs were made more complex and others, often part-time, became more routine, leading to 'an increasing polarisation of skills' (Thompson *et al.*, 1993, p. 19). Gallie (1994) found that 'a polarisation of skill experiences' (p. 75) became apparent in the 1980s, and was closely associated with technological change. Moreover, Elger (1990) concluded that greater work flexibility in manufacturing in Britain in the 1980s was dominated by labour intensification and the horizontal enlargement of tasks. Gallie (1994) investigated the service sector and found evidence to associate its growth in the private sector with the presence of a particularly large and exceptionally low-skilled category of non-manual work. Thompson *et al.* (1993) reported the use of information technology to introduce automation and routinization in jobs in the service industry traditionally performed by youth; these jobs became simplified and repetitive. Overall, therefore, where the trend towards new technology was apparent, there were fewer jobs, and a bipolar situation with a small amount of high-skill jobs which youth could not enter and many very low-skill jobs. Roberts (1995) concluded that 'the type of dead-end juvenile jobs that had existed before the

Second World War, but which had been driven off the labour market in the subsequent conditions of full employment, began to be recreated in the 1980s' (p. 17).

3. The evidence also suggests that although some jobs with promotion prospects were still available for young people, by the mid-1990s they had declined further. Empirical studies of changes in organizational structures and their effects on youth are very difficult to find. With regard to the short-term promotion jobs which provided a 'practice pitch' for youth before they moved on to long-term work, there is no specific evidence at all. Roberts *et al.* (1987) suggested that most training carried out at the workplace was expected to pay for itself within six months. Payne (1995a) also suggested that on-the-job training was very short. With regard to longer-term career jobs, there seem to be two conflicting and opposing trends. First, there is some evidence that the expansion of the service industry meant that, alongside the low-skill work, there were opportunities for jobs with promotion for a small number of youths in the middle years of the 1980s. For example, Roberts *et al.* (1987) found that in 1984, although very few firms offered management training to early school-leavers, 'financial and public sector organisations were recruiting 16–18 year olds into clerical trades from which those suitable for management were eventually selected' (p. 49). Metcalf (1988) reported the following: some banks and insurance companies wanted school-leavers for clerical and future management and some chain stores selected them as management trainees. The public sector selected some future managers from 16/17-year-old entrants. In the health industry there were few substitutes for youth as management trainees for nursing. She found that some organizations recruited young people for these positions only because they thought that they could not get enough recruits from other sources, especially graduates; but others saw school-leaver paths to management as different from more qualified, older groups – moving up career ladders more slowly and therefore providing valuable expertise in the future through long service at the lower levels. Graduates were considered unsuitable in these circumstances because with slow career progressions they were expected to leave. She concluded: 'school leavers' roles in the career structure of organisations were complex and in many organisations school leavers were one of the sources of future managers, particularly low-level managers' (Metcalf,

1988, p. 18). Thompson *et al.* (1993) maintained that the growing service sector of the 1980s typically over-recruited youth, anticipating high turnover and variations in the quality of labour, in a 'sink or swim model' (p. 14) and that for, say, banks or the retail industry, youth was 'cannon fodder', with just a few 16/17-year-olds progressing through the hierarchy to management level in 'youth-based internal labour markets' (p. 14).

Second, there was also a flattening of hierarchies within some service enterprises (Thompson *et al.*, 1993) and this effect seemed to predominate after the initial expansion of the service sector. Thompson *et al.* found that fewer school-leavers were recruited in the service industry in the 1990s and that 'those leaving at 16 years old are more likely to be recruited into the lower skilled area of flatter, as opposed to career ladder structures, without much opportunity to progress' (p. 19). They were left, with women returners, to the routine, unskilled tasks, while the better-educated 18-year-olds were more likely to staff junior and middle management jobs at the bottom of career hierarchies.

Nevertheless, they concluded that some internal labour markets did provide for the transfer of talented 16-year-olds into the 'fast track' areas normally open to 18-year-olds when they reached that age. It is difficult to arrive at any firm conclusions, but the evidence suggests that, though there were some long-term career opportunities available to 16/17-year-olds in service areas, despite the expansion in that sector in the 1980s, they remained very small in number. They were subject to decline in the 1990s (Thompson *et al.*, 1993).

In summary, on the demand side there was a higher level of unemployment and fewer jobs available than in the post-war decades. There was a loss of full-time jobs in manufacturing, previously the most important area of youth employment for both males and females and which, moreover, had provided craft training opportunities, which were correspondingly less available. These jobs were replaced only in part and increasingly by work of non-standard hours, often in the expanding service sector. New technology led to a polarization of skills in some areas, and youth was increasingly restricted to the lower levels with poor pay and conditions. Although these changes must not be over-emphasized, nevertheless they directly affected those with no skills, especially early school-leavers whose traditional areas of work and training (for males) were in decline. Overall, there were fewer job opportunities available to youth; they were more homogeneous, often part-time, and offered worse pay and conditions than previously.

Competition from Other Workers

For those young people intent on finding work on leaving school, there was increasing competition from adult workers. Adult male unemployment remained at higher levels than prior to 1979 and young adult unemployed, older redundant workers, and female returners were more in evidence. Women, in particular, were increasingly competitors for some youth work because of their willingness to work for low pay, their lack of skill, and constraints on mobility.[10] Between 1985 and 1995 the economic activity rate for women with at least one child aged under 5 rose from 39 per cent to 52 per cent (Labour Market Trends, March 1996a). By summer 1997 women made up 45 per cent of the people in employment (Labour Market Trends, December 1997).

The changes in the workplace caused some firms to prefer these older workers. For example, Roberts *et al.* (1987) found that some employers wanted young people who were slightly older than early school-leavers because they were better qualified or perceived to be more reliable. However, the usual conclusion drawn overall is that an inflow of females took up jobs that would normally have been available for unskilled young people, many of whom instead took up Youth Training Schemes, or returned to full-time education. Thompson *et al.* (1993), for example, noted a deliberate move on the part of employers in the service sector to recruit women returners and older workers. McEwan Scott (1995) reported that in the retail industry, employers distinguished between skilled and unskilled sales workers, viewing married women as the former and school-leavers as the latter, and employed married women when they needed expertise, in the form of experience. Hart (1988) claimed that the strong, upward trend in employment of married women, mainly part-timers, and largely in the distributive and service industries, mostly affected the unskilled, untrained sector of school-leavers. Using Labour Force Survey data, Spilsbury (1990) maintained that the dominant trend was that young people were being displaced by adult female workers, mainly part-time. Maguire (1991) also reported evidence which demonstrated the displacement of youths by married women in sales, cashier, and waitress-type jobs in the service sector in the 1980s.[11]

Nevertheless, there are some problems with this interpretation of events. In particular, Hakim (1995) reported that until the late 1980s, the increase in the numbers of women did not lead to an increase in total hours worked by females. Only from 1987, she claimed, did female employment, in terms of full-time equivalent jobs, rise for the first time, as absolute levels of full-time work rose alongside the existing increase in part-time work.[12]

Thus, the general assumption made is that the reason for this apparent usurpation is that much of the new work was in the form of non-standard hours, and women were more likely than youth to be available for part-time jobs. Part-time work was undertaken by only 12.4 per cent of 16–18-year-olds in 1994/5 (*Labour Market Quarterly Report*, 1996) while in 1995, 43 per cent of women in employment worked part-time, compared to 6 per cent of men (Labour Market Trends, 1996a). Nolan and Walsh (1995) reported that the increased number of part-time jobs in the private sector of the service industry in the 1980s was predominantly filled by women; and that in the public sector part-time non-manual women were an increasing share of the total. Thompson *et al.* (1993) claimed that in the service industry some employers only considered youth for full-time work in readiness for a career.

However, all youths may not have been pushed out of this work. They may have taken the option available to their age group of returning to school, faced with new trends in the workplace.

First, there is evidence that some employer preference for early school-leavers over other groups persisted. Roberts *et al.* (1987) claimed that 'most firms wanted their staffs to be trained and fully conversant with in-house methods, and raw beginners were almost invariably considered ideal candidates for such training' (p. 46). They reported that some employers saw definite advantages in cultivating company loyalty in young people. They found examples of where 16-year-olds were recruited, for instance, in an hotel: 'we need people who don't ask questions and who can be trained in our ways of doing things' (p. 32). Metcalf (1988) reported that some service organizations 'saw school leavers as having certain desirable traits, notably that they would be absorbed into the culture quickly, they had no bad habits ... their motivation was high, and they were adaptable' (p. 19). Ashton and Maguire (1986b) reported that some employers did not want to offer work without prospects to young people and that some still preferred to recruit 16/17-year-olds for training rather than 18–24-year-olds. Even with regard to the introduction of new technology, there is evidence of some preference for youth. Roberts *et al.* (1987) found that some companies mistrusted qualifications, especially small computer firms. Ashton and Maguire (1986b) reported that many employers thought that adults were difficult to retrain and would only recruit young people for jobs which involved working with new technology. Metcalf (1988) reported that some employers preferred to recruit school-leavers because they were quick learners, especially of information technology skills. Finally, there was evidence of the influence of customary practices. Most employers surveyed by Metcalf (1988) claimed that 'tradition' played a part in their recruitment of young people as they could get most of the features they wanted from other age groups.

Second, youth wages had fallen relative to adult wages since the 1970s. Before 1979, youth pay had been protected by collective bargaining, some legislation, and Wage Councils (Metcalf and Richards, 1983); during the Conservative era the influence of each was weakened. The decline in union membership after the 1970s meant that collective bargaining arrangements failed to cover young people as extensively as before. With regard to legislation, in 1979 the Conservative government announced a decision to rescind the fair wages clause of the Employment Protection Act (see Chapter 2). Finally, in 1986, the powers of Wage Councils were reduced, taking those aged under 21 out of their scope; i.e. all employees aged 16–20 were excluded from minimum wage protection. Prior to this, minimum wages generally applied at 18 and younger workers received a lower but regulated minimum wage. In 1995, the Councils were abolished. As a result of all of these measures, according to Rubery (1995) 'there is no longer a web of industry-level minimum rates and wage council rates setting a floor to wages in the labour market' (p. 561) and there has been a significant widening of the differential between adult and youth pay. Unsurprisingly, therefore, wages for both men and women under the age of 18 were falling when wages for adults were rising[13] (*New Earnings Survey*, 1992–5). Moreover, these conclusions may be based on youth figures which are an understatement: a survey of wage rates for workers under 25 undertaken by the General, Municipal and Boilermakers Trade Union (GMB) in 1994 demonstrated that the *New Earnings Survey* excludes most people earning below the income tax threshold – in 1993, £66.50 per week – and that only 20 per cent of jobs for young workers gave remunerations of more than £4 per hour (Chatrik and Madagan, 1995).

Interestingly, however, the likelihood is that a fall in the wages of youth, relative to adult competitors, brings about a preference for them only in the low-paid sectors of the market where training is unavailable. For example, Marsden and Ryan (1986) argued that the removal of Wage Councils would help bring about this situation by 'intensifying the orientation of youth employment towards low wage industries' alongside women workers as those adult males who could leave moved to higher-paying industries (p. 97).

Moreover, Snower and Booth (1996) argued that young workers may be unwilling to accept relatively low wages precisely in this situation where training is unavailable because they recognize they have poor chances of acquiring the skills necessary to generate significantly higher wages in the later years. Consequently, at least part of the increase in the participation rate of youth was probably due to the reaction of some young people against the availability of dead-end work offering part-time rates, rather than full-time jobs, and especially those which offered opportunity. There is recent empirical work which provides direct evidence of the unwillingness of some young people to supply themselves for dead-end work. Biggart and Furlong (1996) identified a group of pupils who stayed on at school after 16 who would not have remained in education in earlier times, instead 'following routes into short term careers' (p. 262) but the demise of the apprenticeship system and 'trainee positions in the white collar sector' (1996: 259) made it necessary for them to pursue academic credentials. Paterson and Raffe (1995) analysed a large survey of Scottish school-pupils and found an unwillingness to take the jobs currently available manifest in the following response: 'there were no jobs available that I wanted'. This conclusion about a flight from the new jobs of the labour market, rather than a usurpation, is supported by evidence which suggests there was some labour shortage in low-skill areas for a while during the expansion of the 1980s. Thompson *et al.* (1993) found instances where employers claimed that the lack of availability of youth forced employers to search for substitutes. Metcalf (1988) claimed that employers turned to A-level applicants and adults when they faced a shortage of youth. In fact, Dawkins and Norris (1995), as a result of their empirical analysis, argued that the increase of non-standard work may have been in part a response to perceived married female preferences[14] rather than determined wholly by cost-cutting 'flexible practice' motivations.[15]

Unsurprisingly, the rising proportion of adult workers into some unskilled areas affected the 'youth' character of some jobs. There were some continuities. Payne (1995a) claimed that, as in the post-war decades, relative to adults, youth were still under-represented in some jobs and over-represented in others. She reported patterns similar to the earlier era. In relationship to the rest of the working population, she found fewer youths in high-level jobs and working as plant and machine operatives, but more in craft and professional services, personal and protective services, security, clerical and secretarial, and selling jobs. She also found that the proportions of youth in 'other miscellaneous low skill jobs is pretty much the same as adults'.

However, the evidence also suggests that jobs in which youths previously formed a high proportion of the workforce were being diluted in terms of their youth character by the greater employment of other groups of worker. Gray *et al.* (1994) claimed that adult workers were seen by employers as suitable for what were once perceived as 'youth jobs'. Metcalf (1988) reported from her investigations in the service industry that 'few posts recruited school-leavers exclusively or predominantly, i.e. few were "school-leaver jobs", except technical trainees (apprentices) and nurses. In most other occupations, married women were the other major source of recruits' (p. 1). A 1995 *Labour Force Survey* report indicated that many women worked in the same jobs as young people: half (51 per cent) of all working-age women worked in just four occupational groups – clerical, secretarial, sales and personal service – compared to 16 per cent of men; 85 per cent worked in service industries compared to 59 per cent of men (*Labour Force Survey*, 1995). This dilution was only to be expected with regard to unskilled work. However, in 1983 the Conservative government introduced reform to the apprenticeship system which aimed to replace traditional time-serving by testing standards, and to remove restrictions limiting age of entry to 16-year-olds (Keep and Mayhew, 1995). This system had provided clear-cut 'youth jobs' in the post-war period, conferring entry port advantages on those who were admitted to such positions.

Overall, the picture that emerges is that the early school-leaving pattern of the post-war period was disrupted by unemployment towards the end of the 1970s. Youth, of course, unlike adults, had the options of school or Youth Training (YT). As lack of opportunity persisted throughout the 1980s, more young people stayed in education or took up YT. After controlling for the effect of government training schemes,

Whitfield and Wilson (1991) found that growing unemployment tended to increase the staying-on rate. However, in terms of numbers, very few were unemployed when the benefit was available – about 7 or 8 per cent in the 1980s – once again belying the view of youth as 'workshy'. But in 1988 the withdrawal of the general entitlement of 16/17-year-olds to income support (in the main, social security and unemployment benefits) had a profound and immediate effect which accelerated existing changes in the participation rate for 16-year-olds (see Table 9.1).

'Pull' Factors

The 'pull' factors of education and training were also very influential in the changes seen in the youth labour market during the 1980s and early '90s. The increase in the participation rate was the result of a number of features.[16] In relation to the labour market, however, Payne (1995a) concluded that staying on at school as a response to lack of opportunity was because qualifications were seen as important in gaining work, especially amongst poorly qualified and low-skill workers whose unemployment rates were particularly high. Gray *et al.* (1994) reported changes in attitudes to education and expectations of staying on at school. These were partly engendered by educational developments, in themselves largely a response to the consequences of unemployment and structural changes. Raffe (1992) argued that the replacement in 1988 of earlier examinations by the GCSE, a common examination for all school-leavers, including those pupils considered less able, was an important factor. Ashford and Gray (1993) explicitly linked GCSE, the introduction of new courses and qualifications and an expansion of places in higher education to the increase in numbers staying on at school. Moreover, the government was intent on educational reform: in 1988 the Education Reform Act introduced national testing in schools. There was also a policy of 'new vocationalism'.[17] It was important, of course, that examination success was attainable and Sime (1991) reported a decrease in the proportion of pupils obtaining no graded results and an upward shift in the proportions of those who gained four or more higher grade passes. For those aged 15 in the August preceding the examination, in 1980/1, 13.5 per cent obtained no graded result, while by 1990/1 this figure had almost halved (7.5 per cent) (Roberts, 1995). However, despite these changes, Yates (1996) reported that many stayed on at school merely to defer labour market entry, and Roberts and Parsell (1992b) claimed that many of those taking the non-academic courses after the age of 16 did so merely as a response to lack of availability of work.

Training programmes were also an alternative to lack of opportunity, and a major response to youth unemployment in the 1980s had been to further vocational qualifications via government training initiatives.[18] In the 1980s, government training schemes had been an option for young people without work, and by 1988 a suitable place was 'guaranteed' with an allowance.[19] However, numbers enrolled declined in the 1990s because there was less provision for funding from Training and Enterprise Councils (TECs) and employers (Raffe, 1992). As YT continued to decline in the 1990s even more young people stayed on at school. The likelihood is that YT had been an alternative form of unemployment (Raffe, 1987; Roberts *et al.*, 1992a). When it was less easy to gain a training place, and state benefits were unavailable, young people who would formerly have entered the labour market or YT now had no other option except to stay on at school since unemployed job-search was no longer viable. Thus, by 1995 two-thirds of 16-year-olds were in full-time education, only 8 per cent in employment, 10 per cent in training, and 7 per cent 'other' (Yates, 1996).[20] The 'other' category included part-time jobs or withdrawal from the labour market, but most were looking for a job or a place on YT (Payne, 1995a).

In fact, these figures provide evidence of a disturbing trend. Payne (1995a) reported that the group unidentified in official categories ('other') had grown. Yates (1996) also identified the existence of a small but growing number of young people opting out of the recognized education, training and employment market. It was estimated in July 1993 that there were 95,600 unemployed young people of whom 65,505 had no job, no training, and no benefits (Youthaid, 1993). This 'other' group included a visible element, sufficiently large in number to draw attention to the plight of the young. The removal of unemployment and social security benefits from youth meant that those who did not or could not stay with the family were often without homes. A survey of homeless young people admitted by Centrepoint in London during a one-year period from April 1991 to March 1992 collected data from over 93 per cent (753 young people) of total first-time admissions. There had been a 35 per cent increase in numbers since 1987, i.e. just before the removal of state benefits. Of those aged 16 to 19, 54 per cent were aged 16 and 17, compared to 40 per cent in 1987. Thirty-six per cent were from ethnic minority households, and just over a third were from outside London and the South-East, clearly young people from the provinces without work. Youth homelessness was a phenomenon which became visible on the streets in the Conservative era.

Overall, the proportion of economically active 16-year-olds had declined dramatically since the 1970s. For most 16-year-olds, full-time education replaced full-time work. There is a clear link between declining work opportunity and rising participation rates. In brief, lack of opportunity pushed young people out of work, and the development of examinations pulled them into school. This trend accelerated as state benefits were withdrawn and Youth Training declined. Gray *et al.* (1994: 29) concluded: 'during the 1980s, a combination of so-called "kicks" to the system ... finally ... succeeded in breaking the ingrained habit amongst young people in this country of reaching the age of 16 and leaving [school]'.

Conclusions and Implications

The major themes that emerged from the empirical work on the youth workforce in the Conservative era have demonstrated that, since the 1979–81 survey, the labour market for young people has changed considerably as a result of market forces, institutional and legislative changes, and the disturbance of customs and traditions. Since 1979, there has been a higher plateau of unemployment, a sharper decline in manufacturing – formerly the largest employer of 16-year-old males and females – and a concomitant fall in craft training opportunities. Some jobs in the expanding services area have become available for youth, especially in the private sector, and largely in the form of part-time work. In a limited way, new technology has brought about a polarization of skills but this trend has had important adverse consequences for youth which was excluded from the higher level. By the mid-1990s there were very few 16- and 17-year-olds in the labour market: most stayed on in full-time education. The appearance was that they had been displaced by married women, but the evidence suggests that, with persisting lack of opportunity, the shift to non-standard hours, a decline in the availability of YT, the absence of the unemployment benefit, and developments in education, many preferred to stay in full-time education.[21]

These findings help illuminate controversies about the causes of youth disadvantage (Makeham, 1980; Ashton and Bourn, 1981; Jones, 1984; Raffe, 1985, 1986, 1990; Ashton *et al.*, 1990). By examining these trends over the 1980s and '90s it is possible to include arguments about recessionary forces, structural change, recruitment and training patterns, displaced workers and women returners into an explanation in which apparently conflicting themes can be absorbed. First, after the watershed years of 1979–81, there were fewer jobs available overall, despite short-term periods of growth and recession. The effect on new entrants, including youth, was that recruitment fell relative to the post-war years and there was more competition from displaced and added workers. Second, there was a decline in manufacturing, traditionally the largest employer of youth. It affected males more than females in terms of traditional training opportunities. The service industry expanded but there was a move from standard to non-standard hours. Throughout the period, there was an increase in women workers, many of whom were available for this part-time work. Consequently, young people faced strong competition for these jobs. Third, within these long-term patterns, there were short-term periods of growth and recession: as new entrants, youth were particularly susceptible to downturns. In summary, there were fewer jobs and training opportunities available, a move from manufacturing to the service industry, and a partial replacement of full-time for part-time work.

Overall, from the evidence presented, the likelihood is that recession pushes youth down the employment hierarchy and out of jobs, while structural change pushes them across into different industries. It is difficult to disentangle the effects quantitatively. Moreover, young adults, displaced older workers, and married returners compete with youth for opportunities previously more freely and sometimes exclusively available to school-leavers. Sixteen-year-olds responded by enrolling in training schemes and full-time education. A new set of norms had emerged. By the mid-1980s, Roberts (1995) reported that 'most employers and young people seemed to have adjusted to and thereby normalised the exclusion of 16- and 17-year-olds from full-time employment' (p. 10).

A comparison with their 1970s' counterparts demonstrated strong continuities in terms of the occupations and industries in which youth of the 1990s worked. Nevertheless, in relation to the main argument, 'in the small labour market that survives for 16/17 year olds' (Payne,

1995a), early school-leavers at the end of the 1990s face greater dis-advantage. A smaller group of 16-year-olds have taken jobs which are less heterogeneous and lower paid than those of the 1970s. The evidence therefore suggests that, by the 1990s, the labour market for youth has lost much of the heterogeneity of the post-war years and is converging towards a model of unskilled, dead-end jobs with low incomes, poor conditions, and few entry ports to long-term careers.

Notes

1 The decline in the numbers of school-leavers was only in very small part a result in demographic changes. 1983 marked the zenith for numbers of 16-year-olds in the population, and thereafter there was a decline: numbers have fallen sharply since 1985 to reach a low point in 1993; the subsequent increase is expected to continue to 2010 but numbers are still lower than in the 1970s and early 1980s (Deakin, 1996).

2 There have been several major on-going studies of young people conducted in Britain during the 1980s and 1990s. The England and Wales Youth Cohort Surveys began in 1985 with a longitudinal survey of a nationally representative sample of young people who had been in their final compulsory year of schooling, normally fifth forms, in secondary schools. The Scottish Young People's Survey began in 1976 as biennial surveys of national samples of school-leavers. During the 1980s they became longitudinal. The Economic and Social Research Council 16–19 Initiative was a major programme of research conducted between 1987 and 1989 and consisted of longitudinal surveys of representative samples of 16–19-year-olds in Kirk-caldy, Liverpool, Sheffield, and Swindon, and contained some ethnographic accounts.

3 Byford (1983) compared 16-year-olds in inner London and nationally in 1982 and reported respective full-time education participation rates of 46 and 48 per cent, employment rates of 17 and 28 per cent and YOP rates of 5 and 10 per cent.

4 For detailed figures of school-leaver destinations for England, Wales, Scotland and Northern Ireland, see Yates, 1996.

5 In terms of numbers employed, manufacturing had been declining since the latter half of the 1960s, but in 1980 it experienced the beginning of a sharper decline which persisted throughout the decade (Nolan and Walsh, 1995).

6 The Youth Opportunities Programme (YOP) developed into the Youth Training Scheme (YTS) in 1983 then Youth Training (YT) in 1990. YT

operated through Training and Enterprise Councils (TECs) in England and Wales, and Local Enterprise Councils (LECs) in Scotland. From 1991, YT began to be replaced by Youth (or training) Credits, which enabled young people to buy approved forms of training up to a certain value.

7 This is the total figure of all those undertaking apprenticeships, including several cohorts, not just the number available in one particular year.

8 These lead to level-3 NVQs; see Note 17 below.

9 In the late 1970s there were eighteen million full-time workers. By 1993, there were less than fifteen million. Almost two million of these jobs had been lost since 1989. In 1971 only one in six employees worked part-time; by 1993 the ratio was 1 : 3 (Nolan and Walsh, 1995).

10 Gallie (1994) reported the existence in the 1980s of 'a major sector of part-time female work in which existing levels of skill are typically low and which has remained untouched by the processes that have elsewhere contributed to skill enrichment' (p. 76).

11 Certainly adult female unemployment was low relative to youth unemployment, though many women may not have registered if they were not eligible for benefits.

12 She also claimed that this trend was temporarily halted and reversed in the recession of 1990–3 (Hakim, 1995).

13 In 1995 the gross weekly earnings for under-18 males were £113.4; for females £117.1. For all ages, the respective figures were £370.6 and £267.8 (New Earnings Survey, 1995).

14 It is argued either that they wanted to work part-time to accommodate family responsibilities (e.g. Hakim, 1995), or wanted to work full-time but offered themselves part-time for a number of reasons: lack of childcare facilities in Britain; the relatively long working week of the British adult male (e.g. Ginn *et al.*, 1995); lack of training because of childcare activity (e.g. Dex, 1985). Hart (1988) offered a financial reason: that some married part-time women paid neither income tax nor national insurance contributions if their earnings were under the threshold. This argument was supported by Casey's findings, which demonstrated that 70 per cent of all part-time workers have jobs of less than 16 hours per week, some as low as eight hours (Casey, 1991).

15 Hart (1988) argued that tax and national insurance contributions could be avoided by employers by the use of non-standard hours.

16 For a fuller discussion of social and educational factors outside the brief of this book see Raffe (1992), Paterson and Raffe, 1995; Biggart and Furlong, 1996; Foskett and Hesketh, 1997.

17 For example, in 1983 the Technical and Vocational Education Initiative was announced, and in 1986 the National Council for Vocational Qualifications

was established. National Vocational Qualifications (NVQs) recognize skills relevant to particular occupations or industries. General NVQs are relevant to more general vocational preparation. Level-2 passes were said to be about equivalent to good GCSEs, level-3 passes to about two A-levels. In 1992, the Further and Higher Education Act gave Further Education Colleges a wider role than previously. In 1993 the National Commission on Education reported a need for the workforce to be more adaptable, highly skilled and better trained.

18 The Youth Opportunities Programme developed into the Youth Training Scheme in 1983, then Youth Training (YT) in 1990 with Youth Training Credits. YT operated through Training and Enterprise Councils (TECs) in England and Wales, and Local Enterprise Councils (LECs) in Scotland.

19 Under the Guarantee, every young person who fell into this category should be offered at least two YT places during the Child Benefit extension period (12–17 weeks after leaving school) then one YT place every 8 weeks.

20 Official figures produce similar results, though lower estimates: the *Labour Market Quarterly Report* (May 1996) demonstrated that participation in full-time education for 16–18-year-olds had risen from 28.9 per cent in 1980/81 to 56.6 per cent in 1994/5, mainly in schools and colleges of further education.

21 As a postscript to the survey context, changes in London were similar but more adverse for young people than in Britain generally. In retrospect, the time of the survey had marked a catching-up period for London in terms of unemployment. In the fifteen years afterwards, unemployment rates continued to be higher than for Britain in general. In fact, the North of England and London had the highest rates of claimant unemployment in the country: 10.1 and 9.2 per cent respectively, with unemployment in inner London higher than the outer boroughs (*Labour Market Quarterly Report*, May 1996). London also had the highest proportion of its unemployed out of work for twelve months or more: 42 per cent of claimants unemployed (Office for National Statistics, 1996). Structural changes also reflected those in Britain generally. Buck and Gordon (1986) reported a decline in manufacturing in London accentuated by the movement of manufacturing firms out of London. Hart (1988) claimed that jobs in London were becoming increasingly biased towards the non-manufacturing types which required qualifications and skills. A study of the London Docklands Development Corporation found that, for 16–21-year-olds in the area, there was a move to non-manufacturing jobs by males as manual work declined (Church and Ainley, 1987). The Association of London Authorities conducted a survey in 1992 (ALA, 1992) and reported a polarisation trend: jobs were concentrated at the very specific higher-skill levels and the lower-skill levels with

jobs that 'commonly offer relatively low pay or unattractive working conditions or hours of work' (p. 1).

Participation rates in full-time education also reflected national trends. In 1996, nearly three-quarters of London's 16-year-olds stayed on in full-time education with only 5.5 per cent in employment (*Labour Market Quarterly Report*, May 1996). The number of vacancies in Careers Offices (i.e. suitable for under-18-year-olds) was only 1100 (Office for National Statistics, May 1996). Although since 1993 the growth in employment has been greatest in London, it has mainly benefited part-time adult women (*Labour Market Quarterly Report*, May 1996).

11 JOBS, UNIONS AND STABILITY PATTERNS AT THE END OF THE CENTURY

Introduction

It has been demonstrated that, although young people are heavily represented in low-skill work, the level of purposeful labour-market behaviour that they display is closely related to context. The aim of this chapter is to examine the effect of the changed context of the 1980s and 1990s on the experience and behaviour of youth at that time by an analysis of investigations similar to those apparent in the 1979 survey, as far as this is possible. In this way, an appraisal can be made of the valuable youth studies conducted in the 1980s and 1990s. It will be argued that the changes that took place in the Conservative era had greatest negative impact on those groups already at a disadvantage, while the mechanisms and institutions of the labour market to ameliorate such a situation were further constrained.

Labour Market Patterns: The Relevance of the 1979 Survey Findings in the 1980s and 1990s

Job Search
In a situation where fewer jobs were available, and there had been some move to low-skill work alongside the survival of a smaller craft area, it was expected that job search would be more difficult for young people and that the influences outside the school-leavers' control which were so important in 1979, would play a greater role in the Conservative era, leading to an increase in group disadvantage in such circumstances.

This proved to be the case. Roberts and Chadwick (1991) found, in the 1980s, that that 'the old predictors of occupational attainment ... were in sound working order' (p. 48). More than this though, the evidence suggests that some of them had a stronger influence in this changed panorama.

Job Opportunities: Local Labour Markets and Inner-City Residence

Opportunities in local labour markets remained an important factor for young people (Ashton and Maguire, 1986b; Roberts *et al.*, 1987; Roberts and Chadwick, 1991; Bynner and Roberts, 1991; Sime, 1991; Banks *et al.*, 1992). This was unsurprising as, after 1988, youth no longer had access to unemployment or social security benefits so its mobility for purposes of job search was further constrained. Moreover, inner-city residence remained a distinct influential factor (Gray *et al.*, 1989). In London, youths who were resident in the inner-city areas faced competition from commuting adults. However, it has also been suggested that generally a decline in employment in and close to some city centres may affect young residents of those areas, who cannot easily travel or move out to places where jobs are available (Roberts, 1995).

Employee Characteristics

Overall, with regard to entry to the labour market, the research suggests that those groups of school-leavers who did not go on to higher education and experienced disadvantage in the 1979 survey suffered more in the changed situation of the 1980s and 1990s.

Gender

Gender segregation persisted (Roberts and Chadwick, 1991; Payne 1995a). The same qualifications led to different job opportunities according to gender (Roberts *et al.*, 1987) and findings demonstrate that girls are still less likely than boys to receive training, and when they do it is for shorter periods (Courtenay and McAleese, 1993a; 1993b). For example, Payne (1995a) reported that the proportion of females aged 16 and 17 who received no off-the-job training was about a third more than the proportion of males. Blanchflower and Lynch (1992) found that male apprenticeships in Britain were of 43 months duration on average, while for females the corresponding figure was 34 months. But, more than this, there was evidence of greater disadvantage to young women relative to young men compared to the immediate post-war decades. A more recent occurrence was that young women participated more than young men in most forms of compulsory education. In 1980/1 the female full-time education participation rate, at 48 per cent had been lower than the male rate (54 per cent) for the 16–18-year-old group, but by 1996 the rate was 70 per cent for young females and 50 per cent for males[1] (*Labour Market Quarterly Report*, May 1996). Payne (1995a) also reported that young women were more likely than young men to stay on in full-time education after the end of compulsory schooling. This is related to gender *per se*: Drew, Gray and Sime (1992) and Gray *et al.* (1994), using logit analyses, demonstrated that, controlling for other factors, females were more likely to stay on at school or colleges of further education than males.

The reasons for this may lie in part in changes in socialization forces, educational opportunities and examination success for young women, in which case young females may have been deliberately trying to improve their employment chances by the acquisition of more qualifications. Certainly, in England and Wales by the 1990s females were more likely than males to gain GCSEs and A-levels (*Social Trends*, 1996), and Payne (1995a) demonstrated that girls had improved in their GCSE results more than boys. But she made a further very important finding: she also showed that this did not lead in general to long-term advantage because girls who stay in full-time education were also more likely than males in the same situation to leave after Year 12, and less likely to transfer to GCE A-levels/AS courses after resitting the GCSE examination. She concluded that this was because the boys who gained apprenticeships left school at 16, while, since the late 1980s, their female counterparts who wanted to take up clerical and secretarial jobs had to stay on an extra year, either in full-time education or in YT, to take up these courses. In other words, by the mid-1990s early school-leaving young women were delayed a year before they could take up traditional female work. The likelihood is that staying in education was for many a response to lack of opportunity in the labour market.

This viewpoint is supported by other evidence. Female youth unemployment had been rising faster than that of young males from the mid-1970s (Atkinson and Rees, 1982; Metcalf and Richards, 1983), and

Makeham (1980) found that recruitment cuts, so important with regard to youth unemployment, affected young women more than young men. Drew (1995), using logit analyses for the 1985 and 1986 YCS cohorts (i.e. before unemployment benefit was withdrawn from youth), found that being a male conferred an advantage on the job-seeker. By the end of the 1980s, however, after the benefit was withdrawn, Sime (1991)[2] found that gender *per se* was unimportant for school-leavers regarding the probability of finding work: clearly, rather than undertaking unemployed job search, girls stayed in education to gain further qualifications in response to declining opportunity in 'female' jobs in the context of the withdrawal of state benefits.

The implications are twofold. First, the influx of older women in the youth labour market affected girls more than boys because young females were competing not just for jobs in which all unskilled participate, but also in traditional female occupations where older women were already more experienced or qualified. Webster (1993) claimed that dedicated word-processing technology, diffused throughout offices in Britain in the 1970s and early 1980s, meant that computer literacy became important for typists in all industries during that time. Unlike the new specialist training in 'male' manufacturing industry, female early school-leavers were not excluded from word-processing techniques because, as Liff (1990) reported, most office technology is being used for little more than enhancing the productivity of routine tasks. But although upskilling was available from firms for women returners who were already experienced in keyboard skills, employers still relied on schools and colleges of further education to impart to school pupils the old manual skill now embedded in the new technology. Returners, therefore, might have acted to keep out 16-year-old young women. However, by the end of the Conservative era the girls' investment seems to have paid off in terms of gaining work: unemployment rates in spring 1997 for 18–19-year-old females were lower than those for males at 10.6 per cent and 18.2 per cent respectively (Labour Market Trends, December 1997). This is a neglected area which needs research for verification[3] but it does seem that competition from adult women for traditional, albeit unskilled, female jobs led to a situation where, as a group, girls stayed on an extra year at school, partly perhaps for upskilling purposes with the advent of new technology, but also because they faced competition from older women for jobs in traditional female sectors.

Second, the evidence also suggests that many young women preferred to stay on at school to undertake this form of skill acquisition,
rather than to participate in the low-skill jobs that many older women
undertook. This is because skilled work provides opportunity for
advancement: Webster (1993) reported that, with the advent of word-
processing techniques, 'instead of all office workers being reduced to
uniform de-skilled automatons, the differential between secretarial and
typing workers ... persists' (p. 49). Moreover, typing is not enterprise-
based and provides an ideal opportunity for career progression for
those who wished to leave the labour market temporarily: Roberts *et al.*
(1987) found that, in general, young women were 'still interested in
their occupational career for aspects of full-time parenting' (p. 49).

Race

Racial disadvantage for young people who did not go on to higher
education also continued throughout the 1980s and 1990s (e.g. Roberts
et al., 1986; Connolly *et al.*, 1991; Drew *et al.*, 1992; Jones, 1993; Drew,
1995). Figures for ethnic minorities in the labour market were still
likely to be highly representative of opportunities for their young
people.[4] Black unemployment levels were similar to those of the early
1980s, while the Pakistani/Bangladeshi levels seemed to be slightly
lower (Labour Market Trends, 1996c). The *Labour Force Survey Quarterly
Bulletin* (1984), produced disaggregated unemployment figures for
ethnic groups (not seasonally adjusted) estimating 7 per cent unemployment for whites, compared to 17.2 per cent for all ethnic minority
groups; by autumn 1986, for whites it was about 7 per cent and for all
other groups about 18 per cent (Sly *et al.*, 1997). 'The unemployment
rate of ethnic minority people as a whole remains around double that of
white people'[5] (Labour Market Trends, 1996c, p. 26).

Jones (1993) concluded that there was 'a continuity of patterns which
developed after the first wave of immigration in the 1950s ... ethnic
minority people remained in the low status jobs in distinct parts of the
economy, they still suffered substantially higher rates of unemployment
than existed in the white population' (p. 149). Roberts *et al.* (1986)
reported that 'ethnic minority respondents ... [are] ... less successful
[than whites] in the competition for every single grade of employment'
(p. 139).

This apparent continuing trend of disadvantage, however, conceals the fact that a greater proportion of ethnic minorities relative to whites was staying on at school, and that this was an increasing trend in response to declining employment opportunities. The increase in participation in full-time education since the mid-1980s was particularly marked amongst young people from ethnic minorities (Labour Market Trends, May 1996) and there is disaggregated material available for 1991: Slade (1992) reported that 78 per cent of Africans/Caribbeans, 77 per cent of Asians, and 63 per cent of whites remained in education that year. Drew *et al.* (1992), Gray *et al.* (1994), and Drew (1995) used logit analyses and found that there was a racial influence *per se*: non-whites, especially Asians,[6] were more likely to stay in full-time education. Unsurprising, therefore, were the findings of Roberts *et al.* (1987) that Asian young people were more ambitious than both whites and blacks, who shared similar job aspirations.

This is a similar trend to that apparent amongst females relative to males, but it was much more likely, especially in the case of West Indians, that this marked a form of concealed unemployment and an inability to gain a YTS place, rather than deliberate skill acquisition because increased participation has not been reflected in examination success. A government study (Education Statistics for the UK, 1992) indicated that blacks are still less qualified than whites when they leave school. It may well be that they are aware that the disadvantage caused by the racial factor alone and apparent in the London survey,[7] cannot be removed by better qualifications, so a feeling of hopelessness sets in (Foster, 1992). In fact, successful attempts by Asians to increase their qualifications have not led to greater success in the labour market: Sime (1991) found race unimportant with regard to gaining work, except in the case of Asians, and Jones (1993) found an increasing disparity between the labour market experience of ethnic groups, with Pakistani/Bangladeshis at the bottom. Roberts *et al.* (1987) claimed that qualifications achieved at school, plus the YTS, are doing little, if anything, to overcome non-white disadvantage. For example, black school-leavers were more likely to be without a YT place than whites (*Starting Right*, 1994), and black youths were concentrated in schemes with the poorest job prospects (Cross and Smith, 1987). Moreover, Wrench and Virdee (1995) reported that 'there is a growing category of black/migrant workers who are under-unionised. These are the workers in the expanding sector of low-paid, unregulated marginal work' (p. 6).

There was, however, evidence of one interesting change that had occurred since the post-war period. There semed to be evidence of a slight upward trend in the economic activity rates of Pakistani/ Bangladeshi women (Labour Market Trends, 1996c).[8] It is likely that this is associated with high levels of male unemployment – at 28 per cent in autumn 1996, the highest level for the main ethnic groupings (Sly *et al.*, 1997) – and with changing cultural values. If it is the latter case, it may well be most pronounced among the young. However, participation rates are still very low at about 25 per cent (Labour Market Trends, 1996c) and though in general a higher proportion of men than women have a qualification, the difference is still the largest among Pakistani/ Bangladeshis (Education Statistics for the UK, 1992). Further research is needed to see if this trend persists and grows stronger.

Parental Unemployment

Household unemployment also remains an important determinant of disadvantage in the form of living in a household with an unemployed parent (Furlong, 1992) or having both a mother and father unemployed (Roberts *et al.*, 1987). Roberts *et al.* (1987) reported that 'some companies were suspicious of school-leavers with unemployed parents: the young people could have grown accustomed to idleness' (p. 32). These are disturbing findings in a situation where unemployment levels have been persistently higher than the post-war period for two decades. It means that, over time, unemployment can become a family heritage.

Examinations

Individual effort or ability, in the form of examinations, seemed to be more important in the 1990s than the 1970s. Educational attainment at 16 was a major determinant of some starting opportunities (Roberts and Chadwick, 1991; Sime, 1991; Drew *et al.*, 1992; Roberts and Parsell, 1992b; Gray *et al.*, 1994; Drew, 1995). Ashton and Maguire (1996) reported that 'over the last decade there has been an overall contraction in the demand for labour of young people aged 16 and 17. This has been specifically significant for those with minimum educational qualifications' (p. 52). Payne's findings (Payne, 1995a) were more detailed and suggest that, reflecting the polarization of work and changes in job types available to those at the age of 16/17, there were some young people with higher levels of fifth-form qualifications for the craft jobs, and others with relatively lower levels for the expanding low-skill areas.

By the late 1980s, Roberts *et al.* (1991) claimed that young people had a realistic set of expectations and aspirations: they had adjusted to the context of persisting unemployment and there was clearly a deliberate attempt by some to increase human capital and their own job chances. But in view of the kind of jobs available for 16/17-year-olds, it seems unlikely that much of the extra education was necessary upskilling. Despite some employer complaints about lack of training and education, there is no clear evidence that there was a skill deficit generally (Shackleton, 1993). Only a minority of firms in the 1980s reported recruitment difficulties and this proportion was no higher than in the 1970s (IFF Research, 1990). It is unsurprising, therefore, that there is evidence of a general examinations inflation. Although some early school-leavers were displaced by slightly older workers in a move to A-level qualifications (Roberts *et al.*, 1987; Thompson *et al.*, 1993), Sime *et al.* (1990), reported that school-leavers needed higher qualifications than fifteen years previously to get the same kind of work. Roberts (1995) also claimed that 'as more young people have obtained them, all qualifications have been occupationally devalued' (p. 52). Certainly, unlike the recent evidence, the 1979/81 survey results found that exams were only important with regard to skilled work, but not for getting a job in general. The new trend may have been in part a response to changes in work organization. But Roberts (1995) argued that 'the pace at which young people have become better qualified in recent years has been faster than any occupational upgrading' (p. 34). Moreover, there is evidence that some of the new vocational qualifications were not very valuable either intrinsically, or in terms of gaining work. The Smithers Report (Smithers, 1993) claimed that NVQs were of a low standard relative to their academic 'equivalents'. Roberts (1995) claimed that by the mid-1990s, lower level NVQ was widely taken as standing for 'not very qualified' (p. 65). Bennett *et al.* (1992) reported that wage and employment returns were nil on NVQs below Level 3. Roberts and Corcoran-Nantes (1994) reported that NVQs were only valuable when gained within a given firm. Whatever the case, those who did/could not increase their qualifications in both absolute and relative terms were more disadvantaged than previously in a context of high youth unemployment. Unsurprisingly, therefore, Payne (1995a) reported that staying-on rates had increased most for those with the least qualifications, for the group with low or no GCSE passes, clearly those who failed to gain work (Maguire, 1991) or a YT place.

Personal Characteristics

There was some evidence that some employers still took account of individual characteristics. For example, Ashton and Maguire (1986a) reported that, in general, employers offering manual jobs attached more weight to attributes such as personality and attitude to work than straightforward academic ability. Roberts *et al.* (1987) reported the kinds of qualities searched for by employers in specific jobs taken up by these young people: builders looked for physical strength, shops and hairdressers for smart dress and appearance; most employers of youth wanted good health, enthusiasm, keenness to learn, communicativeness and an appearance that was not 'scruffy'. MacEwan Scott (1994) reported that employers in retailing sought personality and social rather than technical skills; moreover, that ability was important only for jobs which led to management.

Overall, factors over which young people had no control were more apparent in the 1980s and1990s than in the 1970s. In combination, the group features of parental unemployment, inner-city residence and race, are very powerful and are often shared by young people from low-income households. Garner *et al.* (1988), for example, reported that high local unemployment rates owed more to the characteristics of the locality's inhabitants, usually in the form of lack of qualifications and skills, than to local job opportunity levels. Moreover, by the mid-1980s, of those that lived in city areas, 31 per cent were white and 68 per cent non-white. Of the latter, 85 per cent of West Indians and non-Chinese Asians, the two largest minority groups, were city residents (Rajan *et al.*, 1990). According to Jones (1993), 'ethnic minority people were more likely to be living in lower standard accommodation' (p. 149).[9]

Ironically, in the main area where young people could affect their destiny, examination success, they had to 'run in order to stand still'. Those least able to pass examinations, including the discouraged, were even further disadvantaged in the 1990s.

Quits and Unions: Mechanisms of Amelioration

It is expected that, in a situation of lack of opportunity and prevalence of low-skill work, both the purposeful role of job swapping and recruitment to union membership will have declined. Thus, the mechanisms and institutions to ameliorate conditions are more constrained.

Quits and Job-Swapping

In relation to the incentive-opportunity quit model (see Chapter 8), it was expected that young people would be less likely to embark on purposeful job-shopping in a situation of low opportunity and greater homogeneity, especially where state benefits could not be used to finance unemployed job search. In fact, Elias and Blanchflower (1989) reported the difficulty of getting a job after a quit. Payne and Payne (1994) found, at the beginning of the 1990s, that if a young person left employment whether voluntarily or otherwise, he/she was more than two and a half times more likely to end up without a job as with one. They concluded that, as a consequence, the labour market cannot operate efficiently because 'job sampling is the luxury of the very few' (p. 94).

Nevertheless, there is some evidence that young people did indulge in quit behaviour. In the early 1980s, Roberts *et al.* (1987) investigated 17/18-year-olds of mixed leaving cohorts, some of whom were early school-leavers, and reported that in less than two years, 7 per cent of the sample had experienced three or more jobs since leaving school, although 63 per cent were still in their first job. Payne (1995a) found evidence of many quits among early school-leavers in the early 1990s. She observed 16/17-year-olds at that age and a year later, and of those who held a job at both times, about 25 per cent had changed their occupation. Moreover, Payne and Payne (1994), using *Labour Force Survey* data for 1979, 1981, 1982–1991, found that the overall separation rate declines rapidly with increasing age, and this in a period when youth unemployment rates were consistently much higher than adult rates. Consequently, although some of these voluntary separations may be rent-seeking activity, others may be quits engendered by the job, perhaps through frustration, or as a conscious means of gaining respite from deadly work, in the manner predicted by Doeringer and Piore (1971). In support of this explanation are findings from Payne (1995b) which indicate that the lowest rates of loss were in clerical work and processing, and the highest in selling. Where job search could not lead to better work, quits could not increase market efficiency.

However, there was some evidence of the efficacy of purposeful job-swapping as she identified two quite common trends: a move from selling to 'clerical and related' (13 per cent), and a move from 'routine operative' to 'processing, making and repairing'. She claimed that both of these paths suggest possible upward mobility achieved through 'practical work experience'. This is a very important finding as it suggests not just that rent-seeking is efficacious for some, but that early work might act as a 'practice pitch' and/or provide a work record for future employers. It lends empirical support to the argument that indirect entry ports to work in 'adult' sectors exist within traditional youth areas.

Union Membership

If young people found it more difficult to ameliorate their situation by rent-seeking quit behaviour, fewer of them partook in the voice option. A *Labour Force Survey* report demonstrated an 'association between increasing age and the likelihood of union membership but in 1995 only 6 per cent of employees under the age of 20 years were union members, compared with over a third among those aged 30 years or more' (LFS, 1995, p. 288). It also concluded that there was no difference between younger men and younger women. These gender results for young people reinforce the 1979 survey findings. In summary, adult membership had halved since the 1970s, but youth membership had fallen by two-thirds.

Using the strands of argument developed in the new trade union model (see Chapter 6), it might be possible to explain this decline. The new trade union theory asserted that the 'core' members of a union joined for positive reasons and the remainder 'or neutral', were put under pressures from union and employers respectively to join/leave/not join/not leave, subject to the norms of the workplace. Most school-leavers in the survey did not join, and a third (the largest group) of these were not asked; most of the others were neutral or unaware. The likelihood is that, in the 1980s and 1990s, two factors became important. First, trade unions were less available to the minority of young people who actively wanted to join and, second, the norms and pressures of the workplace meant that even fewer of the remainder were recruited. There is some evidence to substantiate these arguments.

With regard to trade union availability, young people had been particularly affected by structural change and, thereby, policies of employer recognition. Their traditional main employer, manufacturing, was in decline, and they were being employed in increasing proportions in the service industry, especially in the private sector. Workplace size was found to be unimportant with regard to union membership in the 1979–81 survey. However, results from the 1990 Workplace Industrial Relations Survey demonstrated that this was probably no longer the case by the end of the 1980s. By that time, in general there had been a widespread decline in the number of union representatives, 'the most basic building blocks of the local trade union organisation' (Millward *et al.*, 1992, p. 43). In particular, smaller workplaces were affected and those with low levels of union membership (Millward *et al.*, 1992). There was also evidence from the 1980s that fewer shop stewards were permitted to spend all their working time on trade union activities (Millward and Stevens, 1986). In view of the high representation rate of youth in those areas of work, it was likely they would number among the most adversely affected groups of workers in terms of the availability of a union.[10]

With reference to the norms and pressures of the workplace, there were important effects of structural change. Many young people worked in the private sector of the service industry, and Cully and Woodland (1996) reported that such employees were much more likely to report union recognition than those in the public sector. Gallie (1996) also reported the powerful influence on union membership of working in the public sector. Moreover, for those young people left in manufacturing industry, Waddington and Whitston (1995) reported that between 1979 and 1991, membership of the three craft unions, the Amalgamated Electrical Union (AEU), the Electrical, Electronic, Telecommunications and Plumbing Union (EEPTU), and the Union of Construction, Allied Trades and Technicians (UCATT), declined sharply because of developments in new technology and multi-skilling. There were fewer apprentices and fewer union members to recruit them.

In fact, regardless of structural change, the effect of the general decline in union density meant that there was a smaller number of adult unionists and less finance for recruitment purposes. Cully and Wood-land (1996) reported that union membership in Britain was estimated to be 7.3 million in 1995. Union membership had fallen by 3 per cent each year from 1989, when the *Labour Force Survey* series began, repre-senting a fall of about 1.7 million. Union density had declined from 39 per cent in 1989 to 32 per cent in 1995. This decline was particularly marked in the areas where the young found work: Cully and Woodland claimed that the fall had been particularly apparent among manual employees, and those in production industries, all of which once formed 'the core' (p. 215) of union membership. In response to union density and membership decline, there were some attempts at recruit-ment drives. Results from the London survey showed that recruitment was particularly important in the case of young people. In the early 1980s, the 1985 Workplace Industrial Relations Survey found that only 10 per cent and 15 per cent of unorganized establishments experienced recruitment activity among manual and non-manual workers, respec-tively (Millward and Stevens, 1986). But McIlroy (1988) claimed there was an increase in activity after 1984–5. Some of these drives were aimed at youth or at the kind of jobs they undertook. He reported the following examples. The Union of Shop, Distributive and Allied Work-ers (USDAW), which during the 1980s lost a third of its membership each year through high turnover, launched a campaign against poverty pay and attempted to involve shop stewards rather than full-time officials in recruitment. The Trades and General Workers Union (TGWU) initiated a 'Link-Up' campaign in 1986, aimed primarily at temporary and part-time workers. He also found evidence of some unions targetting the lower-paid including the offer of cut-rate sub-scriptions for certain categories of member and a new category of associate membership by which those employees would only pay part of the normal fee and receive limited union services in return. However, the 1979 survey findings concluded this type of policy would have little influence on youth membership. In fact, overall, these activities had little general effect and McIlroy (1988) described them somewhat disparagingly as 'talk about action' (p. 219).

With regard to pressures from the employer, Gallie and Rose (1996) reported evidence from the 1980s of a widespread growth of a more hostile attitude to unions on the part of employers, especially in small-sized establishments. In terms of workplace norms, Conservative trade union legislation with regard to the closed shop[11] may also have been an important factor, although there was a spread in check-off arrangements.

Structural change took place within a context of higher unemployment, and Waddington and Whitston (1995), analysing theories of union decline in Britain, suggested that business cycle theories were most important. Unfortunately, they generally fall prey to the free-rider problem. Nevertheless, they may be effective through the core-remainder arguments. The likelihood is that persistent levels of high unemployment did make some youth look askance at union membership if they feared employer victimization. Moreover, the low level of strike activity in such a climate meant that the excitement and recruitment drives that may result from such cohesiveness were not apparent. In 1994, the number of working days lost from labour disputes in the UK was at its lowest level since records began, at about 280,000 (*Social Trends*, 1996). In part, this may have been due to the 1984 Trade Union Act whereby both secondary and unballoted strikes were no longer immune from court action.

In summary, the likelihood is that employer recognition changed in some workplaces, recruitment pressures fell sharply, fear of employer reaction rose, and workplace norms changed. This occurred within the framework of Conservative trade union legislation, persisting unemployment, and a change in political attitudes for those with rising wages. This led overall, but more than proportionately for young people, to a decline in union density.

This decline seems to have had a relatively large impact on one of the most disadvantaged groups. Wrench and Virdee (1995) reported that there was a growing category of black/migrant workers who were under-unionized: 'These are the workers in the expanding sector of low-paid, unregulated marginal work' (p. 6).

Factors Which Affect Future Prospects

In the changed situation of the mid-1990s it is expected that, nevertheless, the declining craft option is still the best route for increased rewards while job-swapping may be counterproductive where much work is homogeneous and quits/lay-offs are likely to lead to unemployment without benefit. Moreover, it is suggested that the scope for individual effort and ability to make an impact will have lessened.

The findings which were available replicated those of the survey years. Unsurprisingly, the apprenticeship option still remained important (Roberts and Parsell, 1992a) and the best opportunity of long-term job training for early school-leavers (Payne, 1995a). However, relative to 1979, this was available to fewer young people. Moreover, it remained largely restricted to young males. Payne (1995b) reported lower returns for training (including apprenticeships) to women than men at ages 23/4. Blanchflower and Lynch (1992) found that apprenticeships offered a higher rate of return to men but not to women.

Moreover, initial unemployment continued to cast its long shadow (Furlong, 1992). There is some recent evidence which suggests how this comes about. Payne and Payne (1994), using *Labour Force Survey* data of 1979, 1981, 1982–91, concluded that, in an upturn, to meet their increasing labour needs, employers turned first to school-leavers before they began to consider young people who had been in the labour market for a year or more. That is, employers turned first to those without labour-market histories. This has serious implications in a situation of unemployment levels persistently higher than the post-war period. Furthermore, if parental unemployment helps bring this about, as the findings suggested, it not only helps to disadvantage children in their initial quest for jobs, but casts a long shadow on their later chances. In such a situation, the long-term unemployed are particularly disadvantaged as they are poor and amongst the least able to finance children who are unable to gain work yet cannot gain non-insurance benefits.

Finally, this book has not been directly concerned with youth training schemes, but since the survey period, especially during the 1980s, they became a major source of vocational training for school-leavers. With regard to future prospects, however, there is evidence to suggest that many of them were little more than a substitute for non-insurance benefits. For example, Wells (1983) reported that the expansion of YOP after 1980 had an immediate impact on youth unemployment. In a recent major survey, Mizen (1995) concluded that Youth Training is 'defined by unpleasant and alienating types of work. It means a protracted period of work experience which offers little personal or financial reward, and it means suffering the insecurity and threat of unemployment that being a trainee usually entails.' Begg *et al.* (1991) claimed that YTS contributed 'only peripherally to meeting aggregate demand for skilled labour' (p. 234). Ashton *et al.* (1990) reported that it offered low standards of training. Employers seemed to recognize this. Sime *et al.* (1990) found that the chances of being employed by the age of 19 for those who completed their YT course were very similar to direct entrants. Banks *et al.* (1992) concluded that YT was the least favourable route for young people in their school-to-work transition. More disturbingly, Dolton (1993) claimed that by the end of the 1980s there were negligible wage effects and possibly negative employment effects of YTS experience. However, there is also evidence which suggests that there was a hierarchy of schemes, though very few of them endowed credentials valuable in the wider labour market (e.g. Raffe, 1986; Lee *et al.*, 1990; Roberts and Parsell, 1992a).

Conclusions

Investigations in the 1980s and 1990s have demonstrated that the survey results, in general, have been replicated but with different implications in the changing youth labour market. By the mid-1990s, 16-year-old school-leavers had even less control over their own destiny than previously. Group disadvantage was more apparent than in the post-war period, and increased qualifications and job-swapping did not seem to ameliorate the situation for the cohort in general while union membership was not as available. Moreover, the important group characteristics reinforced each other so the disadvantaged become easily identifiable: non-white, poorly-qualified, parent(s) unemployed, inner-city residents. Ashton *et al.* (1990) claimed that the cost of the impact of Thatcherite policies and global influences has been the growth of a large group of sub-employed young adults and long-term unemployed adults who have carried the costs of change. Over time, the long shadow of young people's initial disadvantage is building up a heritage of disadvantage and poverty and 'a growing underclass of unemployed' (Roberts and Chadwick, 1991).

Notes

1 These figures are supported by data from 1991 which disaggregates by sex; with regard to males and females respectively, 56 per cent and 70 per cent returned to full-time education, 12 per cent and 8 per cent gained work, and 17 per cent and 12 per cent took up YT (Slade, 1992).

2 Gray *et al.* (1994) found gender unimportant, but their sample consisted of cohorts from 1986, 1988, and 1990, i.e. from before and after the benefit was withdrawn.

3 Jenson (1989) claims it is ignored in much of the literature because women are regarded as having talents rather than skills, yet 'a secretary's job is probably the ideal-typical form of flexible specialisation' (p. 151).

4 The latest available information on the British population based on 1995 mid-year estimates by the Office of Population Censuses and Surveys reports that 68 per cent of non-whites are under the age of 16, compared to 20 per cent of whites, while only 3 per cent are over 60 compared to 19 per cent of whites (Rajan *et al.*, 1990).

5 The LMT survey also reported trends in unemployment broadly similar to all labour market participants, but with increases and decreases more pronounced than among white people: following the findings of Payne and Payne (1994), this is probably reflecting the high proportion of youth among non-whites. In 1984, within the ethnic minority groups, rates for blacks, Indians and Pakistanis/Bangladeshis were 20.7, 12.8 and 22.5 per cent respectively. By autumn 1996, the rates were 22, 12 and 27 per cent respectively (Sly *et al.*, 1997).

6 Drew *et al.* (1992); Banks *et al.* (1992).

7 In the 1979/81 survey, the most disadvantaged group was non-white females, and further analysis showed that Asian females (excluding Chinese), were most disadvantaged. Numbers, however, were very small so it was difficult to draw conclusions. Nevertheless, more recent findings support these results. Official figures demonstrate that, in general, a higher proportion of men than women have a qualification, but the difference is smallest among blacks and largest among Pakistani/Bangladeshis (Education Statistics for the UK, July 1992). The latter group of females had a very low proportion of economically active members in the post-war era. Interestingly, it is the only ethnic female group which might demonstrate an increase, from approximately 10 per cent in the early 80s to about 25 per cent in the mid-90s (Sly *et al.*, 1997). This may be a result of the assimilation of cultural values by younger women and/or a response to Asian male unemployment but it is too early to establish a definite trend.

8 LFS estimates for 1979: female economic activity rates for Europeans were 46.6 per cent; West Indians/Guyanans, 49.8 per cent; Indians, 49.8 per cent; Pakistanis/Bangladeshis, 15.7 per cent. Corresponding male rates were 78.3, 79.3, 83.8 and 86.5 per cent.

9 But within the ethnic minorities he also found disparities, with African–Asians, Indian and Chinese populations at the top, Pakistani/Bangladeshi at the bottom, Afro-Caribbean in between, and Africans with more varied experience (Jones, 1993).

10 Interestingly, check-off arrangements had grown in workplaces with lower union membership (Millward *et al.*, 1992).

11 Kessler and Bayliss (1992) reported that employers did not make full use of the new union legislation and, indeed, check-off agreements increased in the 1980s. Millward *et al.* (1992) confirmed that they remained widespread. This is easily explained by suggesting that those firms faced with unions were likely to make use of them, while new firms avoided them.

12 WHAT IS THE YOUTH LABOUR MARKET? CONCLUSIONS AND POLICY IMPLICATIONS

Introduction

The aim of the final chapter is to draw together the findings and derive policies from them which will ameliorate the condition of youth in the labour market at the start of the new century when individual, purposeful behaviour has been constrained in a situation of greater job homogeneity and persisting unemployment. The main theme of the book is that labour market experience and behaviour are closely related to context. This has been empirically sustained within two different contexts in the last half-century. It will be proposed in this chapter that context and related experience/behaviour determine not only the character of the youth labour market, but also the paths and ease of youth transition from school to work. This transition has become more difficult since the post-war era, causing problems not just for youth but for the national interest. It will also be proposed that the character of the youth labour market can be manipulated by government intervention to bring about a transition period which gives greater benefit to both school-leavers and the nation than that afforded by a context of dead-end work and unemployment. Finally, policy changes will be discussed to help remedy a situation in which youth is becoming more vulnerable and less able to help itself.

The Character of the Youth Labour Market

It has been argued that many factors influence the character of the youth labour market and thereby affect the proportions of youth, relative to other groups, represented in different jobs and industries. Some of them are constant, defining and central. There are distinctive age-related characteristics: in particular, early school-leavers lack training and experience and are willing to work for low pay. This means that they can only participate in unskilled work or in jobs which offer training. However, the youth labour market is also a dynamic construct. This is because many of the factors from which it is shaped are subject to change, such as market forces and legal/institutional requirements. Consequently, in some contexts, young people may also be in the lower echelons of short-term promotion or even some adult career jobs when needed by employers in a time of labour scarcity. If there is overall stability in the influences which affect the labour market, then 'youth' areas of such work may become apparent over time as traditions of recruitment emerge. Nevertheless, these areas are not necessarily exclusive to young people as unskilled workers of other ages may also be represented there.

These arguments were established empirically, but in a dynamic panorama. Although change was occurring continually, two distinct periods emerged which were termed the post-war period and the Conservative era. The post-war period provided job availability, an established apprenticeship system, and jobs with training and some prospects. Young people responded by leaving school early. Although they were largely restricted to certain occupations and industries, many of these jobs were meaningful, and provided a 'training ground' for the future. The cost to youth and the nation was a shortage of tertiary educated graduates, but expansions in higher education in the 1960s were beginning to overcome this disadvantage.

However, a higher plateau of unemployment, structural shifts, work organization changes, and a new political stance brought about a situation in which job and training opportunities diminished and much of the work available to school-leavers was low-skill, poorly paid, and increasingly part-time. This resulted in a decline in job heterogeneity and in possibilities of purposeful job-shopping. The removal of some legislation, especially with regard to unemployment benefit, and the loss of influence of unions took away protective devices in a situation where the market no longer operated adequately to provide a period of adjustment. Most young people chose to stay at school or enter Youth Training, and by the 1990s the 16-year-old youth labour market had nearly vanished. Moreover, the youth character of some jobs, with prospects and otherwise, was diluted by an increasing representation of adult workers in the areas in which they were based.

In general, these changes led to a worse experience for those who left school in the 1990s compared to the earlier period. The 1979/81 survey data demonstrated the existence of a variety of jobs with some ports of entry confined to youth, a range of young people, and a matching process via job search. Most young people were stable, but purposeful job search was evident among the job-swappers. Only a small minority of 'mavericks' was identified. Reflecting this commitment to work, there were some mature attitudes in those positive about union membership. Training, ability, job-swapping, and union membership led to higher wages overall. The market and its institutions were operating in a situation of some heterogeneity and job availability.

Nevertheless, from the beginning of the 1980s, increasing lack of opportunity and continuing decline in job and training opportunity constrained market mechanisms from ameliorating conditions of lower incomes and more unpleasant work. In other words, the shift towards homogeneity in a situation of high youth unemployment meant that purposeful job search was impeded and union strength diminished, particularly as craft unions declined. Lack of jobs also meant that groups already disadvantaged faced greater difficulties, and the acquisition of qualifications may have merely been part of a qualifications inflation rather than an upskilling process. Consequently, as labour market experience worsened in general, individuals lost control over their destiny.

These findings help to resolve an important controversy about whether or not there is a separate youth labour market. Ashton and Bourn (1981), for example, claimed there is a clear youth segment and challenged Raffe (1983), who disputed its existence in the late 1970s. He portrayed youth and adult labour markets as undifferentiated, arguing that there was more competition than segmentation between young people and adults. By the 1980s, he claimed that there might be a part of the labour market reserved for some youth, but that young people were broadly in the same markets as adults and affected by the same factors but more strongly (Raffe, 1985). Griffin, Kalleberg and

Alexander (1981) and Brown (1987) also challenged the notion that there is a separate youth labour market. Garonna and Ryan (1991) maintained that, because of its distinctive characteristics, 'youth may constitute an important socio-economic category without there being any separate youth market' (p. 27). Jones (1984) argued that analyses which emphasize the difference between youth and adult labour markets may be misleading predictors because there are changes in employers' recruitment patterns. Even in the USA, with its narrower range of early school-leavers, Hills and Reubens (1983) denied the appropriateness of the concept of a youth labour market, suggesting there were overlaps between youth and adult experiences and heterogeneity among youth categories of jobs: 'differences among groups of young people emerge as a more significant feature of our analysis ... than differences between youth and adults' (p. 310).

The crucial point is that, if youths *per se* are not immature, then the level of opportunity they are offered depends on other factors. Although their lack of skill and experience means they will be represented in jobs which offer training or require no skill, at any point in time, the volume, character, and mix of these jobs is determined by market forces in the context of historical, legal, and institutional factors and any influence of custom or tradition. By the same process, some jobs might be restricted to youth, say, for example, where apprenticeship-like schemes are age-related. If there were little competition for unskilled work then recruitment traditions might emerge in some industries and occupations which result in what are perceived to be youth jobs. The same applies to jobs which offer short-term promotion. Moreover, in a tight labour market, one might expect youth to encroach into 'adult' areas, some perhaps leading to long-term careers because of a general need for labour. This was the case in the post-war years in Britain. By the mid-1990s, however, the situation seems to have been reversed in part.

This state of affairs and its consequences can be explained in terms of segmentation analysis. Many studies of young people rest on the notion that the labour market is segmented (e.g. Ashton and Maguire, 1986b; Marsden and Ryan, 1986; Ashton, 1988; Marsden and Germe, 1990) or stratified (Roberts *et al.*, 1987). In general, their analysis builds on Osterman's dualist model (Osterman, 1980) but takes account of the heterogeneous nature of jobs available to youth in Britain. In Osterman's account, the youth labour market is essentially part of the secondary labour market. There are no entry ports within it to enable youth access to primary work. Young people must wait until they are old enough to enter the primary sector directly. Studies associated with both Ashton and Roberts, however, suggest that though the youth labour market consists largely of unskilled work, it also offers important entry ports to long-term careers. Indeed, the major example of 'youth jobs' in Britain is apprenticeships, part of the primary segment and most advantageous to youth at the expense of older workers. The strong implication is that if entry ports in the form of training and promotion opportunities are not taken advantage of by young people in the early years, they may well be excluded from the primary segment in adult life, as age and institutional regulations etc. may restrict them to secondary work in the future. In the context of decreasing opportunity, Roberts *et al.* (1987) argued that those who failed to gain early entry into jobs with prospects 'may find themselves permanently excluded from routes up the occupational structure, confined to unemployment or secondary occupations' (p. 30). Ashton and Maguire (1986a) also maintained that those who had not obtained a formal training by the age of 18 were excluded from large parts of the labour market.

In a situation of continuity and stability where norms in recruitment patterns prevailed, it was useful to analyse in terms of segments; but the effect of change on the labour market has been to eradicate some of the existing rigidities and bring into existence different constraints on youth. In segmentation terms, the effect of the changes has been to provide fewer entry ports for early school-leavers and a conventional youth labour market of the Osterman type has arisen for many young people. This outcome has fulfilled the prophecy of Marsden and Ryan (1986) of 'an intensified crowding of youth employment into a "ghetto" of secondary jobs' (p. 97). However, in the absence of a flourishing primary segment, these jobs may not act as a transit lounge in which youngsters adjust and mature. Rather, they may be the port of final destination for many young people.

Youth Transition

The changes that occurred in the Conservative era were important, not just in terms of their effect on the character of the youth labour market but also on the character of the transition period of new entrants.

Transition to the adult labour market in terms of gaining a settled job involves an adjustment to the workplace. On entry to the workplace, most young people need a process of familiarization to absorb the realities of work. This can involve aimless and/or mature behaviour and results in the characteristic high instability of the group. Providing the school-leaving cohort does not merely consist of a minority of high-school drop-outs, a smooth transition for many of the cohort can be achieved by purposeful search behaviour to achieve a suitable job–individual match. This, however, needs work availability and variety, especially of jobs which involve opportunities for betterment.

The transition process is also important in terms of the national interest. First, any early process of job-swapping increases market efficiency by resolving initial mismatches which occurred, say, as a result of poor information (Elias and Blanchflower, 1989). Second, the early years in the labour market can provide young people with a 'training ground' or 'practice pitch' for their long-term careers. This can be achieved by the availability of skill acquisition opportunities in these early years and the provision of jobs that offer chances of responsibility. These may be of short-term duration in industries from which young people later move or entry points to long-term jobs in the same firm or industry. Consequently, the facilitation of such a process is engendered by the existence of a heterogeneity of jobs and mechanisms which foster choice and purposeful job-swapping. For those who are 'immature', this period can, alternatively, provide a 'moratorium stage', in the Osterman (1980) tradition in jobs where instability is expected and has little impact on productivity. This was the pattern of the post-war years.

In the recent literature, it is claimed that periods of transition in adolescence 'may involve changes that enhance adjustment and abilities to cope with life stressors or that diminish adjustment and coping' (Lerner *et al.*, 1996). With regard to the transition from school to work, the length and character of this adjustment period depends on the characteristics of the young person and the opportunities available, even stretching into a life otherwise characterized by adult experiences. Since the 1970s, changes in the labour market have deleteriously affected this process. This is because lower levels of opportunity and heterogeneity have constrained the matching process. Roberts (1984) claimed that the post-war decades had merely proved an exception to the general rule that throughout the industrial age, the transition to work had been a problem for most young people. By the end of the century, his forecast was realized. Entry to the labour market had returned to Miller and Form's theme of the school-to-work transition as a time of stress (Miller and Form, 1951). Although Roberts and Chadwick (1991) found 'massive continuities in patterns of transition in the early 80s' (p. 48), by the latter half of the decade, Sime *et al.* (1990) found that, in general, 'young people's transitions from school into the labour market have become lengthier and more complex' (p. 19). Brown (1987) argued that there had been a collapse of the transition to work at the age of 16, and Payne (1995a) concluded that routes had profoundly altered. Thompson *et al.* (1993) claimed that 'the transition from compulsory education is now dominated by a period of further study' (p. 3), and Sime *et al.* (1990) reported that YTS had emerged as a major stepping-stone from school to work. Overall, the transition for youth, and for disadvantaged groups within that age cohort, had become more difficult by the mid-1990s than in the post-war period. It had become increasingly hard for young people to ameliorate their condition by their own efforts in a situation where there was a decline in job opportunities for the entire age group. For many young people, the transition process merely performed the function of 'scaling down their dreams' (Borman and Reisman, 1986: 24). Moreover, the national interest was affected adversely, in ways which have yet to be calculated, by the increasing length of transition and its final outcomes. These issues have been recognized and there has been increasing state intervention, largely in the form of the provision of vocational education and training.

Policy Implications

In a situation of persisting unemployment and a decline of work with prospects for young people, there are two main views with regard to policy.

Conservative policy

The first set of policies aimed to alter the characteristics of the school-leaving cohort. Roberts (1995) reported that an employer ethos emerged in the 1970s in which young people were said to have the 'wrong' attitudes to authority. They were said to be 'unprepared to knuckle down and accept the routine of much employment' (p. 85). This viewpoint is based on the assumption that young people are aimless in their labour market behaviour merely by virtue of their age. Because they are young, in general they lack a work ethic and do not search hard enough for jobs. They also lack sufficient skills for the modern world. The reaction to lack of work should be the involvement of relatively under-qualified young people in Britain in new education and training systems which can provide them with the 'right' attitudes and with skill opportunities appropriate to the changed circumstances making Britain more competitive. Consequently, if youths continue in full-time education after the age of 16, or take up YT, etc. then they will become older (i.e. more mature) when they enter the workforce and be more adequately equipped in educational and skill terms. They must be encouraged to do this by taking away state benefits and developing new academic and vocational courses. The normal school-leaving age should now be regarded as 18, and, it is argued, this older cohort is better equipped for the modern labour market than the 1979 school-leavers and will find adjustment easier than at the age of 16. Roberts (1995) reported that 'a constant body of opinion has argued that youth employment should not be regarded as a problem, but as an opportunity' (p. 11), and policy based on this kind of attitude was pursued in the Conservative era.

However, there is little empirical support for its efficacy. The evidence available suggests that, in the 1990s, many 18-year-olds seemed to have merely delayed their entry to the workplace by continuing in training and education and then left school to find similar opportunities to their 16-year-old counterparts without the availability of traditional male apprenticeships. State benefits were available to the unemployed from the age of 18 so unemployment rates can be realistically compared to those of school-leavers pre-1988. They were persistently high: 21 per cent in 1996 (*Labour Market Quarterly Report*, May 1996). The shift to part-time and low-skill work also affected 18-year-old school-leavers. In 1994/5, 12.3 per cent of 19/20-year-olds had part-time work (*Labour Market Quarterly Report*, May 1996). A measure of the plight of these young adults is the fact that in 1991, for the first time in the YCS series, 18-19-year-old unemployed's average reservation wage exceeded the age-group's average pay (Park, 1994). This was partly because the least able were over-represented in the 18-year-old leaver cohort. There are two reasons.

First, the evidence suggests that those most disadvantaged amongst this age cohort were young people who had only achieved modest or poor attainments earlier on. Roberts and Chadwick (1991) reported that post-16 educational and training opportunities were not improving their relative prospects. These were the very people who formed a large part of the 18-year-old school-leaver cohort because many of the least qualified who could not gain work or training opportunities stayed on at school at 16 (Payne, 1995a) and left as soon as they became eligible for state benefits. Although participation has increased in education for all age groups between 16 and 24, for the 19–20 age group, only 4 per cent were in schools or colleges of education (Department of Education and Science, 1996).

Second, at least in part as a response to their disadvantaged situation, more young adults who were sufficiently qualified took up tertiary education than previously. The numbers of young people in higher education nearly doubled in the 1980s, from 34,900 to 67,200.[1] By the early 1990s, the student population in higher education was equivalent to one-third of the 18–21-year-old age group, at a time when the government was shifting the cost to parents through a reduction in grants and benefits, and the introduction of loan schemes (Roberts, 1995). In 1996, 26 per cent of 18-year-olds took up higher education (Department of Education and Science, 1996).

Moreover, although those at 18 with A-levels or who had undertaken vocational courses had average or better prospects of work than the less qualified (Sime *et al.* 1990) some employers now looked to graduates (Pike, Connor and Jagger, 1992). In fact, more students gained A-levels or the equivalent in the mid-1990s than in previous times: in 1980/1, 17 per cent of school-leavers gained one or more A-levels (or the equivalent). The proportion rose steadily over the 1980s, until in 1990/1, the figure was over 23 per cent (Roberts, 1995). Consequently, many young people who acquired extra qualifications may have been 'running just to stand still' in the qualifications inflation.

By the end of the Conservative era, the 18-year-old school-leaver experience, in general, was worse than that of their 16-year-old contemporaries and of those in the post-war period. Traditional apprenticeships were still the most valuable job for early school-leaver males in terms of later success (Payne, 1995a) but continued to be confined to 16-year-olds in most cases. The jobs available to 18-year-old school-leavers consisted largely of increasingly low-level and part-time unskilled work offering poor pay and conditions. Better/more qualifications were needed than previously for any work which offered prospects. Individuals could improve their chances only at the expense of others in the queue. Moreover, the character of this 18-year-old group is different from that of the wide-ranging group of early school-leavers in 1979 with a bias towards the lower-ability group who faced competition from other unskilled workers, young and old alike, and had little alternative to unemployment or underemployment. Thus, in the absence of unemployment benefit for 16- and 17-year-olds, the two-year waiting period may merely be acting as a proxy for unemployment for many. Roberts (1995) suggested that some sections of post-16 academic education in Britain seem to have taken on a 'cooling-out' function which merely demonstrates to some pupils that they lack ability. In this way, their aspirations are subdued. More than this, Roberts *et al.* (1992a) claimed that the results of their findings in the late 1980s demonstrated that the Conservative government's education and training policies 'sidetracked' the most disadvantaged young people. They were a 'huge success' in that they concealed economic and political failures 'by convincing the wider society and even the young victims themselves that the latter were to blame for their own difficulties in becoming established in the workforce' (p. 751).

Overall, Conservative policy consisted of the pursuit of downward wage flexibility at the same time as an expansion of the skilled labour force by an investment in training. Chapman and Tooze (1987) claimed that such an investment is wasted in the absence of effective demand management policies, and it is not clear whether any government is likely to carry these out on a scale sufficient to create the requisite number of jobs offering standard hours of work.

A new policy for a new century

The second set of policies is based on implications derived from the findings of this book. It aims to change the character of the youth labour market. By the start of the new century, the labour market for youth and young adults is converging to a hybrid of the conventional model of dead-end work. However, for many young people the outcomes are different from those observed by Osterman (1980) because, in a situation of job scarcity and polarization, many early school-leavers may never enter career jobs – they are trapped in work without ports of entry. Their youth experience is the same as the adult experience. Low-skill work is not an ephemeral experience restricted to their early years. The jobs of the dead-end youth labour market are also the jobs of their adult world.

In this situation, the existence of entry ports to career jobs, in the form of skill acquisition or a work history of job progression, take on a greater significance as they decline relative to the availability of dead-end work. A new pattern of stratification may emerge if the current polarized situation persists, with unemployment as a major segment. This pattern may further disadvantage the long-term hopes of many young people already disadvantaged, including the least able, non-whites, inner-city residents, and those with unemployed parents. The new apprenticeships which are not exclusive to 16-year-olds may weaken the most important entry port for 16-year-old males, while helping young adults previously excluded.

Moreover, there are implications more far-reaching than a less than optimal allocation of resources and social inequity. The findings of the book demonstrate that labour market maturity is, in part, based on the availability of meaningful work. Thus, the provision of dead-end work for a large group of young people in search of full-time, long-term careers, with no provision for purposeful search, might mean that 'immature' behavioural traits emerge in a group that is, in fact, of an older age than early school-leavers. One of the most profound implications of Doeringer and Piore's seminal work (Doeringer and Piore, 1971) was that job-induced behavioural traits gave misinformation to employers about already disadvantaged groups of workers. Such a process would impede the future chances of this school-leaving age cohort and those visible, disadvantaged groups over-proportionately represented within it. New customs, traditions, and segments might emerge, based on changed attitudes.

However, it has been demonstrated that the character of the youth labour market is dynamic. Therefore, it can be manipulated by a change in its causal factors, say, legislative, institutional, or customary devices, which in turn affect the attitudes of participants – employers and employees. The implication is that government policy can affect youth transition. This viewpoint has received some support. Raffe (1988a) reported differences in transition patterns between England/

Wales and Scotland due to the influence of institutional differences. Bynner and Roberts (1991) argued that 'it is crucial to examine the transition from compulsory education to the labour market within the contemporary political and historical context' (p. 5). Kerckhoff (1990), in a comparative US/UK study, concluded that there are 'ways in which a society structures the transition process' (p. 83). In terms of the national interest, both economic and social, the transition period needs to be one which eventually allows young people to become productive over their lifetime in the most efficient way. In this way, there should be a congruence of national and individual interest.

The policy has several aims which, it is proposed, can help reverse the convergence apparent at the end of the century and to adapt youth transition to the changed economy to promote both the welfare of young people and, thereby, the national interest.

1. To provide ports of entry to long-term jobs, either through direct skill acquisition, or the opportunity to take responsibility in firms and industries which may provide short- or long-term work.

2. To provide a system where continuous job search and matching can prevail, via job-swapping.

3. To allow clearing mechanisms to operate so segments do not become embedded in the labour market, especially in the early years, in relation to age, gender, race, etc.

4. To promote disadvantaged groups.

5. To provide meaningful work to end the transition.

6. To provide legislative protection and information about trade unions to the most vulnerable members of the workforce.

7. To avoid the displacement of other workers.

In these ways, individual satisfaction, market efficiency, and social goals might be met in a changing labour market.

The nub of the policy is simple. The manipulation of the character of the labour market can be triggered by a reorganization of the post-16 education and training system in which non-standard hours of work are embedded. It builds on existing trends in the workplace and makes them a feature of strength: by the end of the 1980s, over 90 per cent of secondary schools were arranging work experience in which over 70 per cent of pupils were involved (National Curriculum Council, 1991). The policy can be developed alongside existing educational developments.

It consists of two main features: work of non-standard hours and day-release from full-time education. The main recommendation is for the establishment of a large-scale day-release system for young people of 17+ to work blocs of non-standard hours in local firms on a routine basis, perhaps increasing incrementally over time. In time, this system might replace YTS and receive its funding. Snower and Booth (1996) argued that equal training support, in pro rata terms, for those in full-time and part-time education and training, would usually be in the public interest.[2] Employers should pay the young employees directly at the market rate to provide information to the young person about the workplace and to avoid displacement. Firms can recruit by direct observation: mismatched entrants merely return to school or college of further education, rather than to unemployment, until another position becomes available. At any stage, the employee can be released from the job. To some extent, the idea is a mirror image of the apprenticeship system with its day-release to colleges of further education. The inversion is a response to the changed context of job scarcity, and the use of part-time jobs takes advantage of the availability of work of non-standard hours. Moreover, the current apprenticeship system, with most of the time spent at work rather than college, can be adapted to such a scheme.

The system can comfortably coexist in a situation where many young people continue in full-time education. All students should complete a year of education at 16 before they decide which route to choose, and there should be possibilities to switch between routes – to higher education or work-based training. Moreover, the option of unemployed job search should be available. Consequently, for those who leave school, unemployment benefits should be restored, allowing them to job-swap even within the restricted context of the 1990s. Some may be the immature, but they need time to explore the low-skill market, perhaps to realize that such work may no longer be of temporary duration.

Direct involvement by employers with new entrants will help disadvantaged groups. If selection is carried out by employer and employee choice with recommendation from the school/CFE, then there will be less reliance on personal contacts. Once in the job, a continuation of the employment contract will be by direct information rather than screens and signals. Inner-city residents gain an advantage over commuters. Household unemployment is no longer as important where direct contacts do not matter. Racial prejudice should be countered. There are still problems, particularly in terms of local labour markets, and it may be that regional grants are essential, or boarding/travelling allowances paid to young people. However, if the training received is part of a recognized accreditation programme with a system of national qualifications, it will give employers fuller information and allow employee transferability.

In terms of the transition period, the system provides possibilities of adjustment and job-matching before full entry to the labour market. Young people can be eased into the labour market. The scheme can become a training ground and practice court by a dovetailing transition process between school and work. Young people can be encouraged to job-swap without a period of paid unemployment. They can merely stay in school until a new job is arranged. Familiarization with the workplace can take place in easy stages. The period can act as a training ground for employers also, and help them perceive once again that young people can be responsible, if given meaningful job opportunities. In this way, youth might gain access to a wide range of industries and skill opportunities. Marsden and Ryan (1986) argued that in such a situation, youth unemployment rates would be correspondingly lower.

However, training should be available for young people for as long as they require. It must be meaningful and employers therefore must be involved. At the end, there may not be 40-hour a week jobs, but 'part-time' work, in which training is still embedded where wanted. In this way the work can be shared without either legislation or union opposition because an acceptance of fewer hours of work may grow with the young generation as it passes into adulthood. Moreover, through this system, less work guarantees more training, and a possibility to swap occupations throughout life, thereby breaking down segments. In order to avert the mere displacement of older workers, the suggestion is that this scheme should not be reserved only for young people, but should also be available to older workers and returner women, say through colleges of further education, so can they can be upskilled also.[3] In fact, Snower and Booth (1996) claimed that there was no good case for giving favourable treatment to young people in support for their training and education: 'the forces of technological change …

continuously make skills obsolete and make it necessary for people of all ages to retrain' (p. 347). Mitterauer (1992) argued that the static view of an adult as a fully developed personality was being replaced by the concept of the 'lifelong learner' (p. 40), prepared to accept changes and work them into his/her personal development. Mobility across the traditional gender-based jobs might be encouraged through schools and colleges of further education for all age groups.

Clearly the system requires the co-operation of school-leavers, employers, unions, and schools. It can be argued that it is in their joint and separate interests. First, young people are likely to welcome it. They do not lack a work ethic. The results of this book make that abundantly clear. Even before the benefit was removed, most preferred to return to full-time education or take up YT courses, rather than be unemployed. This scheme builds on such a positive attitude. For young people, training is relevant and paid and may even tempt the small minority that preferred unemployment to education. It gives them a chance because it guarantees them access to some work. Second, it is in the interest of firms to be involved because of the constant complaint of skill shortage. The advantage to the employer is that, initially, some of the training is provided by state finance, though it can be tailored to the firm's needs by on-the-job training.[4]

Third, it is in the interests of unions, because they have lost their traditional areas of recruitment in manufacturing and the skilled crafts. Unions can recruit young people and sow the seeds of future membership and leadership, especially important in a period of general union decline. They can carry this out in part perhaps by an education scheme in schools, which the findings of the London survey suggested might be a valuable method of recruitment. Unions can reach young people who are based in places of education, rather than working in small, unorganized workplaces. In this way they can help monitor and ameliorate conditions for youth in the workplace; this might be necessary to avoid exploitation of the young. Finally, schools no longer need to police youth who stay on because they cannot find work. They are more likely to be happy with purposeful youth. The consensual aspect of the employment relationship needs to be emphasized and reinforced when the interests of the nation's future are so closely tied to those of one of its most vulnerable groups. The 'social partnership' systems of Germany and Denmark, for example, have demonstrated the success of such an approach (Snower and Booth, 1997).

The system affects the national interest in its broadest sense and can have far-reaching social and economic effects. If employers can recruit young people to work of non-standard hours, they may well repackage their tasks into different bundles of jobs with a mix of skills, thereby reducing polarization and making use of the training in new technology available in schools. It can provide ports of entry to all ages and help break down segments. It clearly adapts to the changing needs of the economy, making the acquired skills particularly relevant to the available jobs, but evolves out of the current youth labour market context, allowing change without statutory imposition. It could become a permanent feature, adjusting skill levels and hours of work to changes in demand, technology, and demography. It could also just act as a bridging or interim measure until a more advanced scheme is constructed, say on the German or Japanese model, or following the prescriptions of Layard *et al.* (1994).[5]

There is, however, a great danger that if training in schools and colleges is not meaningful, and does not lead to appropriate jobs, young people will be crowded into what might become a lifetime of institutionally determined low-skill, low-wage, part-time jobs. Consequently, legislation with regard to a minimum wage for youth and the low-paid should be reintroduced to induce employers to repackage their bundles of tasks and make full use of the training offered. In the absence of such measures, union opposition is guaranteed.

The evidence that has been presented since the survey period demonstrates that for most young people, labour market entry has become more hazardous and less rewarding than in those years. Circumstances outside their control continue to influence their initial experience and cast a long shadow. Market mechanisms, institutions, legal and otherwise, and prevailing ideologies are constrained from ameliorating their situation. A failure to identify young people's aims and aspirations with the national interest defined in both economic and social terms, may have long-term consequences for Britain. In a continuing situation of long-term, dead-end work, the transition to the workplace might become an idling or adjustment time in which learning of a different nature takes place. So-called 'wrong' attitudes to work identified in youth from the 1970s might in fact, at least in part, be determined by job characteristics. The survey findings unequivocally showed that most young people are not workshy. They demonstrated positive, mature, and purposeful attitudes. Young people wanted to work and they liked work. More recent studies show they hate being unemployed: school-leavers described unemployment as an ordeal (Hendry *et al.*, 1984). Young people want jobs, almost any kind of jobs, even on modest wages (Coffield *et al.*, 1986). The desire for work is strongest amongst the least qualified (Banks *et al.*, 1992). They are angry, not demoralized (Willis *et al.*, 1988). These attitudes have implications for the wider national interest: McRae (1987) argued that 'without employment ... young people are effectively excluded from the mainstream of society' (p. 151).

During the course of the survey period, a series of riots erupted in Britain's inner-city areas, mainly involving young people. In the debate in the House of Commons that followed the publication of the official enquiry into their origins (the Scarman Report) a member of Parliament said: 'It is no coincidence that the first outbreak of violence in 1980 and 1981, in Bristol and Brixton, took place in April, in the week before Easter, at the end of the Spring term, as the first crop of the year's school leavers found themselves outside their classrooms and on the dole queue' (*Hansard*, 10 December 1981, pp. 1042–3). The protection of the young is not just a moral imperative. In the absence of opportunities to enhance life chances, an older group might respond with less mature job-induced behaviour than their 16-year-old counterparts of 1979. It might be interesting to see the effects of a longer wait in a queue in a labour market which offers even less hope for the future.

Notes

1 During the 1980s, there was a small increase (just 8 per cent) in the number of young students in Britain's older universities. In the polytechnics, which became the new universities, there was an increase of 93 per cent between 1980 and 1990 (Roberts, 1995).

2 There are those who argue that the market should decide who bears the costs of training and that the state should not intervene except in cases of clear market failure (e.g. Booth and Snower, 1996). However, in the case of disadvantaged youth in a historical context of state support for apprenticeships and tertiary education, it seems unlikely that early high-school leavers will take out loans unless work is available at the end of the training period. Moreover, young people are generally restricted to local labour markets so jobs/training opportunities are likely to be least available in those places

where there is high unemployment. Consequently, state finance should be targeted at such areas. Nevertheless, if sufficient government finance is available and there is adequate provision in workplaces to provide sub-sidised jobs/training to young people while they are at school, then firms may be encouraged to relocate to such areas to take advantage of the skilled cohort of school leavers who cannot find work in the locality.

3 The older unemployed could be financed through training vouchers pro-vided through government revenues, or a levy system. For a fuller discussion, see Booth and Snower (1996).

4 The market failure brought about by the transferability of early workplace training which acts as a 'practice pitch' may result in the need for state financial intervention in the long term. See Stevens (1996) for an analysis of such a situation.

5 The authors also have a firm belief in the importance of part-time employment-based training for 16–19-year-olds, but based at the workplace rather than the place of education.

APPENDIX 1: THE LOGIT MODEL

The logit equation is an additive model of the form:

$$\ln \frac{p_i}{1-p_i} = \alpha + \beta X_i \dots$$

where p is the probability of getting a job. Therefore, the coefficient b is the effect of a change in an independent variable upon

$$\ln \frac{p_i}{1-p_i}$$

The coefficients are estimated using the maximum – likelihood method: those that make the observed results most likely are selected (Norusis, 1993).

The amount of increase in the probability, p_β, depends upon the original probability and thus upon the initial values of all the independent variables and their coefficients, i.e.

$$\frac{\partial p_i}{\partial X_i} = \beta \frac{e^{\alpha + \beta X_i}}{(1+e^{\alpha + \beta X_i})^2}$$

Thus, while the sign of the coefficient does indicate the direction of the change, the magnitude depends on the original probability and is not directly interpretable as the effect of a change in an explanatory variable on the mean, or expected value of the dependent variable (Maddala, 1983).

The results from the job regression (Table 4.3) will be used as an example of how to interpret the findings.

An observation of the residuals showed that the model fits the data reasonably well. The Pearson chi-square goodness of fit test, which for large groups is akin to the log likelihood statistic, is calculated as

$$\chi^2 = \frac{\Sigma(\text{residual}_i)^2}{n\hat{p}_i\,(1-\hat{p})_i}$$

where $\hat{p}$ is the predicted proportion.

The chi-square of the job model is not significant. (This is the case throughout, unless reported otherwise.) This means that the unexplained part of the model is statistically unimportant.

Since the observed significance level for the chi-square statistic is reasonably high ($p = 0.46$), there is no reason to doubt the model.

Although the coefficients cannot be simply interpreted, Seltzer (1995) has adapted Maddala's analysis (1983) to produce a way in which the variables can be ranked in their effect on the probability of gaining in this case a job and, following him.

$$p_i = e\,(\Sigma\hat{\beta}\mu X_i)\,[1 + e\,(\Sigma\hat{\beta}\mu X_i)]$$

Thus, the coefficients from the JOB regression can be interpreted.

	$\hat{B}$	Increase	Decrease
EXAMS	0.30	0.03	-0.03
COMPREHENSION	0.11	0.01	-0.01
ATTITUDE	0.35	0.03	-0.03
RACE	0.84	0.05	-0.06
SEX	0.15	0.01	-0.01
AREA	0.51	-0.05	0.05
WORRIED	0.48	0.34	-0.04
PREVIOUS WORK	0.13	0.01	-0.01
PARENTAL HELP	0.43	0.04	-0.04
HOUSEHOLD	-0.56	-0.05	0.05
UNEMPL. ADVICE	-0.37	-0.12	0.12
OCCUPATION	-0.04	-0.01	0.01

Note: $p_i = 0.740562$

The number in the Increase/Decrease columns is the change in probability caused by a one-standard deviation change in the independent variable. In this case, for example, not only is race significant, but it has the greatest effect on chances of gaining work.

Appendix 2: Data Dictionary

Unless stated to the contrary, the variables are dichotomous, usually based on a positive response to the question (1) or otherwise (0). The questions are from the survey questionnaire.

ABSENTEEISM: *Are you absent from work for reasons other than sickness?*

ADVICE: *Have you been given advice by school, careers guidance, or government agencies?*

APPRENTICESHIP: *Are you/will you be an apprentice or are you/will you be on some other sort of training scheme that leads to a certificate or qualification?*

AREA OF RESIDENCE: Inner city (1) outer city (0)
These following dummy variables were set up as reference categories in turn:
AREA1 Tower Hamlets
AREA2 Hammersmith
AREA3 Lambeth
AREA4 Hounslow
AREA5 Bromley

CHANGE IN INCOME: A simple calculation was made, subtracting weekly income at the beginning of the survey from weekly income at the end and the dependent variable was constructed accordingly.

COMPREHENSION: The professional interviewers were asked to make an assessment of whether the young person displayed a good understanding of the survey questions (1) or otherwise (0).

DURATION: *How long do you intend to stay in your first job?*
The dummy was constructed on the basis of a response which indicated an intention to stay less than a year (1) or longer (0).

EXAMS: Examinations taken while at school, GCE (1) or otherwise (0).

GENERAL TRAINING: *Are you/will you be an apprentice? Or are you/will you be on some other sort of training scheme that leads to a certificate or qualification?*

HOUSEHOLD UNEMPLOYMENT: *Is anyone in your household currently unemployed?*

IDEAL SKILL: *Ideally, what kind of job would you like to do?*
Skilled manual (1) otherwise (0).

INCOME: *How much are you earning/about to earn?*
Youngsters were asked how much they were earning on a weekly basis at the beginning of their first job and the continuous variable was set up according to the response.

INTENTION TO LEAVE: *Are you seriously considering changing your job at the moment?*

INTEX: Employer interview or exam.

JOB: Definite job offer accepted and taken up by September 1979 (1) or not (0).
During the summer holidays, in July and August 1979, the school-leavers were asked if they had been offered a job which they were planning to take or had already started.

JOB LOCATION: Location of job
Youngsters were asked where they worked. Responses were categorized according to inner or outer location.

LATENESS: *Are you late for work?*
Very often, often, occasionally, never (coded 1,2,3,4).

NUMBER OF PEOPLE AT THE WORKPLACE : *About how many people work at the place you work?*
A continuous variable was constructed based on the response. Specific numbers given ranged from 2 to 450. A few said 'over five hundred' (26) or 'over a thousand' (49) and the corresponding variables were allocated values of 1000 and 1500 respectively.

OCCUPATION: Occupation of head of household.
The occupational categories developed by Stern (1981) for this data-set were used to determine the socio-economic status of the head of household (which in 81 per cent of the cases was the father). These

were further divided into four major categories: managerial, skilled, semi-skilled, and unskilled.

PARENTAL HELP: *Have you (the parent), or has anyone else here (i.e. in the home), done anything to help the young person get a job when he/she leaves school?*

PREVIOUS WORK: *Have you ever done any part-time or voluntary work?*

PROMOTION: *Do people who do your job normally get promotion?*

QUIT: Voluntary turnover.
The dummy was set up on the basis of the division of these respondents into those who had quit by the end of one year after leaving school, i.e. by October 1980, and those who were still in the same job.

RACE: White (1); non-white(0).

SEX : Male (1); female (0).

SEPARATIONS: Number of job separations experienced over the period July 1979–January 1981.

SOCWEF: A dummy was constructed based on the employed (1) and those unemployed and eligible for receipt of social security payments (0).

TAKE ANY JOB: *Would you take a job that wasn't really what you wanted, just so you would have a job?*

UNION: *Have you joined/do you intend to join a union in your job?*

WORRIED: *Are you worried about being unemployed?*

APPENDIX 3: ENGLAND AND WALES YOUTH COHORT SERIES

Gray, J., Jesson, D., Pattie, C. and Sime, N. (1989) *Education and Training Opportunities in the Inner City.* Youth Cohort Series No. 7 (1985 school-leaving cohort)

Sime, N., Pattie, C. and Gray, J. (1990) *What Now? The Transition from School to the Labour Market among 16 to 19 Year Olds.* Youth Cohort Series No. 14 (1985 school-leaving cohort)

Roberts, K. and Chadwick, C. (1991) *Transitions in the Labour Market: The New Routes of the 1980s. A Study of Transitions 1984–87.* Youth Cohort Series No. 17 (1984 school-leaving cohort)

Sime, N. (1991) *Constraining Choices: Unemployment among Sixteen and Seventeen Year Olds in the Late Eighties.* Youth Cohort Series No. 18 (1984, 1985, 1986, 1988 school-leaving cohorts)

Drew, D., Gray, J. and Sime, N. (1992) *Against the Odds: the Education and Labour Market Experiences of Black Young People.* Youth Cohort Report No. 19 (1985, 1986 school-leaving cohorts)

Courtenay, G. and McAleese, I. (1993) *Cohort 5: Aged 16 and 17 in 1991. Report on Sweep 1.* Youth Cohort Report No. 22 (1991 school-leaving cohort)

Ashford, S. and Gray, J. (1993) *Young People in Training: Towards a National Picture in the Late 80s.* Youth Cohort Report No. 25 (1986 school-leaving cohort)

Gray, J., Jesson, D. and Tranmer, M. (1994) *Local Labour Market Participation: Evidence from the End of the Eighties.* Youth Cohort Report No. 26 (1986, 1988, 1990 school-leaving cohorts)

Park, A. (1994) *Young People 18–19 Years Old in 1991.* Youth Cohort Report No. 29 (1988, 1989 school-leaving cohorts)

Payne, J. (1995) *Routes Beyond Compulsory Schooling.* Youth Cohort Report No. 31, (1988, 1990, 1991 school-leaving cohorts)

BIBLIOGRAPHY

Albanese, R. and Van Fleet, D. D. (1985) Rational behaviour in groups: the free-riding tendency. *Academy of Management Review*, Vol. 10, No. 2, 244–55.

Althauser, R. (1989) Internal labor markets. *Annual Review of Sociology*, Vol. 15, 143–61.

Angle, H. J. and Perry, J. L. (1986) Dual commitment and labor–management relationship climates. *Academy of Management Journal*, Vol. 29, No. 1, 31–50.

Ashenfelter, O. and Pencavel, J. H. (1969) American trade union growth: 1900–1960. *Quarterly Journal of Economics*, Vol. 83, 434–48.

Ashford, S. and Gray, J. (1993) Young People in Training: Towards a National Picture in the Late 80s. Youth Cohort Report No. 25. Sheffield: Department of Employment.

Ashton, D. N. (1973) The transition from school to work: notes on the development of different frames of reference among young male workers. *Sociological Review*, Vol. 21, No. 1, 105–25.

Ashton, D. N. (1975) From school to work: some problems of adjustment experienced by male workers, in Brannen, P. (ed.) *Entering the World of Work: Some Sociological Perspectives*. London: Manpower Intelligence Unit, HMSO.

Ashton, D. N. (1988) Sources of variation in labour market segmentation: a comparison of youth labour markets in Canada and Britain. *Work, Employment and Society*, Vol. 2, No. 1, 1–24.

Ashton, D. N. and Bourn, C. J. (1981) *Education, Employment and Young People*. Vaughan Paper No. 26. Leicester: University of Leicester Department of Adult Education.

Ashton, D. N. and Field, D. (1976) *Young Workers*. London: Hutchinson.

Ashton, D. N. and Lowe, G. (eds) (1991) *Making their Way. Education, Training and the Labour Market in Canada and Britain*. Milton Keynes: Open University Press.

Ashton, D. N. and Maguire, M. J. (1986a) *Young Adults in the Labour Market*. Department of Employment Research Paper No. 55. London: HMSO.

Ashton, D. N. and Maguire, M. J. (1986b) *The Vanishing Youth Labour Market*. London: Occasional paper, Youthaid.

Ashton, D. N., Maguire, M. J. and Garland, V. (1982) *Youth in the Labour Market*. Department of Employment Research Paper No. 34. London: HMSO.

Ashton, D. N., Maguire, M. J. and Spilsbury, M. (1983) Local labour markets and their impact on the life chances of youths, in Coles, R. (ed.) *Young Careers*. Milton Keynes: Open University Press.

Ashton, D. N., Maguire, M. J. and Spilsbury, M. (1990) *Restructuring the Labour Market: The Implications for Youth*. Basingstoke: Macmillan.

ALA (1992) *The Great Skills Divide. The Jobs–Training Mis-match in London*. London: Association of London Authorities.

Atkinson, P. and Rees, T. L. (1982) Youth unemployment and state intervention, in Rees T.L. and Atkinson, P. (eds) *Youth Unemployment and State Intervention*. London: Routledge and Kegan Paul.

Bain, G. S. and Elias, P. (1985) Trade union membership in Great Britain: an individual-level analysis. *British Journal of Industrial Relations*, Vol. 23, 71–82.

Bain, G. S. and Elsheikh, F. (1976) *Union Growth and the Business Cycle: An Econometric Analysis*. Oxford: Blackwell.

Bain, G. S. and Elsheikh, F. (1979) An inter-industry analysis of unionisation in Britain. *British Journal of Industrial Relations*, Vol. 17, 137–57.

Baker, G. and Holmstrom, B (1995) Internal labor markets: too many theories, too few facts. *American Economic Association Papers and Proceedings*, Vol. 85, 255–65.

Banks, M., Breakwell, G., Bynner, J., Emler, N., Jamieson, L. and Roberts, K. (1992) *Careers and Identities*. Milton Keynes: Open University Press.

Barling, J., Wade, B. and Fullagar, C. (1990) Predicting employee commitment to company and union: different models. *Journal of Occupational Psychology*, Vol. 18, 49–61.

Baxter, J. L. (1975) The chronic job changer: a study of youth unemployment. *Social and Economic Administration*, Vol. 9, No 3, 184–206.

Becker, G. S. (1962) Investment in human capital: a theoretical analysis. *Journal of Political Economy*, supplement, Vol. 2, no. 5, part 2, 9–49.

Becker, G. S., (1971) *The Economics of Discrimination*. Chicago: University of Chicago Press.

Becker, G. S. (1975) *Human Capital: A Theoretical and Empirical Analysis, with Special Reference to Education*. Chicago: University of Chicago Press.

Begg, I. G., Blake, A. P. and Deakin, B. M. (1991) YTS and the labour market system. *British Journal of Industrial Relations*, Vol. 29, 223–36.

Beloff, H. (1986) Making Ourselves, in Beloff, H. (ed.) *Getting into Life*. London: Methuen.

Bennett, R., Glennester, H. and Nevison, D. (1992) Investing in skills: to stay on or not to stay on. *Oxford Review of Economic Policy*, Vol. 8, 130–45.

Berger, S. and Piore, M. J. (1980) *Dualism and Discontinuity in Industrial Societies*. Cambridge: Cambridge University Press.

Biggart, A. and Furlong A., (1996) Educating 'discouraged' workers: cultural diversity in the upper secondary school. *British Journal of Sociology of Education*, Vol. 17, No. 3, 253–66.

Blackburn, R. M. and Mann, M. (1979) *The Working Class in the Labour Market*. London: Macmillan.

Blanchflower, D. G. and Lynch, L. M. (1992) *Training at Work: A Comparison of US and British Youths*. Discussion Paper No. 78, June: London: London School of Economics Centre for Economic Performance.

Blau, F. and Kahn, L. (1981). Race and sex differences in quits by young workers. *Industrial and Labor Relations Review*, Vol. 34, No. 4, 563–77.

Blau, P. M. and Duncan, D. D. (1967) *The American Occupational Structure*. New York:

Wiley.

Booth, A. (1983) A reconsideration of trade union growth in the United Kingdom. *British Journal of Industrial Relations*, Vol. 21, 377–91.

Booth, A. (1986) Estimating the probability of trade union membership: a study of men and women in Britain. *Economica*, Vol. 53, 41–61.

Booth, C. (1981) *Labour Force Information from the NDHS*. Department of Employment Research Paper No. 17. London: HMSO.

Booth, A. L. and Satchell, S. (1996) On apprenticeship qualifications and labour mobility, in Booth, A. L. and Snower, D. J. (eds) *Acquiring Skills: Market Failures, their Symptoms and Policy Responses*. Cambridge: Cambridge University Press.

Bordieu, P. and Passeron, J-C. (1977) *Reproduction in Education, Society and Culture*. London: Sage.

Borland, J. and Ouliaris, S. (1994) The determinants of Australian union membership. *Journal of Applied Econometrics*, Vol. 9, 453–68.

Borman, K. M. (1991) *The First "Real" Job: A Study of Young Workers*. Albany: State University of New York Press.

Borman, K. M. and Reisman, J. (1986) Becoming a worker, in Borman, K. M. and Reisman, J. (eds) *Becoming a Worker*. Albany: New York University Press.

Bowles, S. and Gintis, H. (1976) *Schooling in Capitalist America: Educational Reform and the Contradictions of Economic Life*. New York: Basic Books.

Bradshaw, J., Lawton, D. and Cooke, K. (1987) Income and expenditure of teenagers and their families. *Youth and Policy*, Vol. 19, 15–19.

Brannen, P. (ed.) (1975) *Entering the World of Work: Some Sociological Perspectives*. London: HMSO.

Brown, P. (1987) Schooling for inequality? Ordinary kids in school and the labour market, in Brown, P. and Ashton, D. N. (eds) *Education, Unemployment and Labour Markets*. Lewes: Falmer Press.

Brown, P. and Ashton, D. N. (eds) (1987) *Education, Unemployment and Labour Markets*. Lewes: Falmer Press.

Buck, N. H. and Gordon, I. (1986) *The London Employment Pattern*. Oxford: Oxford University Press.

Byford, D. (1983) *Comparison between the Educational and Economic Activity of Young People in Inner London and Nationally*. ILEA Research and Statistics Report, 877/83, May, London: ILEA.

Bynner, J. and Roberts, K. (1991) *Youth and Work: Transition to Employment in England and Germany*. London: Anglo-German Foundation.

Carter, M. J. and Carter, S. B. (1975) Internal labor markets in retailing: the early years. *Industrial and Labor Relations Review*, Vol. 38, 586–98.

Carter, M.P. (1962) *Home, School and Work: A Study of the Education and Employment of Young People in Britain*. Oxford: Pergamon Press.

Carter, M. P. (1966) *Into Work*. Baltimore: Pelican.

Carter, M. P. (1975) Teenage workers: a second chance at 18 ?, in Brannen, P. (ed.) *Entering the World of Work: Some Sociological Perspectives*. London: HMSO.

Cartwright, D. (1968) The Nature of Group Cohesiveness in Cartwright, D. and Zander, A. (eds) *Group Dynamics: Research and Theory*. London: Tavistock.

Casey, B. (1991) Survey evidence on trends in 'non-standard' employment, in Pollert, A. (ed.) *Farewell to Flexibility?* Oxford: Blackwell.

Casson, M. (1979) *Youth Unemployment,* London: Macmillan.

CBI (1983) Special Programmes Unit, Confederation of British Industry, Wolverhampton Community Action Programme.

Chaison, G. N. and Dhavale, D. G. (1992) The choice between union membership and free-rider status. *Journal of Labor Research,* Vol. 13, 355–69.

Chapman, P. G. and Tooze, M. J. (1987) *The Youth Training Scheme in the United Kingdom.* Aldershot: Avebury.

Chatrik, B. and Madagan, I. (1995) *Taking their Chances: Education, Training and Employment Opportunities for Young People.* London: The Children's Society and Youthaid.

Cherry, N. (1976) Persistent job changing. Is it a problem?. *Journal of Occupational Psychology,* Vol. 49, 203–22.

Church, A. and Ainley, P. (1987) Inner city decline and regeneration: young people and the labour market in London's Docklands, in Brown, P. and Ashton, D.N. (eds) *Education, Unemployment and Labour Markets.* East Sussex: Falmer Press.

Clark, K. and Summers, L (1982) The dynamics of youth unemployment, in Freeman, R. B. and Wise, D. A. (eds) *The Youth Labour Market Problem: Its Nature, Causes and Consequences.* New York: National Bureau of Economic Research.

Clarke, L. (1980a) *The Transition from School to Work: A Critical Review of the Literature.* London: Department of Employment Careers Service Branch, HMSO.

Clarke, L. (1980b) *Occupational Choice: A Critical Review of Research in the UK.* London: Department of Employment Careers Service Branch, HMSO.

Coffield, F., Borrill, C. and Marshall, S. (1986) *Growing up at the Margins.* Milton Keynes: Open University Press.

Connolly, M., Roberts, K., Ben-Tovim, G. and Torkington, P. (1991) *Black Youth in Liverpool.* Culemborg: Giordano Bruno.

Connolly, S., Micklewright, J. and Nickell, S. (1992) *The Occupational Success of Young Men who Left School at Sixteen.* Economics Working Paper No. 92/61, November 1991. Florence: European University Institute.

Courtenay, G. and McAleese, I. (1993a) *Cohort IV: Young People 16–17 Years Old in 1989. Report on Sweeps.* Youth Cohort Report No. 21. Sheffield: Department of Employment.

Courtenay, G. and McAleese, I. (1993b) *Cohort 5: Aged 16 and 17 in 1991. Report on Sweep 1.* Youth Cohort Report No. 22. Sheffield: Department of Employment.

Cregan, C. (1991) Young people and trade union membership: a longitudinal analysis. *Applied Economics,* Vol. 23, 1511–18.

Cregan, C. M. (1992) Young workers and the job-swapping phenomenon in the school-to-work transition. *Work, Employment and Society,* Vol. 5, No. 3, 417–36.

Cregan, C. M. and Johnston, S. (1990) An industrial relations approach to the free rider problem: young people and trade union membership in the UK. *British Journal of Industrial Relations,* Vol. 28, 84–104.

Cregan, C. M. and Johnston, S. (1993) Young workers and quit behaviour. *Applied Economics,* Vol. 25, 5–33.

Cross, M. and Smith, D. I. (eds) (1987) *Black Youth Futures*. Leicester: National Youth Bureau.

Cully, M. and Woodland, S. (1996) Trade union membership and recognition: an analysis of data from the 1995 Labour Force Survey. *Department of Employment Gazette*, May, p. 201.

Dalton, A. H. and Snelling, E. C. (1983) A note on salary variations in an academic internal labor market. *Atlantic Economic Journal*, Vol. 11, 70–8.

Dawkins, P. and Norris, K. (1995) The growth of part-time employment in Australia and the UK, 1978–93. *Labour Economics and Productivity*, Vol. 7, No. 4, 1–28.

Deakin, B. W. (1996) *The Youth Labour Market in Britain: The Role of Intervention*. Cambridge: Cambridge University Press.

Department of Education and Science (1980) *Statistics of Education, Education for 16–19 Year Olds*. London: HMSO.

Department of Education and Science (1996) *Department of Education and Science Bulletin*. London: HMSO.

Department of Education Statistical Bulletin (1992) 14/92, July. London: HMSO.

Department of Employment Gazette (1979, 1995 and 1996) August 1979, February 1995, December 1995, May 1996, June 1996.

Department of Employment Gazette (1980) First-off. 16 year olds entering employment in 1978. September. London: HMSO.

Department of Employment Gazette (1982a) Learning the job: apprenticeships and training in manufacturing industries. London: HMSO.

Department of Employment Gazette (1982b) First employment of young people. Vol. 3, March, pp. 117–20. London: HMSO.

Department of Employment Gazette (1983) Vol. 1, January, s59. London: HMSO.

Department of Employment Gazette (1990) Ethnic origins and the labour market. March, pp. 125–37. London: HMSO.

Deshpande, S. P and Fiorito, J. (1989) Specific and general beliefs in union voting models. *Academy of Management Journal*, Vol. 32, 883–97.

Dex, S. (1982) *Black and White School-leavers: The First Five Years of Work*. Department of Employment Research Paper No. 33. London: HMSO.

Dex, S. (1985) *The Sexual Division of Work*. Brighton: Wheatsheaf.

Disney, R. (1990) Explanations of the decline in trade union density in Britain: an appraisal. *British Journal of Industrial Relations*, Vol. 28, No. 2, 165–81.

Doeringer, P. and Piore, M. J. (1971) *Internal Labor Markets and Manpower Analysis*. Lexington Mass.: Heath.

Dollard, J. *et al.* (1939) *Frustration and Aggression*. New Haven, Conn.: Yale University Press.

Dolton, P. J. (1993) Youth Training in Britain. *The Economic Journal*, Vol. 103, 1261–78.

Drew, D. (1995) 'Race', Education and Work: The Statistics of Inequality. Aldershot: Avebury.

Drew, D., Gray, J. and Sime, N. (1992) *Against the Odds: The Education and Labour Market Experiences of Black Young People*. Youth Cohort Report No. 19. Sheffield: Department of Employment.

Education Statistics for the UK (1992) *Educational Statistical Bulletin*, July. London: HMSO.

Edwards, P. (ed.) (1995) *Industrial Relations: Theory and Practice in Britain*. Oxford: Blackwell.

Elger, T. (1990) Technological innovation and work reorganisation in British manufacturing in the 1980s: continuity, intensification or transformation? *Work, Employment and Society*, Special Issue, May, pp. 67–102.

Elias, P. and Blanchflower, D. (1989) *The Occupational Earnings and Work Histories of Young Adults. Who Gets the Good Jobs?* Department of Employment Research Paper No. 68. London: HMSO.

Esland, G. *et al.* (eds) (1975) *People and Work*. Edinburgh: Holmes McDougall.

Eyraud, F., Marsden, D. W. and Silvestre, J. J. (1990) Occupational and internal labour markets in Britain and France. *International Labour Review*, Vol. 129, 501–18.

Fiddy, R. (ed.) (1983) *In Place of Work*. Lewes: Falmer Press.

Foskett, N. H. and Hesketh A. J., (1997) Construing choice in contiguous and parallel markets: institutional and school leavers' responses to the new post-16 marketplace. *Oxford Review of Education*, Vol.23 , No. 3, 299–319.

Foster, P. (1992) Teacher attitudes and Afro-Caribbean achievement. *Educational Studies*, Vol. 18, No. 3, 269–81.

Freeman, R. and Pelletier, J. (1990) The impact of industrial relations legislation on British union density. *British Journal of Industrial Relations*, Vol. 28 (2), 141–64.

Freeman, R. B. and Wise, D. A. (1982) *The Youth Labour Market Problem: Its Nature, Causes and Consequences*. New York: National Bureau of Economic Research.

Furlong, A. (1987) Coming to terms with the declining demand for labour, in Brown, P. and Ashton, D.N. (eds) *Education, Unemployment and Labour Markets*. Lewes: Falmer Press.

Furlong, A. (1992) *Growing up in a Classless Society? School to Work Transitions*. Edinburgh: Edinburgh University Press.

Gallagher, D. G. (1998) Youth and labor representation, in Barling, J. and Kelloway, E. K. (eds) *Youth and Employment*. Washington DC: APA Books.

Gallie, D. (1994) Patterns of skill change: upskilling, deskilling or polarisation? in Penn, R., Rose, M. and Rubery, J. (eds) *Skill and Occupational Change*. Oxford: Oxford University Press.

Gallie, D. (1996) Union allegiance and decline, in Gallie, D., Penn, R. and Rose, M. (eds) *Trade Unionism in Recession*. Oxford: Oxford University Press.

Gallie, D. and Rose, M. (1996) Employer policies and union influence, in Gallie, D., Penn, R. and Rose, M. (eds) *Trade Unionism in Recession*. Oxford: Oxford University Press.

Gamson, W. A. (1975) *The Strategy of Social Protest*. Homewood, Ill.: Dorsey.

Garner, C., Main, G. M. B. and Raffe, D. (1988) A tale of four cities: social and spatial inequalities in the youth labour market, in Raffe, D. (ed.) *Education and the Youth Labour Market*, Lewes: Falmer Press.

Garonna, P. and Ryan, P. (1991) The problems facing youth, in Ryan, P., Garonna, P. and Edwards, R. (eds) *The Problems of Youth*. London: Macmillan.

Geary, J. F. (1995) Work practices: the structure of work, in Edwards, P. (ed.) *Industrial*

Relations: Theory and Practice in Britain. Oxford: Blackwell.

Gibson, A. (1985) *Report for the Centre of Caribbean Studies* (mimeo).

Gilman, J. (1975) Initiation into adulthood, in Brannen, P. (ed.) *Entering the World of Work: Some Sociological Perspectives.* London: HMSO.

Ginn, J. *et al.* (1996) Feminist fallacies: a reply to hakim on women's employment. *British Journal of Sociology*, Vol. 47 (1), 167–74.

Ginzberg, E. (1951) Towards a theory of occupational choice: a restatement. *Vocational Guidance Quarterly*, Vol. 20, 169–76.

Ginzberg, E., Ginsburg, S. W., Axelrad, S. and Herma, J. L. (1951) *Occupational Choice: An Approach to a General Theory.* New York: Columbia University Press.

GLC (1980) *London's Economy: Trends and Issues.* Review and Studies Series No. 1. London: Greater London Council.

Glickman, M. J. A. (1975) Education and work: an anthropological view of the transition process, in Brannen P. (ed.) *Entering the World of Work: Some Sociological Perspectives.* London: HMSO.

GMB (1994) Press Release. 6 September, London: General Municipal and Boilermakers' Trades Union.

Goldthorpe, J. H. and Llewellyn, C. (1977) Class mobility in modern Britain: 3 theses examined. *Sociology*, Vol. 11, 257–88.

Goldthorpe, J. H., Lockwood, C., Bechofer, F. and Platt, J. (1968) *The Affluent Worker: Individual Attitudes and Behaviour.* Cambridge: Cambridge University Press.

Gordon, A. (1984) The importance of educational qualifications to employers in the selection of school leaver recruits. *Educational Studies*, Vol. 10, No. 2, 93–111.

Gordon, M. E., Philpot, J. W., Burt, R. E., Thompson, C. A. and Spiller, W. E. (1980) Commitment to the union: development of a measure and an examination of its correlates. *Journal of Applied Psychology*, Vol. 65, 479–99.

Granovetter, M. (1978) Threshold models of collective behaviour. *American Journal of Sociology*, Vol. 83, 1420–43.

Granovetter, M. (1981) Sociological perspectives on labor markets, in Berg, I. (ed.) *Sociological Perspectives on the Labor Market.* New York: Academic Press.

Gray, J., Jesson, D., Pattie, C. and Sime, N. (1989) *Education and Training Opportunities in the Inner City.* Youth Cohort Series No. 7, Department of Employment. Sheffield: HMSO.

Gray, J., Jesson, D. and Tranmer, M. (1994) *Local Labour Market Participation: Evidence from the End of the Eighties.* Youth Cohort Report No. 26, Department of Employment, Sheffield: HMSO.

Green, F. (1992) Recent trends in British trade union density: how much of a compositional effect? *British Journal of Industrial Relations*, Vol. 30, No. 3, 445–58.

Griffin, B., Kalleberg, B. and Alexander, S. (1981) Young people in the labour market. *Sociology of Education*, Vol. 54, 62–81.

Gronau, R. (1971) Information and frictional unemployment. *American Economic Review*, Vol. 61, 290–301.

Guest, D. E. and Dewe, P. (1988) Why do workers belong to a trade union? A social psychological study in the UK electronics industry. *British Journal of Industrial Relations*, Vol. 26, 178–94.

Hagell, A. and Shaw, C. (1996) *Opportunity and Disadvantage at Age 16.* London: Policy Studies Institute.

Hakim, C. (1979) *Occupational Segregation.* Department of Employment Research Paper No. 9. London: HMSO.

Hakim, C. (1995) Five feminist myths about women's unemployment. *British Journal of Sociology,* Vol. 46 (3), 429–55.

Hall, R.E. and Lazear, E. (1984) The excess sensitivity of lay-offs and quits to demand, *Journal of Labour Economics,* Vol. 2, 233–57.

Hamilton, S. F. (1990) *Apprenticeship for Adulthood: Preparing Youth for the Future.* New York: The Free Press.

Hart, P. E. (1988) *Youth Unemployment in Great Britain.* Cambridge: Press Syndicate of the University of Cambridge.

Heery, E. (1997) Review article. *British Journal of Industrial Relations,* Vol. 35, 81–109.

Hendry, L. B., Raymond, M. and Stewart, C. (1984) Unemployment, school and leisure: an adolescent study, *Leisure Studies,* Vol. 3, 115–28.

Hills, S. M. and Reubens, B. G. (1983) Youth employment in the United States, in Reubens, B. G. (ed.) *Youth at Work: An International Survey.* New York: Rowman and Allanheld.

Hines, A. G. (1964) Trade unions and wage inflation in the United Kingdom, 1893–1961. *Review of Economic Studies,* Vol. 31, 221–52.

Hirshleifer, J. (1973) Where are we in the theory of information?, *American Economic Review,* Papers and Proceedings, Vol. 66, 31–49.

Hirschman, A. O. (1970) *Exit, Voice and Loyalty: Responses to Declines in Firms, Organisations and States.* Cambridge, Mass.: Harvard University Press.

Holland, A. (1966) *The Psychology of Vocational Choice: A Theory of Personality Types and Environmental Models.* New York: Ginn.

Holmlund, B. and Laing, H. (1985) Quit behaviour under imperfect information: searching, moving, learning. *Economic Enquiry,* Vol. 23, 383–93.

Horrell, S. and Rubery, J. (1991) Gender and working time: an analysis of employers' working time policies. *Cambridge Journal of Economics,* Vol. 15, 373–91.

Hunt, J. and Small, P. (1981) *Employing Young People.* Edinburgh: Scottish Council for Research in Education.

Huszczo, G. E. (1983) Attitudinal and behavioural variables relating to participation in union activities. *Journal of Labor Research,* Vol. 4, 287–97.

IFF Research (1990) *Skill Needs in Britain.* London: Industrial Facts and Forecasting.

Ito, T. (1988) Labour contracts with voluntary quits. *Journal of Labour Economics,* Vol. 6, 100–31.

Jackson, M. P. (1985) *Youth Unemployment.* Kent: Croom Helm.

Jenson, J. (1989) The talents of women, the skills of men: flexible specialisation in women, in Wood, S. (ed.) *The Transformation of Work: Skill, Flexibility and the Labour Process.* London: Unwin Hyman.

Jim Conway Foundation (1993) *Trade Unions: The Thatcher Years.* Stockton-on-Tees: JCF.

Johnson, W. R. (1978) A theory of job shopping. *Quarterly Journal of Economics,* Vol. 92, No. 2, 261–77.

Jones, B., Gray, J. and Clough, E. (1988) Finding a post-16 route. The first year's experience, in Coles, B. (ed.) *Young Careers: the Search for Jobs and the New Vocationalism*, Milton Keynes: Open University Press.

Jones, P. (1984) *What Opportunities for Youth?* Occasional Paper No. 4. London: Youthaid.

Jones, T. (1993) *Britain's Ethnic Minorities: An Analysis of the Labour Force Survey Since 1982*. London: Policy Studies Institute.

Joshi, H. and Owen, S. (1987) How long is a piece of elastic? The measurement of female activity rates in British censuses, 1951–1981. *Cambridge Journal of Economics*, Vol. 11, 55–74.

Jovanovic, B. (1984) Matching, turnover and unemployment, *Journal of Political Economy*. Vol. 92, 108–22.

Junankar, P. N. (ed.) (1987) *From School to Unemployment?* London: Macmillan.

Keep, E. and Mayhew, K. (1995) *The British System of Vocational Education and Training: A Critical Analysis*. Oxford: Oxford University Press.

Keep, E. and Rainbird, H. (1995) Training, in Edwards, P. (ed.) *Industrial Relations: Theory and Practice in Britain*. Oxford: Blackwell.

Kelly, J. E. (1987) Trade unions through the recession. *British Journal of Industrial Relations*, Vol. 25, 275–82.

Kelly, J. E. (1982) Useful work and useless toil. *Marxism Today*, August, 12–17.

Kerckhoff, A. C. (1990) *Getting Started: Transition to Adulthood in Great Britain*. Boulder Co.: Westview Press.

Kessler, S. and Bayliss, F. (1992) *Contemporary British Industrial Relations*. Basingstoke: Macmillan.

Klandermans, B. (1984) Mobilisation and participation: social psychological explanations of resource mobilisation theory. *American Sociological Review*, Vol. 49, 583–600.

Klandermans, B. (1986a) Psychology and trade union participation: joining, acting and quitting. *Journal of Occupational Psychology*, Vol. 59, 189–204.

Klandermans, B. (1986b) Perceived costs and benefits of participation in union action. *Personnel Psychology*, Vol. 39, 379–97.

Kochan, T. A., Katz, H. C. and McKersie, R. B. (1986) *The Transformation of American Industrial Relations*. New York: Basic Books.

Kreckel, R. (1980) Unequal opportunity structure and labor market segmentation. *Sociology*, Vol. 14, 525–50.

Krueger, A. and Summers, L. (1988) Efficiency wages and the inter-industry wage structure. *Econometrica*, Vol. 56, No. 2, 259–93.

Labour Force Survey (1979, 1981, 1995), London: HMSO.

Labour Force Survey Quarterly Bulletin (1994) No. 8, June. London: HMSO.

Labour Market Quarterly Report (May 1996) 'Trends in education and training'. Department for Education and Employment, Sheffield: HMSO.

Labour Market Trends (March 1996a) *Women in the Labour Market: Results from the Spring 1995 Labour Force Survey*. London: HMSO.

Labour Market Trends (May 1996b) *Trade Union membership and Recognition: An Analysis of Data from the 1995 Labour Force Survey*. London: HMSO.

Labour Market Trends (June 1996c) 'Ethnic Minorities in the Labour Market'. London: HMSO.

Labour Market Trends, December, 1997, London: HMSO.

Labovitz, S. (1977) Some observations on measurement and statistics. *Social Forces,* Vol. 46, No. 2, 23–32.

Landau, N. (1983) *London from the 1979 Labour Force Survey.* Statistical Series No. 22. London: Greater London Council.

Layard, R. (1982) Youth unemployment in Britain and the US compared, in Freeman, R. B. and Wise, D. A. *The Youth Labour Market Problem: Its Nature, Causes and Consequences.* National Bureau for Economic Research.

Layard, R., Mayhew, K. and Owen, G. (1994) Why we need a Training Reform Act, in Layard, R., Mayhew, K. and Owen, G. (eds) *Britain's Training Deficit,* Aldershot: The Centre for Economic Performance Report/Avebury.

Lee, D. J., Marsden, D., Rickman, P. and Duncombe, J. (1990) *Scheming for Youth: A Study of YTS in the Enterprise Culture.* Milton Keynes: Open University Press.

Lee, G. and Wrench, J. (1983) *Skill Seekers: Black Youth, Apprenticeships and Disadvantage.* Leicester: National Youth Bureau.

Lerner, R. M., Lerner, J. V., Von Eye, N., Ostrom, C.W., Talwar-Soni, R. and Tubman, J. (1996) Continuity and discontinuity across the transition of early adolescence: a developmental contextual perspective, in Graber, J. A., Brookes-Gunn, J. and Petersen, A.C. (eds) *Transitions through Adolescence: Interpersonal Domains and Context.* New Jersey: Lawrence Erlbaum.

Lightbody, P. and Durndell, A. (1996) Gendered career choice: is sex stereotyping the cause or consequence? *Educational Studies,* Vol. 22, No. 2, 133–46.

Liff, S. (1990) Clerical workers and information technology: gender relations and occupational change. *New Technology, Work and Employment,* Vol. 5, No. 1, 44–55.

Livock, D. (1983) *Screening in the Recruitment of Young Workers.* Research Paper No. 41, Department of Employment. London: HMSO.

London Research Centre (1986) *GLC Borough Vacancy and Unemployment Rates* (mimeo).

Lynch, L. M. (1983) Job search and youth unemployment. *Oxford Economic Papers,* Vol. 35, 595–606.

Lynch, L. M. (1985) *State Dependency in Youth Unemployment: A Lost Generation? Journal of Econometrics: Annals of Applied Econometrics,* Vol. 28, No. 1, 71–84.

Lynch, L. M. (1987) Individual differences in the youth labour market: a cross-section analysis of London Youth, in Junankar, P. N. (ed.) *From School to Unemployment?* London: Macmillan.

Lynch, L. M.. and Richardson, R. (1982) Unemployment of young workers in Britain. *British Journal of Industrial Relations,* Vol. 20, No. 3, 362–72.

McClure, S. (1979) *Education and Youth Employment in Great Britain.* Berkeley, California: The Carnegie Council for the Advancement of Teaching.

MacEwan Scott, A. (1994) Gender segregation in the retail industry, in MacEwan Scott, A. (ed.) *Gender Segregation and Social Change: Men and Women in Changing Labour Markets.* Oxford: Oxford University Press.

McIlroy, J. (1988) *Trade Unions in Britain To-day.* Manchester: Manchester University

Press.

McKenna, C. J. (1985) *Uncertainty and the Labour Market.* Brighton: Wheatsheaf.

McRae, S. (1987) *Young and Jobless.* Poole, Dorset: Policy Studies Institute/The Blackmore Press.

Maddala, G. S. (1983). *Limited-Dependent and Qualitative Variables in Econometrics.* New York: Cambridge University Press.

Maguire, M. (1991) British labour market trends, in Ashton, D. N. and Lowe, G. (eds) *Education, Training and the Labour Market in Canada and Britain.* Milton Keynes: Open University Press.

Main, B. G. M. and Raffe, D. (1983a) Determinants of employment and unemployment among school-leavers: evidence from the 1979 survey of Scottish school-leavers. *Scottish Journal of Political Economy,* Vol. 30, No. 1, 1–17.

Main, B. G. M. and Raffe, D. (1983b) The transition from school to work in 1980/81: a dynamic account. *British Educational Research Journal,* ix, 57–70.

Mainwaring, T. (1984) The extended internal labour market. *Cambridge Journal of Economics,* Vol.. 8, 161–87.

Maizels, J. (1965) The entry of school-leavers into employment. *British Journal of Industrial Relations,* Vol. 3, 77–89.

Maizels, J. (1970) *Adolescent Needs in the Transition from School to Work.* London: University of London/Athlone Press.

Makeham, P. (1980) *Youth Unemployment: An Examination of the Evidence of Youth Unemployment Using National Statistics,* Department of Employment Research Paper No. 10. London: HMSO.

March, J. G. and Simon, H. A. (1958) *Organisations.* New York: Wiley.

Markall, G. and Finn, D. (1981) *Young People and the Labour Market: A Case Study.* Department of the Environment Inner Cities Research Programme. London: HMSO.

Marsden, D. (1990) Institutions and labour mobility: occupational and internal labour markets in Britain, France, Italy and West Germany, in Brunetta, R. and Dell'Aringa, C. (eds) *Labour Relations and Economic Performance.* London: Macmillan.

Marsden, D. and Germe, D.-F. (1990) Young people and entry paths to long-term jobs in France and Great Britain, in Ryan, P., Garonna, P. and Edwards, R. C. (eds) *The Problem of Youth.* London: Macmillan.

Marsden, D. and Ryan, P. (1986) Where do young workers work? Youth employment by industry in various European economies. *British Journal of Industrial Relations,* Vol. 24, no. 1, 83–102.

Mattila, J. P. (1969) Quit behaviour in the labour market. American Statistical Association Annual Meeting, mimeo.

Mayhew, K. and Rosewell, B. (1978) Immigrants and occupational crowding in Great Britain. *Oxford Bulletin of Economics and Statistics,* Vol. 40, No. 3, 22–248.

Metcalf, D. and Richards, J. (1983) Youth employment in Great Britain, in Reubens, B. G. (ed.) *Youth at Work: An International Survey.* New Jersey: Rowman and Allanheld.

Metcalf, D. and Richardson, R. (1974) Unemployment in London. Paper presented to Royal Economic Society Conference, Durham, April. (Unpublished).

Metcalf, H. (1988) *Employer Response to the Decline in School Leavers into the 1990s.* IMS

Report No. 152. Brighton: Institute of Manpower Studies.

Michael, R.T. and Tuma, N. (1984) Does life begin at 16? *Journal of Labor Economics*, Vol. 2, No. 4, 464–76.

Micklewright, J. (1989) Choice at 16. *Economica*, Vol. 56, 25–40.

Miller, D. C. and Form, W. H. (1951) *Industrial Sociology*. New York: Harper.

Millward, N. and Stevens, M. (1986) *British Workplace Relations, 1980–1984*. Aldershot: Gower.

Millward, N., Stevens, M., Smart, D. and Hawes, W.R. (1992) *Workplace Industrial Relations in Transition*. Aldershot: Dartmouth.

Mitterauer, M. (1992) *A History of Youth*. Oxford: Blackwell.

Mizen, P. (1995) *The State, Young People and Youth Training*. London: Mansell.

Montgomery, B. R. (1989) The influence of attitudes and normative pressures on voting decisions in a union certification election. *Industrial and Labor Relations Review*, Vol. 42, 262–79.

Mortensen, D. T. (1986) Job search and labour market analysis, in Ashenfelter, O. and Layard, R. (eds) *Handbook of Labour Economics*. Amsterdam: New Holland.

MSC (1977) *Young People at Work*, London: Manpower Services Commission.

MSC (1980) *Manpower Review*. London: Manpower Services Commission.

MSC (1981) *London Labour Market Review, 1980–1981*. London: Manpower Intelligence Unit.

MSC (1982a) *School–leavers in the London Labour Market, 1979–1981*. Briefing Note No. 6. London: Manpower Services Commission.

MSC (1982b) *Employment Profile of Hounslow*. Briefing Note No. 10. London: Manpower Services Commission.

MSC (1982c) *ILEA Review of Education Provision for 16–19 Year Olds*. London Regional Manpower Intelligence Unit, Briefing Note No. 12. London: Manpower Services Commission.

MSC (1982d) *London Plan for Special Programmes, 1982/3*. London: Manpower Services Commission.

MSC (1984) *London Employment Review*. London: Manpower Services Commission.

National Curriculum Council (1991) *Work Experience and the School Curriculum*. York: NCC.

National Youth Survey (1983) Youth Service Review Group.

NDHS (1978). *National Dwelling and Housing Survey*. London: NDHS.

New Earnings Survey (1979–1995) London: HMSO (published annually).

Newton, L. A. and Shore, L. M. (1992) A model of union membership: instrumentality, commitment and opposition. *Academy of Management Review*, Vol. 17, No. 2, 275–98.

Nickell, S. J. (1982) The determinants of occupational success in Great Britain. *Review of Economic Studies*, Vol. 49, 43–53.

Nolan, P. and Walsh, J. (1995) The structure of the economy and labour market, in Edwards, P. (ed.) *Industrial Relations: Theory and Practice in Britain*. Oxford: Blackwell.

Norusis, M. J. (1993) *SPSS for Windows. Advanced Statistics Release 6.0*. Chicago: SPSS Inc.

Oberschall, A. (1973) *Social Conflict and Social Movements*. New Jersey: Prentice Hall.

OECD (1991) *Historical Statistics, 1969–1990*. Paris: Organization of Economic Cooperation and Development.

Office for National Statistics (1996) *Labour Market Statistics for April 1996*. Employment Information Service. London: HMSO.

Oliver, P., Marwell, G. and Teixera, R. (1985) A theory of the critical mass I. Interdependence, heterogeneity and the production of collective action. *American Journal of Sociology*, Vol. 90, 522–56.

Olson, M. (1965) *The Logic of Collective Action: Public Goods and the Theory of Groups*. Cambridge, Mass.: Harvard University Press.

Ornstein, M. D. (1976) *Entry into the Labor Force*. New York: Academic Press.

Osborn, A. (1985) *Commission for Racial Equality Paper*, July. London: CRE.

Osterman, P. (1980) *Getting Started: The Youth Labor Market*. Cambridge, Mass.: MIT Press.

Osterman, P. (1982) Employment structures within firms. *British Journal of Industrial Relations*, Vol. 20, No. 3, 349–3.

Osterman, P. (1984) White-collar internal labour markets, in Osterman, P. (ed.) *Internal Labor Markets*. Cambridge, Mass.: MIT Press.

Osterman, P. (1987) Choice of employment systems in internal labor markets. *Industrial Relations*, Vol. 26, 46–67.

Pahl, R. E. (1984) *Divisions of Labour*. Oxford: Basil Blackwell.

Park, A. (1994) *Young People 18–19 Years Old in 1991*. Youth Cohort Report No. 29, Department of Employment. Sheffield: HMSO.

Parsons, D. O. (1973) Quit rates over time: a search and information approach. *American Economic Review*, Vol. 63, 390–401.

Paterson, L. and Raffe D. (1995) Staying-on in full-time education in Scotland, 1985–1991. *Oxford Review of Education*, Vol. 21, No. 2, 3–23.

Payne, C. (1989) Trade union membership and activism among young people in Britain. *British Journal of Industrial Relations*, Vol. 27, 111–32.

Payne, J. (1995a) *Routes Beyond Compulsory Schooling*. Youth Cohort Report No. 31. Sheffield: Department of Employment.

Payne, J. (1995b) *Options at 16 and Outcomes at 24: A Comparison of Academic and Vocational Education and Training Routes*. Youth Cohort Report No. 35. Sheffield: Department of Employment.

Payne, J. and Payne, C. (1994) Trends in job loss and recruitment in Britain, 1979–1991, in White, M. (ed.) *Unemployment and Public Policy in a Changing Labour Market*. London: Policy Studies Institute.

Pencavel, J. (1970) *An Analysis of the Quit Rate in American Manufacturing Industry*. Princeton University Industrial Relations Section Research Paper No. 14, Princeton, NJ.

Pencavel, J. (1972) Wages, specific training and labor turnover in US manufacturing industry. *International Economics Review*, Vol. 13, no. 1, 53–64.

Pike, G., Connor, H. and Jagger, N. (1992) *IMS Graduate Review 1992*. Brighton: Institute of Manpower Studies, University of Brighton.

Raffe, D. (1983) Can there be an effective youth employment policy? in Fiddy, R. (ed.) *In Place of Work*. Lewes: Falmer Press.

Raffe, D. (1985) *Youth Unemployment in the UK, 1979–84*. University of Edinburgh: Centre for Educational Sociology.

Raffe, D. (1986) Change and continuity in the youth labour market. A critical review of structural explanations of youth unemployment, in Allen, S., Watson, A., Purcell, K. and Wood, S. (eds) *The Experience of Unemployment*, London: Macmillan.

Raffe, D. (1987) The context of the Youth Training Scheme: an analysis of its strategy and development. *British Journal of Education and Work*, Vol. 1, 1–33.

Raffe, D. (ed.) (1988a) *Education and the Youth Labour Market: Schooling and Scheming*. Lewes: Falmer Press.

Raffe, D. (1988b) Going wth the grain: youth training in transition, in Brown, S. and Wake, R. (eds) *Education in Transition*. Edinburgh: Scottish Council for Research in Education.

Raffe, D. (1992) *Educational Participation amongst 16–18 Year Olds*. Briefing Paper. London: National Commission on Education.

Raffe, D. and Courtenay, G. (1988) 16–18 on both sides of the border, in Raffe, D. (ed.) *Education and the Youth Labour Market: Schooling and Scheming*. Lewes: Falmer Press.

Raffe, D. and Willms, J. D. (1989) Schooling the discouraged worker: local labour market effects on educational participation. *Sociology*, Vol. 23, No. 4, 559–81.

Ragan, J.F. (1984) Investigating the decline in manuafacturing quit rates. *Journal of Human Resources*, Vol. 19, 53–77.

Rajan, A., Bevan, S., Gordon, A. and Walsh, K. (1990) *British Socio-economic Trends to 1995 and their Employment Implications*. IMS Report No 189. Brighton: Institute of Manpower Studies.

Rees, T. L. and Atkinson, P. (1982) *Youth Unemployment and State Intervention*. London: Routledge and Keegan Paul.

Reubens, B. G. (ed.) (1983) *Youth at Work: An International Survey*. New Jersey: Rowman and Allanheld.

Richardson, R. (1977) Trade union growth. *British Journal of Industrial Relations*, Vol. 15, 279–82.

Richardson, R. (1983) *Unemployment and the Inner City: A Study of School-leavers in London*. Department of the Environment Inner Cities Research Programme No. 10. London: HMSO.

Richardson, R. and Metcalf, D. (1982) Labour, in Prest, A.R. and Coppock, J.D. (eds), *The UK Economy: A Manual of Applied Economics*. London: Weidenfeld and Nicolson.

Richardson, R., Robinson, C. and Smith, J. (1977) Quit rates and manpower policy. *Department of Employment Gazette*, January. London: HMSO.

Roberts, K. (1968) The entry into employment: an approach towards a general theory. *Sociological Review*, Vol. 16, No. 2, 165–84.

Roberts, K. (1975) The developmental theory of occupational choice: a critique and an alternative, in Esland, G. *et al.* (eds) *People and Work*. Edinburgh: Holmes McDougall.

Roberts, K. (1984) *School-leavers and their Prospects. Youth in the Labour Market in the 1980s*. Milton Keynes: Open University Press.

Roberts K. (1995) *Youth and Employment in Modern Britain*. Oxford: Oxford University Press.

Roberts, K. and Chadwick, C. (1991) *Transitions into the Labour Market. The New Routes of the 1980's. A Study of Transitions, 1984–1987.* Youth Cohort Report No. 17. Sheffield: Department of Employment.

Roberts, K. and Corcoran-Nantes, Y. (1994) TQM, the new training and industrial relations, in Wilkinson, A. and Willmott, H. (eds) *Making Quality Critical.* London: Routledge.

Roberts, K. and Parsell, G. (1992a) Entering the labour market in Britain: the survival of traditional opportunity structures. *Sociological Review,* Vol. 40, 727–53.

Roberts, K. and Parsell, G. (1992b) The stratification of youth training. *British Journal of Education and Work,* Vol. 5, 65–83.

Roberts, K., Dench, S. and Richardson, D. (1987) *The Changing Structure of Youth Labour Markets.* Research Paper No. 59, Department of Employment. London: HMSO.

Roberts, K., Parsell, G. and Connolly, M. (1991) Young people's transitions into the labour market, in Cross, M. and Payne, G. (eds) *Work and the Enterprise Culture.* London: Falmer Press.

Robertson, D. and Symons, J. (1990) The occupational choice of British children. *Economic Journal,* Vol. 100, 828–41.

Rubery, J. (1995) The low-paid and the unorganised, in Edwards, P. (ed.) *Industrial Relations: Theory and Practice in Britain.* Oxford: Blackwell.

Rubery, J. and Wilkinson, F. (1994) *Employer Strategy and the Labour Market.* Oxford: Oxford University Press.

Ryan, P. (1987) Trade unionism and the pay of young workers, in Junankar, P. N. (ed.) *From School to Unemployment?* London: Macmillan.

Ryan, P., Garonna, P. and Edwards, R. (1991) *The Problem of Youth: The Regulation of Youth Employment and Training in Advanced Economies.* London: Macmillan.

Sawdon, A., Tucker, S. and Pelican, J. (1981) *Study of the Transition from School to Working Life.* London: Youthaid.

Schools Council Inquiry (1968) *Young School-leavers.* London: HMSO.

Schwarz, M. (1976) *Radical Protest and Social Structure.* New York: Academic Press.

Seltzer, A. J. (1995) The political economy of the Fair Labor Standards Act of 1938. *Journal of Political Economy,* Vol. 103, No. 6, 1302–42.

Sexton, J. J., Whelan, B. J. and Williams, J. A. (1988) *Transition from School to Work and Early Labour Market Experience.* Dublin: ESRC.

Shackleton, J. R. (1993) Investing in training: questioning the conventional wisdom. *Policy Studies,* Vol. 14, No. 3, 29–40.

Sharpe, I. G. (1971) The growth of Australian trade unions, 1907–1969. *Journal of Industrial Relations,* Vol. 13, 138–54.

Shishter, J. (1953) The logic of collective action. *Journal of Political Economy,* Vol. 61, 413–33.

Sillitoe, K. and Meltzer, H. (1985) *The West Indian School Leaver.* London: Department of Employment/HMSO.

Siann, G. (1994) *Gender, Sex and Sexuality.* London: Taylor and Francis.

Sime, N. (1991) *Constraining Choices: Unemployment among Sixteen and Seventeen Year Olds in the Late Eighties.* Youth Cohort Series No. 18. Sheffield: Department of Employment.

Sime, N., Pattie, C. and Gray, J. (1990) *What Now? The Transition from School to the Labour Market among 16 to 19 Year Olds.* Youth Cohort Series No. 14. Sheffield: Department of Employment.

Slade, R. (ed.) (1992) *School-leavers' Destinations: Destinations of Year 11 Pupils Leaving Secondary Schools in 1991.* London: ACC Publications.

Sly, F., Price, A. and Risdon, A. (1997) Trends in labour market participation of ethnic groups: 1984–1996, *Labour Market Trends*, August, London: HMSO.

Smith , C. S. (1975) Entry, location and commitment of young workers in the labour force: a review of sociological thinking, in Brannen, P. (ed.) *Entering the World of Work: Some Sociological Perspectives.* London: HMSO.

Smith, D. J. (1976) *Facts of Racial Disadvantage: A National Survey.* London: PEP.

Smith, D. J. (1977) *Racial Disadvantage in Britain: The PEP Report.* Harmondsworth: Penguin.

Smithers, A. (1993) *All Our Futures: Britain's Educational Revolution.* London: Channel 4 Television.

Snower, D. J. and Booth, A. L. (1996) Conclusions: government policy to promote the acquisition of skills, in Booth, A. L. and Snower, D. J. *Acquiring skills: Market Failures, their Symptoms and Responses.* New York: Cambridge University Press.

Social Trends (1981) No. 10. London: Central Statistical Office/HMSO.

Social Trends (1996) No. 26. London: Central Statistical Office/HMSO.

Spence, M. A. (1973) Job market signalling. *Quarterly Journal of Economics*, Vol. 87, 355–74.

Spilsbury, M. (1990) *Measuring the Effectiveness of Training.* Brighton: Institute for Employment Studies.

Spilsbury, M., Hoskins, M., Ashton, D. J. and Maguire, M. J. (1987) A note on the trade union patterns of young adults. *British Journal of Industrial Relations*, Vol. 25, 267–74.

Springhall, J. (1986) *Coming of Age: Adolescence in Britain, 1860–1960.* Dublin: Gill and MacMillan.

Starting Right (1994) Manchester: Greater Manchester Low Pay Unit.

Stern, J. (1981) *Choice of Pressure of Demand Variables for the Cohort Study of the Unemployed.* Centre for Labour Economics Working Paper No. 26. London: London School of Economics and Political Science.

Stevens, M. (1996) Transferable training and poaching externalities, in Booth, A. L. and Snower, D. J. *Acquiring Skills: Market Failures, their Symptoms and Responses.* New York: Cambridge University Press.

Stewart, M. (1984) *Relative Earnings and Individual Union Membership in the UK.* Centre for Labour Economics Discussion Paper No. 110. London: London School of Economics.

Stigler, G. (1962) Information in the labor market. *Journal of Political Economy*, Supplement, Vol. 70, 94–105.

Stoikov, V. and Ramon, R. L. (1968) Determinants of the differences in the quit rates amongst industries. *American Economic Review*, Vol. 58, 1283–98.

Strathdee, R. (1992) *16 & 17: No Way Back. Homeless Sixteen and Seventeen Year Olds in the 90s.* London: Centrepoint Soho.

Super, D. E. (1957) *The Psychology of Careers*. New York: Harper and Row.

Swann Report (1985) *Education for All*. Committee of Enquiry into the Education of Children from Ethnic Minority Groups. London: HMSO.

Sweeney, K. (1996) Membership of trade unions in 1994: an analysis based on informations from the Certification Officer. *Department of Employment Gazette*, February.

Tajfel, H. (1982) Social psychology of intergroup relations. *Annual Review of Psychology*, Vol. 33, 1–40.

Thomas, R. K. (1979) *Starting Work and After*. London: OPCS.

Thompson, M., Atkinson, J. and Simkin, C. (1993) *Changing Policies Towards Young Workers*. Brighton: Institute of Manpower Studies.

Thurow, L.C. (1979) A job competition model, in Piore, M. J. (ed.) *Unemployment and Inflation*. M E Sharpe.

Van den Berg, G. J. (1990) Search behaviour, transitions to non-participation and the duration of unemployment. *Economic Journal*, Vol. 100, 842–65.

Verma, G. K and Darby, D. S. (1987) *Race, Training and Employment*. London: Falmer Press.

Von Maanen, J. (1977) *Organisational Careers: Some New Perspectives*. New York: Wiley.

Wachter, M. L. and Wright, R. D. (1990) The economics of internal labor markets. *Industrial Relations*, Vol. 29, No. 2, 240–62.

Waddington, J. and Whitston, C. (1995) Explanations of the decline in unionisation, in Edwards, P. (ed.) *Industrial Relations: Theory and Practice in Britain*. Oxford: Blackwell.

Webster, J. (1990) *Office Automation: The Labour Process and Women's Work in Britain*. Hemel Hempstead: Harvester Wheatsheaf.

Webster, J. (1993) Women's skills and word processors: gender issues in the development of the automated office, in Probert, B. and Wilson, B. W. (eds) *Pink Collar Blues: Work, Gender and Technology*. Melbourne: Melbourne University Press.

Wells W. (1983) *The Relative Pay and Employment of Young People*. Department of Employment Research Paper No. 42. London: HMSO.

West, M. and Newton, N. P. (1983) *The Transition from School to Work*. Kent: Croom Helm.

Wheeler, H. N. and McClendon, J. A. (1991) The individual decision to unionise, in Strauss, G., Gallagher, D. G. and Fiorito, J. (eds) *The State of the Unions*. Madison WI: Industrial Relations Research Association, Madison.

White, M. (ed.) (1994) *Unemployment and Public Policy in a Changing Labour Market*. London: Policy Studies Institute.

Whitfield, K. and Wilson, R. A. (1991) Staying-on in full-time education: the educational participation rate of 16 year olds. *Economica*, Vol. 58, 391–404.

Williamson, O. E. (1975) *Markets and Hierarchies*. New York: Free Press.

Williamson, O. (1981) The modern corporation: origins, evolution, attributes. *Journal of Economic Literature*, Vol. 19, 1537–68.

Williamson, O. E., Wachter, M. L. and Harries, J. E. (1975) Understanding the employment relation: the analysis of idiosyncratic exchange. *Bell Journal of Economics*, Vol. 6, 250–78.

Willis, P. (1977) *Learning to Labour.* London: Saxon House.

Willis, P., Bekem, A. and Whitt, D. (1988) *The Youth Review: Social Conditions of Young People in Wolverhampton.* Aldershot: Avebury.

Wrench, T. and Virdee, S. (1995) *Organising the Unorganised: 'Race', Poor Work and Trade Unions.* Research Paper No. 21. University of Warwick: Centre for Research in Ethnic Relations.

Yates, J. (ed.) (1996) *School-leavers Destinations 1995.* London: UK Heads of Careers Services Associations.

Youthaid (1993) *Unemployed 16 and 17 year Olds.* Working Brief, September. London: Youthaid.

Zax, J. S. (1989) Quits and race. *Journal of Human Resources,* Vol. 24, No. 3, 469–93.

Zax, J. S. (1991) The substitution between moves and quits. *Economic Journal,* Vol. 101, 1510–31.

INDEX

adult workers: competition from 156, 159–60, 164, 170, 172, 189; displacement of 200
age: characteristics linked to 3–5, 63–4, 118, 188; used as proxy for maturity 63, 156
A-levels 15, 195
Althauser, R. 67
apprenticeships 11–13, 17–19, 53–5, 58, 65–6, 144, 151–3, 160, 180, 183, 191, 195
Ashenfelter, O. and Pencavel, J.H. 79, 88
Ashford, S. and Gray, J. 161
Ashton, D.N.: and Bourn, C.J. 189; and Field, D. 12, 35–6, 43; and Maguire, M.J. 18, 157–8, 191; *et al.* 15, 17–18, 54, 64
assertiveness 102, 108

Bain, G.S. and Elsheikh, F. 79–81, 94, 112
Baker, G. and Holmstrom, B. 69
benefits, social welfare 5, 15–16, 50–1, 147, 161–3, 170, 172, 194–6, 199
Biggart, A. and Furlong, A. 150, 159
Blanchflower, D.G. and Lynch, L.M. 77; *see also* Elias, P.
Blau, F. and Kahn, L. 119, 130, 132, 134, 138
Blau, P.M. and Duncan, D.D. 35
Booth, A. 81
Booth, A.L.: and Satchell, S. 55; *see also* Snower, D.J.
Bordieu, P. and Passeron, J.-C. 36
boredom at school and work 37–8
Bowles, S. and Gintis, H. 36
Bradshaw, J. *et al.* 15, 40
Brown, P. 190, 193
Buck, N.H. and Gordon, I. 25, 52
Bynner, J. and Roberts, K. 198

career jobs 62–4, 70, 154–5, 197
Carter, M.P. 118
Cartwright, D. 85
Chaison, G.N. and Dhavale, D.G. 98, 101
Chapman, P.G. and Tooze, M.J. 196
class differences 35–6
collective bargaining 119, 158

commuting 26, 40, 52, 170
Conservative policy 193–6
continuity from school to work 35–7

Dawkins, P. and Norris, K. 159
day-release from full-time education 199
Deakin, B.W. 13–14
demand factors in the labour market 3, 39
Dex, S. 53, 108, 116, 118–19, 134, 138
disadvantaged groups 6–7, 53, 145, 164–5, 169–71, 177, 183–4, 189, 195–9; *see also* ethnic minorities
discrimination 42, 50, 56–7, 139, 200
dissatisfaction with present job 126–9
Doeringer, P. and Piore, M.J. 63, 66–7, 178

education, continuing in 11, 15, 147–8, 160, 171, 174, 195; *see also* participation rates; 'pull' into education
educational reforms 161
efficiency wage theory 70–1, 75
Elger, T. 153
Elias, P. and Blanchflower, D. 138
employers, attitudes of 15, 157–8, 183
employment *see* job
employment, lifetime theory of 123
employment protection legislation 16, 158
'entry ports' to long-term careers 61–2, 65, 141, 165, 179, 189, 191, 197–8, 202
ethnic minorities 14–15, 23–4, 26, 29, 32–3, 47–9, 58, 105, 107–8, 119, 130, 133, 143–5, 173–5, 177
exclusion of young people from certain types of work 17–18, 164
expectancy-value theory 82–3
expectations of young people 51, 176

firm-specific routines 66–70
flexible work organization 152–3
free rider paradox 78–84 *passim*, 88–91, 101, 112, 182

Freeman, R.B. and Wise, D.A. 3

Gallie, D. 153
Gamson, W.A. 82
Garonna, P. and Ryan, P. 190
GCSE 161, 171
Geary, J.F. 152
gender differences 11–12, 15, 17–19, 23, 28, 44, 46, 49, 72, 102, 106–7, 110, 127, 130, 134–5, 139–43, 145, 170–3, 183
General, Municipal and Boilermakers Trade Union (GMB) 158
Gibson, A. 49
Gordon, A. 41, 48
Gordon, M.E. *et al.* 87
Gray, J.: *et al.* 160–1, 163; *see also* Ashford, S.
Griffin, B. *et al.* 189–90
Gronau, R. 124

Hakim, C. 14, 157
Hamilton, S.F. 62
Hart, P.E. 23, 153, 156
hierarchy of jobs 58, 144
Hills, S.M. and Reubens, B.G. 190
Hirschman, A.O. 129
homelessness 162–3
Horrell, S. and Rubery, J. 152
Hounslow 25, 51–2
housing 25
human capital theory 56, 123, 130

immature labour market behaviour 1–7, 62–3, 77, 112, 116–20, 135, 197
incentive-opportunity model 121–9, 135, 178
information gathering by young people 44–7, 117–18, 123–4, 130, 134
information theory 123
inner-city residents 144–5, 170, 177, 184, 200
internal labour markets 64, 66–7, 69, 71, 155
interviews for jobs 42, 134

job opportunities 4–7, 11–13, 189: in London 25; in the 1980s and 1990s 150, 164
job progressions 72, 74, 197
job search 34, 39, 42–4, 48, 53, 58, 117, 123, 126, 130, 144–5, 169–70, 189, 192, 198: costs of 123–4
job-swapping 117–20, 135, 138–47 *passim*, 179, 182, 189, 192, 198–9: definition of 116
jobs obtained, attitudes to 55–6
Jones, P. 190

Jovanovic, B. 117

Kelly, J.E. 109
Kerckhoff, A.C. 198
Klandermans, B. 82–3
Kreckel, R. 68

Labour Force Survey 150, 156, 179, 183
labour market: changes in the 1980s and 1990s 149, 163; young people's attitudes to 28–9
Landau, N. 26
Layard, R. 16: *et al.* 202
lay-offs 125–6, 131
Lee, G. and Wrench, J. 50, 54
leisure 125, 129, 133; *see also* respite
'lifelong learners' 201
lifetime theory of employment 123
Livock, D. 48–9
'lock-in' of employees 67–9, 75
logit analyses 31, 171–2, 174, 205–6
London 24–6, 95, 123, 137, 170
Lynch, L.M. 32, 141: and Richardson R. 32; *see also* Blanchflower, D.G.

McEwan Scott, A. 156
McRae, S. 203
Maguire, M. 150–3, 156
Maizels, J. 118
management training 65, 154
manufacturing, employment in 13, 150–1, 155, 163–4
March, J.G. and Simon, H.A. 122–4, 133
market-clearing mechanisms 122–3, 198
Marsden, D.: and Germe, D.-F. 61; and Ryan, P. 3, 17, 159, 191, 200
matching of workers to jobs 40, 43, 47, 56, 69, 120, 144–5, 192, 200; *see also* mismatch
Mattila, J.P. 124
Mayhew, K. and Rosewell, B. 14
Metcalf, D. 154, 157–60: and Richards, J. 13, 16, 18, 115
Miller, D.C. and Form, W.H. 193
minimum wage 158, 202
mismatch between job and worker 110–11, 129, 192
Mitterauer, M. 201
Modern Apprenticeships scheme 152, 197
Montgomery, B.R. 90
'moratorium' stage 63, 116, 192
mutual dependency between employer and employee 69–71

National Child Development Study 55, 138, 145

National Longitudinal Survey 63, 118–19

National Training Survey 16

net present returns from employment 123

new technology 152–3, 155, 158, 163, 172–3

Nolan, P. and Walsh, J. 152, 157

norms of the workplace 90–1, 99–100, 102–3, 110, 179–82

NVQs 176

Oberschall, A. 82

occupational choice 35–6, 39, 42, 50, 144

Oliver, P. *et al.* 85

Olson, M. 82, 91

Osterman, P. 2–3, 62–3, 65, 71–2, 118–19, 125, 132, 138, 145, 190–2, 196

Pahl, R.E. 51

parents: attitudes of 12; help with jobfinding from 44, 47, 53; occupations of 50, 108; *see also* unemployment for households

Parsons, D.O. 123

participation rates 148, 159, 161, 163

part-time work 152, 157, 163–4, 200

Paterson, L. and Raffe, D. 159

Payne, C. 79, 81, 94, 147

Payne, J. 147, 150, 154, 160–2, 193

personal characteristics 177

polarization of skills 153, 155, 163, 175, 197

population of young people 12–13

principal-agent relationships 71

productivity 138–9

promotion prospects 64–5, 76, 154

promotion structures 66–9, 71–3, 75–6, 144

'pull' into education 149, 161–3

'push' out of employment 149–161; *see also* exclusion

qualifications 41–2, 48–9, 158, 161–2, 171–2, 175–6: inflation of 176–7, 189, 195–6; relationship to number of jobs held 133; required by employers 55

quit behaviour 116, 121–9, 135, 178: motivations for 125–8; *see also* incentive-opportunity model

quit-prone young people 128

racial groups *see* ethnic minorities

Raffe, D. 15, 161, 189, 197; *see also* Paterson, L.

recession, effects of 122, 164

redundancy payments 16

redundancy procedures 116

rent-seeking behaviour 4, 8–9, 69, 115, 117, 137, 139, 178–9

replacement ratio 3–4, 15, 50, 116, 124, 129–30

reservation wage 15, 194

respite from work 116, 120, 139, 178; *see also* leisure

Richardson, R. 31–2, 81; *et al.* 130

risk-prone young people 125

Roberts, K. 35, 39, 43, 153, 164, 192–6; and Chadwick, C. 193, 195; and Parsell, G. 162; *et al.* 16, 18, 64, 153–4, 156–8, 191, 196; *see also* Bynner, J.

Rubery, J. 158: and Wilkinson, F. 66, 73; *see also* Horrell, S.

Sawdon, A. *et al.* 118

school leavers: age of 5–7, 10–12, 19, 21, 65, 194; attitudes of 38; cohort study of 27–32; employers' attitudes to 157–8, 183; types of employment entered by 21–3

Schwartz, M. 82

secondary labour market 63, 66–7, 191

segmentation of the labour market 17–18, 66, 190–1, 198

separation: frequency of 121–2; involuntary *see* lay-offs; rates of 3–4, 115–16, 178; voluntary 122–3; *see also* quit behaviour

separation-prone behaviour 117–19

service industries, employment in 13, 25, 151, 153, 155, 164

sex, analyses by *see* gender differences

shift work 18

Shishter, J. 80–1

'shopping around' for jobs 117, 135, 178

Sillitoe, K. and Meltzer, H. 14, 49, 107

Sime, N. 161: *et al.* 193

Snower, D.J. and Booth, A.L. 159, 199–200

Social and Community Planning Research 27, 30

social class 35–6

social movement theory 89

socialization 35–6, 42–4, 46–8, 52–3, 144, 171

Spence, M.A. 41

Spilsbury, M. 156; *et al.* 78–9, 81, 93–6

Springhall, J. 12

Stigler, G. 123

Stoikov, V. and Ramon, R.L. 123–4

stratification of the labour market *see* segmentation

strikes, days lost through 182
structural change 150, 164
sunk costs 69
supply factors in the labour market 3, 108
Swann Report (1985) 15, 49

Tajfel, H. 86
Thompson, M. *et al.* 151, 153, 155–7, 159, 193
trade unions 7, 16, 78–113, 143: attitudes to
      100–4, 107; core members of 85–8, 93,
      97–100, 112, 179; core non-members of
      88–9, 100–1; future of 201–2; impact on
      wages 139, 141, 144; life-cycle of 84–5;
      membership in the 1980s and 1990s
      179–82; membership related to quit
      behaviour 132–3; motivation for joining
      or not joining 85–104, 110–11, 144;
      services supplied by 78–82, 105
Training and Enterprise Councils (TECs) 162
training: for females 46, 142; on-the-job 66–8,
      75; relationship to quit behaviour 130,
      132
training opportunities 11, 19, 23, 34, 55, 58,
      61, 64–5, 123, 139, 141–4, 189
transferable skills 64–5, 73
transition from education to work 35, 191–3,
      200–2: government policy affecting
      197–8
Transport and General Workers Union
      (TGWU) 181
travel to work 40–1, 51–2, 170
turnover rates 115, 120, 134
turnover theory 135

underclass, emerging 184
unemployment: definition of 32; for house
      holds 50–1, 108, 144–5, 175, 177, 183–4,
      200; in London 24–5; long-term effects
      of 59, 141, 145, 183–4; perceptions of
      129, 131, 134; rising levels of 23, 120,
      149–50, 163
unemployment benefit *see* benefits
unfair dismissal 116

union density 80–2, 90, 180–2, 188–9
union recognition 78–9, 180
Union of Shop, Distributive and Allied
      Workers (USDAW) 181
unionization, propensity towards and
      opportun ity for 79–82, 93–7, 112–13; *see
      also* trade unions
unskilled work 13, 37, 147, 153, 159
utility maximization 124

values 98, 103, 105
vocational qualifications 161–2, 176, 194–5

Wachter, M.L. and Wright, R.D. 69–70
wage differentials 56–8, 68: for young people
      relative to adults 158–9
wages: dissatisfaction with 126–9, 131–2;
      impact of job mobility on 137–8, 140;
      impact of trade union membership on
      139, 141, 144
Wage Councils 158–9
Whitfield, K. and Wilson, R.A. 161
Williamson, O.E. 67–9
Willis, P. 36–40, 43, 46, 55, 76
women's employment 13–14, 19, 156–7, 160,
      163–4, 172
word-processing skills 172–3
work experience 198–9
Workplace Industrial Relations Survey 180–1
workshy attitudes and the work ethic 1, 51, 55,
      133, 161, 194, 201–2

Yates, J. 161–2
young people, definitions of 2
Youth Cohort Series 148, 150–1
youth jobs, character of 17–18, 63–5, 144,
      150–1, 153–4, 160, 190–1
youth labour market, separateness of 189–91
Youth Training 5, 149, 151, 156, 160, 162–3,
      183, 189, 193–4

Zax, J.S. 134